The Reminiscences

of

Admiral George W. Anderson, Jr.

U. S. Navy (Retired)

Volume I

U. S. Naval Institute

Annapolis, Maryland

1983

Preface

In the case of any officer who becomes Chief of Naval Operations, it is interesting and productive to trace the course of his career as a junior officer. Such is the opportunity afforded by this first volume in the oral memoir of Admiral George W. Anderson, Jr., who was CNO from 1961 to 1963. Admiral Anderson was the first in a succession of naval aviators who held the office of CNO--with one exception-- from 1961 through 1982. As such they represented the culmination of aviation's long battle for supremacy in the Navy.

In reading Admiral Anderson's recollections, one finds discussion of a number of increasingly important aviation billets he held following his graduation from the Naval Academy in 1927. He was in the aviation detachments of light cruisers, a carrier pilot flying from the old Lexington and the first Yorktown, patrol plane pilot, and navigator in the second Yorktown under the famous Captain "Jocko" Clark. Ashore he served in important positions--in the Plans Division of the Bureau of Aeronautics during the early part of the World War II and later on the staff of Vice Admiral John Towers, one of naval aviation's strongest boosters, later in the war when Towers was ComAirPac. As the war was winding down, Anderson was aviation officer in the Strategic Plans Section of the CominCh staff in Washington. He was later commanding officer of the escort carrier Mindoro and the fleet carrier Franklin D. Roosevelt; the latter was a prize command during the early 1950s and a certified admiral maker.

Along the way, Anderson demonstrated a skill at planning which surely presaged his future high office in the Navy; in this role he was on General Dwight Eisenhower's staff when the NATO command was established in Europe in the early 1950s, and later Anderson was essentially chief of staff to Admiral Arthur Radford, the first naval officer to serve officially as Chairmen of the Joint Chiefs of Staff. Once he had made his stars, Admiral Anderson held two more aviation jobs, as Commander Formosa Patrol Force, which consisted of seaplanes, and as Commander Carrier Division Six in the Mediterranean. The latter assignment was an important stepping-stone to his service, discussed in Volume II of this memoir, as Commander Sixth Fleet. Volume I does contain Anderson's discussion of the establishment of the Sixth Fleet in the early post-World War II period and then his service on the Sixth Fleet staff in 1950. In all, this first volume presents a picture of an officer on the move upward at a time when naval aviation was coming into its own in the U.S. Navy.

Much of the credit for this oral history belongs to my predecessor, Dr. John T. Mason, Jr., who conducted the interviews and prepared the index of the bound volumes as an aid to researchers. The transcripts of the interviews were corrected by Admiral Anderson and then retyped, but they follow closely the words of the interviews themselves.

>   Paul Stillwell
>   Director of Oral History
>   U.S. Naval Institute
>   July 1983

ADMIRAL GEORGE W. ANDERSON, JR., U. S. NAVY, RETIRED

George Whelan Anderson, Jr., was born on December 15, 1906, in Brooklyn, New York, son of George W. and Clara (Green) Anderson. He attended Brooklyn Preparatory School, and entered the U. S. Naval Academy, Annapolis, Maryland, from his native state in 1923. Graduated and commissioned Ensign on June 2, 1927, he subsequently advanced in rank to that of Rear Admiral, to date from August 1, 1954. He served in the rank of Vice Admiral, from May 1, 1957, until January 18, 1958, and on September 14, 1959 he again assumed the rank of Vice Admiral. He took the oath of office as Chief of Naval Operations, with the accompanying rank of Admiral, on August 1, 1961.

Following graduation from the Naval Academy in 1927, he remained there for the short course in aviation, before joining the USS CHAUMONT, for transportation to the USS CINCINNATI in the Asiatic Fleet, in which he served as a junior officer until 1930. He was then ordered to the Naval Air Station, Pensacola, Florida, for flight training and, designated Naval Aviator in October of that year, was ordered to the Atlantic Fleet for duty in the aviation units of the USS CONCORD and USS RALEIGH, flagships of destroyer squadrons, Scouting Fleet, successively.

Between 1933 and 1935 he was assigned to the Flight Test Division of the Naval Air Station, NOB, Norfolk, Virginia, after which he had duty afloat with Fighting Squadron TWO, based on the USS LEXINGTON. He was detached from that squadron with orders to the Newport News (Virginia) Shipbuilding and Dry Dock Company, where the USS YORKTOWN was building, and joined that aircraft carrier on her commissioning on September 30, 1937, as landing signal officer. From the fall of 1939 until early 1940 he was attached to Patrol Squadron Wing FOUR, based at Seattle, Washington.

He was next assigned to the Plans Division, Bureau of Aeronautics, Navy Department, Washington, D.C., and while there participated in the formulation of the American aircraft program for World War II. This included association with war-time agencies charged with production and allocation of all United State aircraft, and planning the aircraft aspects of the expansion of Naval aviation. For this liaison work with the Army Air Force while in that assignment he received a Letter of Commendation from the War Department, with authorization to wear the Army Commendation Ribbon.

In March 1943 he again reported to the Newport News Shipbuilding and Dry Dock Company, this time to assist in fitting out the new USS YORKTOWN (CV-10), and became Navigator and Tactical Officer when she was commissioned on April 15, 1943. He was aboard that aircraft carrier during her early action in the Pacific and received a Letter of Commendation, with authority to wear the Commendation Ribbon, from the Commander in Chief, U. S. Pacific Fleet, for outstanding services from August 15 to November 1, 1943, while attached to the USS YORKTOWN.

He is also entitled to the Ribbon for, and a facsimile of the Presidential Unit Citation awarded the USS YORKTOWN for "extraordinary heroism in action against enemy Japanese forces in the air, at sea and on shore in the Pacific War Area from August 31, 1943 to August 15, 1945...Daring and dependable in combat, the YORKTOWN with her gallant officers and men rendered loyal service in achieving the ultimate defeat of the Japanese Empire."

He next had duty as Plans Officer on the Staff of Commander Aircraft, U. S. Pacific Fleet, and for "exceptionally meritorious conduct...as Head of the Plans Division of the Staff of Commander Air Force, U. S. Pacific Fleet during the period from November 1943 to March 1944..." he was awarded the Legion of Merit. The citation further states:

"In this capacity it was his grave responsibility to prepare plans for the activation and employment of Air Force, Pacific Fleet aircraft units and ships, and to supervise the preparation of plans for the establishment and initial logistic support of advanced air bases. The ultimate success of these plans may be attributed, in large measure, to the highly efficient manner in which he contributed to the compiling and evaluating of the mass of details upon which these plans were based, and to his sound judgment in estimating future requirements and availability of Pacific Fleet aviation units..."

On March 28, 1944 he reported as Assistant to the Deputy Commander in Chief, U. S. Pacific Fleet and Pacific Ocean Areas. He was awarded the Bronze Star Medal for "meritorious achievement (in that capacity)...during operations against enemy Japanese forces in the Pacific War Area, from March 28, 1944 to April 16, 1945..." The citation further states: "Intelligently planning and estimating for the needs of Naval aviation in the Pacific, (he) contributed materially to the improvement in organization, training and logistical support..."

In June 1945 he became Aviation Officer in the Strategic Plans Section on the Staff of the Commander in Chief, U. S. Fleet, with headquarters at the Navy Department, Washington, D.C. As such he also had duty as Deputy Navy Planner on the Joint Planning Staff. Ordered to the Office of the Chief of Naval Operations, Navy Department, he was appointed a member of the Permanent Joint Board of Defense (Canada-United States) in November 1946; was also one of the Navy members of the Brazilian-United States Defense Commission and served with the Joint War Plans Committee of the Joint Staff.

In July 1948 he returned to sea as Commanding Officer of the USS MINDORO, and when detached from that anti-submarine carrier in August 1949, reported for instruction at the National War College, Washington, D.C. Completing the course there in July 1950 he joined the Staff of the Commander SIXTH Fleet as Fleet Operations Officer. In December 1950 he transferred to the Staff of the Supreme Allied Commander in Europe (SHAPE), and remained there until July 1952 as the Senior U. S. Officer in Plans and Operations. He served as Commanding Officer of the USS FRANKLIN D. ROOSEVELT for a year, and when detached from command of that aircraft carrier in June 1953, reported for duty in the Office of the Chief of Naval Operations, Navy Department.

In July 1953 he became Special Assistant and principal staff officer to the Chairman of the Joint Chiefs of Staff, Washington, D.C., continuing to serve in that capacity until July 1955. On August 3, that year, he assumed command of the Formosa Patrol Force with additional duty as Commander U. S. Fleet Air Wing ONE (his title was changed late in 1955 to Commander U. S. Taiwan Patrol Force). He was Chief of Staff, Joint Staff, Commander in Chief, Pacific, from July 1956 until May 1957 when he reported in the rank of Vice Admiral as Chief of Staff and Aide to the Commander in Chief, Pacific.

He served in the rank of Rear Admiral as Commander Carrier Division SIX from July 1958 until September 14, 1959, when he became Commander SIXTH Fleet and Commander Naval Striking and Support Forces, Southern Europe, with the accompanying rank of Vice Admiral. "For exceptionally meritorious service...as Commander SIXTH Fleet from September 1959 to June 1961..." he was awarded the Distinguished Service Medal. The citation continues in part:

"A dynamic leader and skilled diplomat, Admiral (then

Vice Admiral Anderson) developed and maintained an exceptionally high standard of morale and combat readiness within the SIXTH Fleet, and succeeded in elevating his command to a new hgh level of prestige and effectiveness as an instrument for the conduct of the foreign affairs of his country. Keenly aware that the mission of good will was second only to that of readiness, he has been an outstanding exponent of the President's People to People Program and has indoctrinated personnel of his command in its objectives so successfully that the ships and personnel of the SIXTH Fleet have been welcome visitors at each port of call. Through his exceptional diplomatic and political talents, Admiral Anderson has made a major contribution toward encouraging and strengthening the ties of friendship between the United States and the littoral Mediterranean nations, and toward supporting these national in their resolve to resist Communism and Communist infiltration. In bolstering the morale and combat readiness of the SIXTH Fleet, he has been instrumental in enhancing the military posture and prestige of the United States..."

His appointment to be Chief of Naval Operations for a term of two years, with the accompanying rank of Admiral, was approved by the Senate on June 29, 1961 and he was sworn into office at the Naval Academy, Annapolis, Maryland on August 1, 1961. He served in that capacity until relieved of all active duty pending his retirement, effective August 1, 1963. "For exceptionally meritorious service...while serving as Chief of Naval Operations, principal naval advisor to the President, and member of the Joint Chiefs of Staff, from August 1961 to August 1963..." he was awarded a Gold Star in lieu of the Second Distinguished Service Medal. The citation continues in part:

"Admiral Anderson has displayed superb qualities of leadership and professional competence in one of the most responsible positions in the Department of Defense. Under his skillful and effective guidance, the operating forces of the Navy have contributed significantly to our national posture and have carried out their world-wide responsibilities with a view toward enhancing the prestige of the United States and its objective of world peace. Admiral Anderson's consummate knowledge and understanding of the complexities of international relations, his recognition of the requirements generated by swiftly paced, changing world situations, and his dedication to high military standards have been applied effectively toward keeping the Navy strong and maintaining the United States in a pre-eminent position among the maritime powers of the world..."

On May 21, 1963, President John F. Kennedy announced his intention to appoint Admiral Anderson as United States Ambassador to Portugal. The appointment was approved by the Senate on July 31, and he was sworn in as Ambassador by Secretary of State Rusk on September 4, 1963 where he served as Ambassador until July 1, 1966.

In addition to the Distinguished Service Medal with Gold Star, the Legion of Merit, the Bronze Star Medal, the Commendation Ribbon with Combat V (Navy), the Commendation Ribbon (Army), and the Presidential Unit Citation Ribbon with one star, Admiral Anderson has the American Defense Service Medal with Fleet Clasp; the American Campaign Medal; the Asiatic-Pacific Campaign Medal with two stars; the World War II Victory Medal; the Navy Occupation Service Medal with Europe Clasp; the China Service Medal; and the National Defense Service Medal. He has also been awarded the Order of the British Empire, rank of Honorary Officer, by the Government of Great Britain; the Precious Tripod Medal by the Government of the Republic of China; the Maltese Cross; the Order of Prince Henry the Navigator by the Government of Portugal; the Cross of the Knight Commanders, Royal Order George I, by the Government of Greece; the Grand Cross of the Royal Order of Phoenix by the Government of Greece; the Order of Naval Merit (first class) by the Republic of Venezuela; the Order of Naval Merit, in the grade of Grand Official, by the Government of Brazil; Grand Cross of Military Merit by the Government of Portugal; the Legion of Honor (Commander) by the Republic of France; the Great Star of Military Merit by the Republic of Chile; and the Knight of the Great Cross of the Order of Merit by the Government of Italy.

Returning to the United States in 1966, he became involved

in the private business sector as a Corporate Director of National Airlines, Crown Cork and Seal, the Value Line Mutual Funds, the Bird-Johnson Co., and the Lamar Corporation of Baton Rouge, Louisiana of which he served as Chairman. He was also president of the Naval Academy Alumni Association. In 1967 President Nixon appointed him a member of the President's Foreign Intelligence Advisory Board where he served for eight years, six of which as Chairman.

    Admiral Anderson's official address is Washington, D.C. He is married to the former Mary Lamar Sample of Pensacola, Florida, and had two sons, George W. Anderson, III, and Lieutenant Commander Thomas Patrick Anderson, killed in an accident off USS FORRESTAL in 1978; a daughter, Mary Annette (now Mrs. Daniel Coughlin of London, England; and step-daughter, Carolyn Sample (now Mrs. David M. Abshire of Alexandria, Virginia).

Authorization

The U. S. Naval Institute is hereby authorized to make available to individuals, libraries, and other repositories of its choosing the transcripts of sixteen oral history interviews concerning the life and career of the late Admiral George W. Anderson, Jr., U.S. Navy (Retired). The interviews were recorded by Admiral Anderson on 9 June 1980, 19 June 1980, 17 October 1980, 22 October 1980, 29 October 1980, 5 November 1980, 20 November 1980, 25 November 1980, 10 December 1980, 16 December 1980, 7 January 1981, 27 January 1981, 25 March 1981, 2 April 1981, 9 April 1981, and 22 April 1981, in collaboration with Dr. John T. Mason, Jr., for the U.S. Naval Institute.

The undersigned does hereby release and assign to the U.S. Naval Institute all right, title, restrictions, and interest in the interviews. The copyright in both the oral and transcribed versions shall be the sole property of the U.S. Naval Institute. The tape recordings of the interviews are and will remain the property of the U.S. Naval Institute.

Signed and sealed this __18__ day of __April__ 1992.

Mary Lee Sample Anderson, for the estate of Admiral George W. Anderson, USN (Ret.)

Interview No. 1 with Admiral George W. Anderson, Jr.,

U.S. Navy (Retired)

Place: His residence in the Watergate Apartments, Washington, D.C.

Date: Monday morning, 9 June 1980

Subject: Biography

By: John T. Mason, Jr.

Q: Well, Sir, I don't know how many years it has been that I've been waiting for this day, to have you tell me orally the story of your naval career, your very illustrious naval career.

This being a talking biography, I wonder if you'd begin in the proper way by telling me the date and place of your birth and something about your family background.

Adm. A.: I was born in Brooklyn, New York, on 15 December 1906. My father was George W. Anderson. He was a small independent real estate insurance broker in Brooklyn -

Q: Brooklyn not being so small, however!

Adm. A.: In the Williamsburg section of Brooklyn, where I was born -

Q: Oh, I see.

Adm. A.: He had met my mother up in the Catskill regions of New York state. Her name was Clara Green, and I think at the time he met her he was up there recuperating from some respiratory ailment or something of the sort. They were married up in Rockland,

New York. She came from a family that went back to pre-revolutionary days. Actually, her name was Clara Green, her father was Ahira Green, who ran a farm up there which had been in the family for many generations. Her mother was named Margaret Need of the same area. In addition to the farm they had a small country-type resort hotel, in Rockland, New York, just outside of Roscoe in Sullivan County in the lower Catskills, a great trout fishing country. So, when they were married they were married in a church up there in Roscoe.

My father was a Roman Catholic, my mother was a Methodist. She became a Catholic. They were married by a Catholic priest. She moved down to Brooklyn. I was born and then she became ill and died when I was two years old, so my father moved back with his brothers and sisters, none of whom were married, and they brought me up in Brooklyn. It was a very closely knit, loving family. I guess I was a spoiled child because the aunts and uncles always took a great deal of interest in me. As a result, with two aunts who were schoolteachers, one of them was a principal, they did a lot of preschool education for me.

Q: I expect so. You were the only child?

Adm. A.: I was the only child and, as a result, when I did go to school I entered the second grade rather than going through kindergarten, and then skipped a grade or two during the course of - this was in public school.

Q: Sounds a bit precocious!

Adm. A.: And then after I graduated from grammar school, I

shifted to a Jesuit high school as a day student in Brooklyn. Unfortunately, that school has changed and all that section of Brooklyn is no longer a private school.

Q: That's the Brooklyn Prep School?

Adm. A.: The Brooklyn Preparatory School, yes, and that was, I would say, a very comprehensive education at that time because in addition to all the normal reading, writing, and arithmetic in grammar school, my homework was very carefully supervised. In high school, I guess I had four years of Latin and three years of Greek and two years of French plus the usual mathematics and English, with a great deal of emphasis on English. I graduated from that school - actually, the graduation was in January of 1923, so I finished my four years in January and had to wait until June to graduate.

Q: It was certainly a splendid preparation for -

Adm. A.: Oh, it certainly was. When I finally got an appointment to the Naval Academy I did not even have to take examinations because I was admitted on my record, you might say.

During that time, living in Brooklyn, we'd go down to Long Island in the summertime, either on the north shore or, more frequently, on the south shore of Long Island and I'd be around the boats and interested. When I was a very small boy, I guess about six or seven, my aunt had taken me over to visit the USS Vermont at a time when the fleet was visiting in the Hudson River, which leads to the point that interest in the navy can best be generated at a very young age and I always tried in my own naval career to interest youngsters in the navy and the Naval Academy, in particular, because if you get the boy aroused then you automatically get his parents enthusiastic supporters along with him.

In any event, I'd always said, as I recollect, that I wanted to go the Naval Academy. Well, my family were strong Democrats and my father made some efforts to get me an appointment from one of the Democratic politicians and unsuccessfully.

Q: Your father was all for this idea, was he?

Adm. A.: Not enthusiastic but, I guess, passively so.

When I finished high school, before I actually got my diploma in June, I got a position in an export-import firm in New York. I was just sixteen at the time. I remember they paid me sixteen dollars a week and I would translate from French to English bills of lading invoices and -

Q: They were lucky to get you!

Adm. A.: The rule was imposed on me by the family that I could have one-third of my earnings for my own expenses, one-third of it went into a savings account, and one-third of it went into the family pool to help with family costs. Of course, that all came back to me later. But it was sort of a principle of fiscal discipline. Subway fares were five cents in those days and I would walk up to the subway. I think the firm was called Susfeld, Lorche, and Schimmel, actually German Jewish. They were importers and they had optical goods and all sorts of things manufactured in Europe. But it was an interesting experience, particularly when I look now at my grandchildren and see the difference in their attitude towards money. I sort of wish that times had not changed as much as they actually have.

In any event, I had been successful in getting an appointment through my father. The month of March is the annual period of the Novena of Grace to Saint Francis Xavier, a foremost Jesuit of the founding years of the order. It was stressed that if one made a special request and was sincere in making the Novena the request would be granted "if it was in conformance with the will and glory of God". Then at the end of the Novena one day I saw a little notice in the New York Herald that Congressman Ogden L. Mills had five appointments for the Naval Academy from his district and had found nobody that he felt was qualified.

Q: He was Westchester, was he?

Adm. A.: No, he was in a midtown district in New York that bordered on the East Side -

Q: What later was called the Silk Stocking -?

Adm. A.: Then a very high class neighborhood. The better-class people, I suppose, didn't want to go to the Naval Academy and the others couldn't properly qualify by his high standards. So I wrote him a letter and said that I was anxious to go to the Naval Academy and why, and the first thing I knew I got a telegram back saying, "Establish a residence in my district," which I did. It also was closer in to the theater district and so I established a residence at the Flanders Hotel in midtown, the residence being just a mailing address. Then on the 2nd of July my father drove me down to the Naval Academy. I entered there and was sworn in as a midshipman on the 3rd of July, 1923.

Q: He gave you a principal appointment?

Adm. A.: He gave me a principal appointment, yes.

The other day we were down at the Naval Academy, at a Foundation meeting, and they were talking about the fact that the Naval Academy had agreed with the other service academies that they could no longer support out-of-district appointments. Well, we looked a little askance at that, took a sounding around, and you might say the most successful people there, among the trustees, had all had out-of-district appointments, not necessarily athletes at all.

Q: Exactly. This is my experience in talking to them.

Adm. A.: Sure. In any event, I had a very good education. I had a very fine and interesting family. I lived largely in Brooklyn and went out on Long Island, with occasional trips up to Sullivan County, where my mother's people had come from, and it was, I would say, a very fine childhood.

The district where I grew up was St. Mark's Avenue. It's now the Bedford-Stuyvesant section, and it's all completely changed around -

Q: Completely black, too, isn't it?

Adm. A.: Oh, yes. First it was Jewish, then it was black.

So that's how I came to get to the Naval Academy. Oh, one other thing.

My aunt who was a principal had met a book salesman who also was an official for the college football games. At weekends he'd referee football games. He was probably very well known in that fraternity, a man named William R. Crowley. He came from Bowdoin College in Maine, and he used to take me to football games. He always refereed the Army-Navy game, and at that time they alternated between New York and Philadelphia. So I saw Army-Navy games as his guest, you might say, and it made me more interested in Naval Academy sports as well as the navy.

I can't think of any other particular highlights as a youngster. As I say, none of this family had married except my father, and he never married again. The life at home was a very proper one. The family was religious, Catholic. They would go out for drives on Sunday in the country. Gradually, one or the other would die off. There were three generations in the family. Two elderly great-aunts of mine, one was very proper and one was very neglectful of the normal things of life. We used to refer to Aunt Annie as a holy terror and the other as a princess. Their name was Whelan, my paternal grandmother's name from Philadelphia.

Q: You were the only child?

Adm. A.: I was the only young one in the house which also brings a point. I think today that situation has largely changed throughout the country. There is great merit in having three generations in one home. It shares the expense, you have built in babysitters, you have built in counselors, there's good balance in the family.

Q: Yes, built in tolerance, too.

Adm. A.: That's right. Also, in those larger homes the work was shared. It was a very satisfactory arrangement. Of course, modern living in apartments and so forth and the lack of help has made for a great change in our mode of living in the United States. But that period, up until 1923, when I went to the Naval Academy, it was a pretty stable sort of existence. I mention again the neighborhood encroachment, first, of the Jews, and then of the Negroes in that whole area. But our family had no history of any intolerance.

Q: Also, you might address the fact that there were standards by which you lived, which are in contrast with today.

Adm. A.: Oh! Take, for example, you got your report cards from school and if you had a certain standing they would have little cards called honor cards, and if you went to a high standard there was a little gold seal on them, otherwise it was a silver seal on them. I'd bring a good report card or an honor card home and I'd get a reward, and if I didn't, the allowance was cut and the allowance was very small. It was about ten long blocks from home, up the hill and down, to school and I'd walk back and forth. Sometimes I would serve Mass in the morning. I'd go up to the church and serve the six o'clock Mass, come back, and then go to school, which would open, I guess, at about 8:30. In the wintertime they'd flood the tennis courts and we'd play ice hockey.

Ebbets Field, the home of the Brooklyn Dodgers, was only about four blocks away from prep school and we'd go over and look over the fence. We'd stand on the hills of vacant lots there and look down on Ebbets Field. Occasionally on weekends my father would reward me by taking me to a game where we could sit in the grandstand.

There was intense interest in everything that was going on, local situations in politics. The family, as I said, was Democratic but they favored a Republican national administration. There were always discussion on everything, current affairs, at the dinner table. The whole family was there for dinner every night and on Sundays, if we didn't go out to dinner. It was sort of an interesting type of a life for a boy and I guess I did get somewhat spoiled but the benefits of family attention offset the fact that you might say I was spoiled.

Q: Maybe you were spoiled within reason. It seems to me they had control!

Adm. A.: Oh, definitely. For example, the rule was you could never touch a girl if you were going out, you couldn't hold hands or put your hands on a girl. Very strict moral principles were involved, and very strict curfew hours. You couldn't stay out late the way they do today. Language, manners and politeness were strictly observed and enforced by all. No liquor was served in the home.

As I say, I went to the Naval Academy at sixteen, which was the minimum age at that time, and I didn't have to take any examinations because I was accredited. I had good friends in my prep school class, a boy's class. It was not coeducational by a long shot.

Q: No, you said it was a Jesuit school.

Adm. A.: A boys' school and they emphasized current events, dramatics, debating. I learned public speaking from high school, and you had to do a lot of public speaking - speaking, even though you might not be on a debating team. I was on a debating team. At graduation they had a regular ceremony. The students got up - I happened to be the salutatorian, I guess you might call it, of the class and had to give a talk. "Loyalty to Country" was the subject of that particular talk. (I re-read it recently and it still sounds good). I think it was a superb pre-college education.

Now, you might say about education of that sort, at least you knew what was right and wrong. You might not have developed in high school the ability to do always what was right or wrong. You would get that a little better in college. But at least you knew what was right and what was wrong, and it was just a splendid education.

Q: I suppose it was superior to most of your friends at the Naval Academy who came from different parts of the country?

Adm. A.: Oh, yes, there was a great diversity. At that time, usually the people who had the best preparation came from schools in New England and those who came from the West Coast, California, perhaps were second - and the midwest. Those from the south were much below. I remember when we went to the Naval Academy we had a third man in the room and he came from North Carolina. I think he was the first to fail out of the class. My other roommate was much older than I was, W.H.(Bill) Organ. He'd come from out in Nevada and California and he'd been to college before he came to the Naval Academy.

But it was an excellent education process with a combination which they still carry forward in the Naval Academy, I think, a good academic education, physical education, and a reasonable ethical, spiritual, moral ambiance, training, which is I think all too much lost in general education today.

Q: How did you like the life as a plebe at the Naval Academy? Did you enter into it, the control?

Adm. A.: As a plebe at the Naval Academy my biggest challenge, because I think I was six foot two and weighed 118 pounds when I entered and I was sixteen years old, was getting into physical condition and being able to compete in the major sports was totally out of the question against people who were older, more mature, more physically developed than I. On the other hand, I liked the life at the Naval Academy. I was intensely interested in it and, academically, I had no probelm at all.

Q: In fact, it probably was repetitious in many ways?

Adm. A.: In some cases it was, in English and mathematics it was more or less repetitious.

The plebe summer training was tough physically but no particular apprehension from hazing at all. I used to get my tail beat as a plebe. When the upper classmen came back, they'd swing at me with brooms or they'd make you take physical exercises. No, I adapted very well to plebe year. There was no real problem at all, except first of all meeting the strength tests, meeting the swimming tests, and I got off what they called the sub-squad early and passed all the physical tests without too much delay.

Q: Did you begin to put on weight?

Adm. A.: Well, I think I graduated at 149, or something like that, and six foot three.

I remember very well in plebe year the interest in football. All of us went to every football game that was reachable from the Naval Academy. The Army-Navy game in my plebe year was up at West Point, up in New York, at the Polo Grounds. We went up on trains to Jersey, took ferryboats up the Hudson, and then marched from there to the Polo Grounds. It was a misty, rainy day and we were wearing rain clothes and overshoes. When we marched on the field most of the overshoes stuck in the mud and they had to send the grounds keepers out to collect all the overshoes before they could start the game. It was a 0-0 game and the Navy was almost in very serious trouble because we were down on our own goal line with a ball in the fourth quarter and a kicker, a chap named Cullen, a first classman, punted the ball and it was blocked. He punted again and it was blocked. The third time he got it off, but we tied the game (0-0). That year the Naval Academy football team went on to the Rose Bowl and played the University of Washington out there. It was also a tie (14-14).

Throughout the year most of the Naval Academy and the plebes in particular were required to attend every game, unless they were actually participating in some other sport. I played class lacrosse -

Q: That was a new game, wasn't it?

Adm. A.: It was a new game for me and it was interesting. I played four years at lacrosse at the Naval Academy. I tried to go out for swimming but I wasn't a good enough swimmer for that.

The upper classmen were always very fair to us, I felt, even though there was what they called hazing in those days and they did things then that they're not permitted to do now. They made you learn an awful lot about the navy as a plebe. You had to study and answer questions and, of course, you had to sit very upright at the table, and the usual running of the plebes. To me, it was "running in the education sense" rather than bad physical hazing.

We had a lot of fun. We got along pretty well together, classmates. I was thoroughly interested in the Naval Academy, the navy, and I might say that all during my childhood the family was intensely patriotic. On every national holiday, when they would have parades, we'd always go out and watch the parades. During the First World War, they had big parades in New York, and the family would take me over to New York to watch the parades, the Rainbow Division, the 27th Division, the funeral of Mayor Mitchell, former Mayor Mitchell, who'd been killed in an accident - an intensely patriotic background, which also carried along and made the adaption to the Naval Academy for me extremely easy.

Q: Now, at the end of your plebe year you went on a cruise?

Adm. A.: At the end of plebe year we went on a cruise. They had four battleships, the Arkansas, the Wyoming, the Florida, and the Utah, four coal-burning battleships came up the Severn River to the Naval Academy, the day after graduation when we became youngsters, liberated from the stigma of being plebes. We embarked in ships' motorboats on a cruise and divided up among the four ships.

Q: Did you know what you were getting into, these being coal-burning ships?

Adm. A.: Yes, they'd all been coal-burning then.

We made a cruise to Europe. We went down the Chesapeake Bay and we went to England, to France, two ships went to Holland, where I was, and two ships to Belgium, Antwerp. Then we went around to Gibraltar and we had to coal ship several times, and it was a dirty, tough operation. During the cruise we would change from one assignment on deck to engineering. We'd actually get down in the boiler rooms and have to shovel coal into the fires, the boilers. We were taught by the old-hand enlisted men how to make mulligan of corned beef and vegetables and cook it on a shovel, lots of coffee.

We got up to London, I got to Paris. They were liberal on letting us make trips. My family had given me a little bit of money to facilitate those travels because the allowance you got as a plebe, I think, was three dollars a month. As a youngster it was five dollars a month. That was all the spending money we had. Now they get fifty or sixty dollars a month.

We worked. Youngsters worked basically in enlisted roles. The second-classmen and the first-classmen were at progressively higher levels and with more privileges.

We then left Europe and went down to Guantanamo, where they had target practice. From there we went back and then we had the month of September off for what was known as September leave. I think we all enjoyed the European cruise. It was a good system because they had all the classes, the three upper classes, on cruise together. They visited foreign ports, they traveled.

Q: And you were well received, were you not, in these various places?

Adm. A.: Oh, yes, extremely well received around.

Q: Even entertained, were you not, by local people?

Adm. A.: Modestly so, yes, but we went to the Wembley Exposition and we went sightseeing. We did a lot of sightseeing, and felt our way along towards night clubs within the limits of our resources That was in the summer of 1924 and many of the things I saw then I saw subsequently when I went over to Europe on different trips and cruises on assignment for duty. It was very interesting, broadening. We came back, we had a full month's vacation - I guess it was four weeks - then we started in at the end of September to resume the academic year.

Q: How did you utilize your month of vacation?

Adm. A.: Went back to Brooklyn. I went back each year, and occasionally I'd go up in New York State, up on Long Island, go to the beaches in southern Long Island. Quite a few midshipmen came from Brooklyn, New York, around and we'd get together.

I wasn't involved particularly with dates at the time. I'd go to baseball games, listen to the radio - they didn't have TV in those days. They had a lot of radio. But again, it was a wholesome curriculum at the Naval Academy.

Q: After that first cruise, were you confirmed in your desire to be a sailor?

Adm. A.: No question, no question at all. I didn't have any problems as far as I was concerned of making the navy a career. I think at that time it was a little before I made up my mind I wanted to go into aviation. I knew I wanted to go back to Europe, I wanted to travel.

The second year at the Naval Academy was youngster year. I had more difficulty academically that year because all the carryover from high school courses that I had had run out, except in English. I stood quite well in the class but I didn't star, as we called it, that year. The other three years I did star. I had to work harder in youngster year. There were no particular significant changes, except that you had the freedom of not being as restricted as a plebe was.

At the end of that year we made a midshipman cruise to the West Coast, run around through the Panama Canal, up the West

Anderson #1 -17-

Coast. That year I was on the Utah, which was still a coal-burning ship. On the first cruise I made the ships were the Arkansas, Wyoming, New York, and Texas. The second cruise I was on the Utah and that had already been converted to oil, in the summer of '25.

Q: So you were spared -?

Adm. A.: Spared the second cruise of shoveling coal.

The interesting thing on that cruise, as I remember, was we got up off the Columbia River and ran into a really rough storm up there. We'd gone up as far as Seattle, a rough storm up there. Then, on that trip, the people on the West Coast were much more capable of doing a lot of entertaining for us. When we'd come in port - we were in, let's see, San Diego, Los Angeles, Long Beach, San Francisco, and Seattle. I guess we also stopped in Portland. That was lots of entertaining, dances and so forth, and we met some nice people out there. Then we ended up coming back through the Panama Canal to Guantanamo for target practice, and back to the Naval Academy.

The last cruise, what we called the first-class cruise, was up and down the East Coast, where we visited Philadelphia, Newport, New York, and Boston.

Q: That was less thrilling than the others?

Adm. A.: Less thrilling, yes it was, but offset by the fact that you were given the opportunity of acting more as an officer. But again we went back to Guantanamo for target practice.

Q: Did you have instructors on board during these cruises?

Adm. A.: There was a midshipman officer representative on each ship, but basically the instruction was being done by the officers of the ship. They would move over part of the crew to make room for the midshipmen, enlisted personnel, but the instruction was largely done by the ship's officers and the ship's chief petty officers, and by the rotation of your assignments. A great deal of emphasis was put in the phase of rotating you from different divisions and different departments.

Q: I suppose it was an implementation of what you'd been learning in textbooks, too?

Adm. A.: Yes, it was the practical side of what we had in textbooks, particularly on first-class cruise where you actually had to do certain navigation, practical navigation, of the ship, and seamanship as well.

I would say it was a very well-balanced course. Of course, they look on it askance today with the changes in the curriculum at the Naval Academy.

Q: Admiral Hart told me one time that the purpose of training at the Naval Academy was to train a man to be a naval officer and a gentleman.

Adm. A.: I would say so, and that was still the emphasis. We still like to be able to train combat officers, but at that time they had very strict requirements for eyesight and quite a few of my classmates failed to make up on eyes at graduation.

As a result, they went into the Supply Corps. We still had a lot of people who went into the Marine Corps then, as now. We started off 1,074 and I think when my class ended at the Naval Academy we graduated 575 and 525 went into the navy.

Q: One of our mutual friends called it a vintage class.

Adm. A.: Oh, I would say it was a very good class because, among other things, we were the national collegiate champions in football our first-class year. We had that famous football game in Chicago that ended up 21-21 and they took the whole brigade of midshipmen and corps of cadets out to Soldier Field for the dedication of Soldier Field. The people in Chicago were most hospitable to us. It was a superbly organized trip, exceptionally well done.

We had good spirit in our class and good spirit in the Naval Academy, which is always enhanced by good performance by our athletic teams, particularly football. I've said frequently that the two people who realized most the importance of Naval Academy football were the chief of naval operations and the superintendent of the Naval Academy, because first of all, if you have a good football team, it enhances the morale not only of the Naval Academy but of the navy as a whole, it greatly increases the competitive spirit of the midshipmen, and it's a lift from some of the less pleasant sides of the disciplinary, cloistered life that midshipmen have to live down there. Definitely, a winning football enhances the morale, particularly of the Naval Academy, but generally of the navy as a whole.

Anderson #1 -20-

Q: And financially -?

Adm. A.: Oh, financially it's absolutely indispensable. It carries not only the varsity program but the intramural sports as well. Of course, Congress over the years has appropriated very little for athletics at the Naval Academy. That's paid by the Naval Academy Athletic Association.

Q: I recall Admiral Harry Hill during his time as superintendent certainly emphasizing sports as absolutely essential to the development of the sense of teamwork.

Adm. A.: Yes. We had the opportunity to get to know, particularly as first-classmen, we got to know the officers on duty at the Naval Academy, and they were pretty fine officers in our opinion. Of course, to us in those days lieutenants, lieutenant commanders, and commanders were pretty high-ranking people. If you were a commander in the navy it represented a very successful career, and the captains and the flag officers were really something.

We had a very fine, jaunty officer, Henry B. Wilson, as superintendent of the Naval Academy my plebe year, and then we had Admiral Nulton, Louis McCoy Nulton, as the superintendent later. We had Tommy Kurtz as one commandant of midshipmen and Sinclair Gannon was the second commandant of midshipmen. We had good company officers, who were carefully selected. They took an interest in you. There was lots of amusement in the midshipmen describing the officers. The officers knew it. We had nicknames for them all. I think they were, by and large, extremely fair and understanding with us.

My first-class year I was what we called a striper. I had three stripes. I was a battalion subcommander. When we went to Chicago, for example, my midshipman battalion commander, a classmate of mine, a four-striper, was on the football squad so I led the battalion out there, and I think it was very interesting all the way through. I had a pretty good record as far as demerits were concerned until I got to be a first-classman, and being the senior midshipman in the Catholic Church party I got more demerits then than I'd gotten the rest of the time because I'd get put on report for improper performance of duty for the misbehavior of the midshipmen marching out in town to church.

Q: Talk about the program of worship there, I mean the emphasis on chapel attendance and that sort of thing.

Adm. A.: Well, I was appalled and disappointed when the ruling was made that midshipmen and cadets no longer had to attend chapel. I felt that what we had was right. You attended the chapel of your choice. If you had a mandatory reason as an atheist or something of that sort, why, you were dispensed with a church and you'd have to spend your time in some other ethical or moral activity. I didn't know anybody who did that. Everybody went to a church party, as I say, of their choice.

It was an extremely magnificent occasion, the midshipmen marching in, and going to the academy chapel. The Catholic service we had out in town at St. Mary's Church. It was a shame we didn't have our own chapel at the Naval Academy but the efforts of the good Redemptorist fathers who had that church out in Annapolis, they were not about to let them have a Catholic chaplain at the Naval Academy.

But when we had the prisoners of war, particularly some of these people I know quite well, they said the things that made them carry on were their religious training and their survival training and the general training that they had. I belong to a club here in Washington that has three members of the Supreme Court which had voted to eliminate the compulsory requirement as an infringement on personal rights, and I explained to them what the impact was and my experience was with regard to being able to meet the challenges that I had later on in life. They simply never thought of that.

Q: Well, it was pointed out to them.

Adm. A.: Not adequately, apparently. They never thought of the impact of being able to sustain a prisoner of war when they made that decision.

Q: Too bad Jerry Denton wasn't around to tell them about it!

Adm. A.: That's right, Bill Lawrence and Jack McCain, a wonderful group of people, Jim Stockdale.

That's what I say, the balance of the Naval Academy, the academic, the physical, the military training, and the spiritual environment, in my opinion, is better than any other place and I always, in writing to candidates, young people, would say, "If I could have a grandson to influence, I would say 'I heartily

Anderson #1 -23-

recommend you go to the Naval Academy because it's the best you can get and the opportunity is the greatest.'"

Q: When were you introduced to aviation? While you were at the Academy?

Adm. A.: I guess the dramatic thing on aviation was Lindbergh flew the Atlantic -

Q: In 1927, yes.

Adm. A.: - and then we had to stay at the Naval Academy after graduation. They divided the class into two parts, an early summer aviation or a later one. I went on leave right after graduation, went back up to Brooklyn and around New York and New York state, then came back to the academy for aviation indoctrination. They had a squadron of patrol planes that came up there and they gave us various courses and flew us around. At that point I made up my mind I wanted to go into naval aviation.

Q: Had you been intrigued with the idea before that?

Adm. A.: We would talk about it because of the addition of flight pay. An ensign only got one hundred and twenty-five dollars a month, and so flight pay was attractive. But, no, I would say that I would have gone into aviation anyway, even if they had had no flight pay, because I was intrigued with it. It seemed to me that aviation was the coming offensive arm of the navy, and I was reinforced in that belief by the indoctrination training.

Of course, you had to wait two years. We didn't have to wait two years to get married. Some classmates did get married. But basically you had to wait before you could go into aviation. We drew numbers, preference numbers, not dependent upon your academic standing or anything else, purely luck and I drew a number that normally would have let me have a pretty good choice, and I had picked a ship that I thought was going over to Europe, a cruiser. But unfortunately after I'd gotten my preference the ship had gone out to the Asiatic Fleet, and so after aviation summer some fifteen of us went on a train across country, joined the Chaumont, a transport, went all the way out to Manila, where we joined the light cruisers Cincinnati, Richmond, and Marblehead.

All the time I was on the Chaumont I still wanted to go to aviation flight training, but I had to await my turn and wait for the end of my two years, you might say. Then you had also to go to elimination training before you could pass the stage where they would accept you for application to go for flight training.

Q: Yes, to see if you had aptitude.

Adm. A.: To see if you had the aptitude.

So I was interested in aviation particularly towards the end of my Naval Academy course, but I was going to stay in the navy, anyway. You had to do those two years, anyway.

Q: As you say, it was being emphasized more and more. Lindbergh, that was a spectacular -

Adm. A.: That was the dramatic impact for the country as a whole and, of course, for the services, too.

Q: And you had, prior to that, the Billy Mitchell controversy about aviation, and was not Admiral Moffett around publicizing it?

Adm. A.: Not particularly. There was not the competition at the Naval Academy to get people to go into submarines, into aviation, immediately, or the Marine Corps. A lot of classmates of mine, of course, went in the Marine Corps and then there was the consideration of a lot of the people if they were going to get married. There was the usual parade from graduation to the Naval Academy chapel to get married. A lot of them got married and that influenced their choice of duty, too. If they were getting married, whether to go to submarines or to aviation was a very important factor.

Q: Who was the speaker at your graduation?

Adm. A.: Curtis D. Wilbur, the secretary of the navy, tall. I think he was from Stanford originally -

Q: Yes, he was, from California.

Adm. A.: Sort of a stuffed shirt. I can't remember anybody who could remember what he said! I don't think you could find out from a classmate of mine what he said at graduation. Of course, all my family came down, the remaining aunts and uncle, my father. That was a great occasion. They spent June Week down there, at the Naval Academy. It was good weather, gaiety, everybody happy.

I look back on the Naval Academy with tremendous affection, what it did for me. I would say in retrospect, it was probably too dramatic, too significant, an emancipation from the discipline of being a midshipman when you go out into the fleet.

Q: Actually become an officer!

Adm. A.; That's right. Maybe in those days of those who went to junior officers' messes in battleships, it might have been a little bit different, but I think there was a little bit too dramatic a change there, which might have been improved upon, how I don't know. But it was a very significant change, just like finishing plebe year.

Q: Tell me about the Cincinnati. She was the ship you served in?

Adm. A.: She was the ship I served in. She was a light cruiser, there were ten of them, 7,500 ton cruisers. They had a battery of 6-inch guns, main battery, 3-inch antiaircraft guns, practically no fire-control system as such. They were 30-odd-knot ships, oil, would roll quite a bit, organized in two divisions, right through division 2, right through division 3.

Then they had the other two ships as the commanders of the destroyer squadrons, Atlantic and Pacific Fleets, and -

Q: They didn't have catapults, did they?

Adm. A.: Yes, they had two catapults and two O2U Vought Corsair seaplanes when they were on board ship, convertible to land planes ashore.

As I say, I joined the ship out on the Asiatic station. The Cincinnati, the Richmond, and the Marblehead had been sent out there late in the spring of 1927, I guess as a show of force to reinforce the Asiatic Fleet, and due to the conditions prevailing on the mainland of China, primarily.

I joined the ship in the Philippines and actually it went up to Olongapo and went in the old floating dry dock Dewey as soon as I'd gotten on board to have the hull cleaned. The Richmond and the Marblehead were up in China at the time. Then the Richmond and the Marblehead came back down and from - I guess it was October when we actually got on board the ship, we operated in and out of Manila, Cavite, until after Christmas, and then we made a cruise - we had a wonderful time in the Philippines, met lots of nice people. Incidentally, an important part of your graduation outfit from the Naval Academy was all your full-dress clothes, a mandatory part of the uniform was a civilian tuxedo. We normally went out on Saturday nights to dances. We had a very, very pleasant life, met lots of good people in the Philippines.

About January of 1928, they sent the three ships on a cruise around the southern Philippines, really to look at potential anchorages and fleet bases -

Q: Hydrographic work?

Adm. A.: Semi-hydrographic work. We'd come into one of these places like Olongapo, like Malanipa Sound, Zamboanga, different places like that, and the boats would go out, and we had certain requirements we'd have to fill in for the Hydrographic Office and for the Office of Naval Intelligence. Then we ended up in Shanghai.

My skipper was Tommy Johnson, who was a very strict officer who really didn't believe that officers should go ashore very much. He had the feeling that if the bachelors went ashore they just went ashore to raise hell. The married officers had no wives out there at the time because they were temporarily deployed and they shouldn't be going ashore, anyway.

Q: Shouldn't go ashore and be tempted!

Adm. A.: That's right.

We made this cruise around the southern Philippines and ended up in Shanghai, at the old Standard Oil Docks in the river below Shanghai. Of course, that was a very interesting experience. From there, we went up to Tsingtao, which was occupied at that time, the old German fort, by the Japanese and where we would anchor, why, we could smell the cremations of people who had been executed down there. There were Japanese patrols all over the city.

We had to go to certain parties at which there were officers from the Japanese ships.

Some people got up to Peking. I did not. But it was an interesting experience.

Q: What was the attitude of the Japanese at that time towards Americans?

Adm. A.: Formal. The few parties I was at with them they would get very drunk. There'd be geisha girls and they'd play these silly games that geisha girls do play.

We had done some target practice in the Philippines but basically it was normal shipboard work. I did not in the Cincinnati get up the Yangtze River to Nanking. The Marblehead was on its tour up there. The Cincinnati had been before. I would say that the Cincinnati was not a particularly good ship in terms of overall efficiency, but we were ordered back to the Hawaiian Islands. Light Cruiser Division 3 was replaced by another light cruiser division out there. We went to fleet concentration, fleet maneuvers, in the Hawaiian Islands.

I had one very amusing experience. Of course, these were the days of Prohibition -

Q: This was in 1928?

Adm. A.: This was in '28. They had what they called cigar messes on board and we'd have near beer, but the near beer came from the San Miguel Brewery in the Philippines. We would order the near beer but then we would go out to the brewery and have them put the near beer labels on the right beer, and got away with that for a while. Finally that was discovered and -

Q: By your results!

Adm. A.: Yes. Oh, I had many amusing experiences out in China. Everybody bought a lot of things. I got a lot of things for the family, Minton service plates, pretty good investments in chinaware, linen, and things of that sort.

Then we went on to San Francisco to pick up a bluejacket battalion that was to be transported down to Nicaragua to supervise the elections down there.

Q: Was Sandino still operating down there?

Adm. A.: Yes.

So we took our share of those and dropped them off at Nicaragua, then went on through the canal and came back to the East Coast.

In the summer of 1928 we were sent on a cruise to visit most of the ports in the New England area to "sell" the navy, to enhance the vote, you might say, for better naval appropriations, to win friends and influence people. We went from Newport to Newburyport, to Portland, to Gloucester, to Lynn, Nahant, Salem, and up to Bar Harbor for tennis week in September, the first week in September, I think it was, and we'd bring ships in there. Then we came back.

Q: What techniques did you employ in going to these ports, just appear?

Adm. A.: Oh, they had a modest sort of public-relations program. Local towns would entertain us. We met lots of local people and were invited to their homes. In Newport, we were invited to The Breakers, you know, with the Vanderbilts, who entertained us. Particularly in Bar Harbor we met lots of nice people there and had a marvelous cruise.

Then we came on down to the Virginia Capes, Hampton Roads, and did target practice, and then went up to the Navy Yard in New York for maintenance work.

Right after January, down we went to Guantanamo to stay there until about the first of April. That year we also went back up to New England, the Newport area -

Q: In 1929?

Adm. A.: In '29, and that year my turn came up for elimination flight training down in Norfolk, and I passed that successfully.

Q: What did that comprise, elimination flight training?

Adm. A.: Elimination flight training comprised primarily training in a seaplane, a training seaplane, so many flights and checked, and then, if you passed your dual instruction, then you were given one solo flight, and if you passed that you were put on the list to go to flight training in Pensacola. I passed it in October of '29.

Q: That demonstrated your aptitude?

Adm. A.: It demonstrated your aptitude.

Q: There were no gliders or anything like that involved in this?

Adm. A.: Oh, no, and not too much ground school because you had ground school at the Naval Academy before.

We had a captain, later a vice admiral, Gilbert J. Rowcliff, whom we used to call Uncle Horse Collar, who was a big stuffed shirt. He saw my orders detaching me and he said:

"You goddamned fool. You're going down to fly one of those goddamned airplanes. I hope you break your goddamned neck."

Very antiaviation, but he couldn't do anything else except let me go. He said once, "Why don't you get your orders changed and stay on here?"

That ship was sort of a floating psychopathic ward by that time with some of the officers we had. I don't know whether Admiral Carney ever told you about the Cincinnati. He wasn't on board then but he came aboard later as the gunnery officer and he said he's never been on such a ship in his life. It was really a screwball ship, with Rowcliff and the executive officer, who was a screwball. There was generally a lack of any sense of loyalty up or down among the officers. There were some hard-working, decent officers but thoroughly disgusted with what they were exposed to on that ship.

Q: Rowcliff must have been one of the last gasps in being so antiaviation, wasn't he? Because it began to change, didn't it?

Adm. A.: Oh, yes, it changed greatly. We had very fine aviators on the Cincinnati, neither of whom were Naval Academy officers. One was La Verne Pope and the other one Eddie Dolachek, non-Naval Academy, very high-type officers. When we'd go in the navy yard, of course, they'd stay down at Norfolk. But they also enhanced interest, certainly on my part, in naval aviation.

Q: I should think they would, yes.

Adm. A.: Although I think I was the only one of six classmates who had come to the Cincinnati out of the Naval Academy who went into aviation. None of the others had a distinguished career.

I was fortunate, in my opinion, to have gone to Penscola at that particular time. I would have liked to have gone down a little bit earlier but in retrospect it was very good that I had those two years at sea, because in that time I had a rotation of duty which enabled me to qualify as an officer of the deck at sea and in port and be a division officer, of an exposure to fire control, such as it was in those days, and also to be qualified as an engineering watch officer in the engineering department.

Q: That underscores the wisdom of that system, doesn't it?

Adm. A.: Oh, terrific, yes. and that carried on until after I'd finished at Pensacola and went back to another light cruiser which, at that time, was the Concord, which was the flagship of the destroyer squadron, flying O2U convertible landplanes-seaplanes. After a very short time in the Concord, the flagship was changed and the Raleigh became the flagship of the destroyers. There, I was immediately qualified as an officer of the deck at sea and also they used me as an engineering watch officer, as an aviator.

So, in my opinion, the ability to go from Pensacola to a cruiser - the same situation would apply in a battleship the same billet at the time, although we didn't like it so much at the time, it was very useful for the preparation for a longer-term career.

Then, at Pensacola, you had preliminary training in training planes, primary training planes, seaplanes. Then you went into land planes, then you went into fighters, and you had a certain amount of exposure to patrol planes. So you got a wide exposure to aviation as a whole, in contrast now to the far more cost-efficient specialized training that they have.

Q: Yes. Well, that's across the board in life.

Adm. A.: That's right, and then also the Bureau of Aeronautics would control the aviation personnel at that time, rather than the Bureau of Personnel. If you had your first tour of duty in a cruiser squadron, then your second tour of duty would be in a carrier squadron, then your third tour of duty would be in a patrol squadron. So, they gave you at that time and this carried on right up to the opening of World War II a very diversified experience.

Then, of course, you had to do your tour of purgatory, so to speak, as a ship's officer in some capacity.

So, I had as a junior aviator, a cruiser's scouting squadron, seaplanes at sea, land planes for training ashore, then I had a fighter squadron and I had a patrol squadron. My first shore duty was at the Naval Air Station, Norfolk, in what they called the experimental division, which was a sort of flight test division. Finally, I had a tour as a landing signal officer on a carrier, the Yorktown.

Anderson #1 -35-

So you had a wide range of diversified aviation, naval aviation, experience which, to me, is exceptionally valuable and which is not possible today. Too bad.

Q: Would you focus on Pensacola and the course of sprouts there?

Adm. A.: In Pensacola I had no difficulty in the flying part. I enjoyed the flying. I had good instructors, primary instructors. When you went down, you had to spend a lot of time in ground school, which none of us were particularly interested in. I and most of us did not do very well in ground school because-

Q: Half a day, was it?

Adm. A.: Yes, right - we didn't pay much attention to it, which was too bad. It wasn't made sufficiently attractive, in my opinion, and wasn't emphasized enough, because the overemphasis on flying. It was a sort of a factorylike procedure because there were new classes coming in all the time. You'd solo and then you'd go on for your primary training, and then you'd pass through another squadron, and others would come in the pipeline. And when all your flight class, I think mine was No. 25, or something, had soloed, we had a solo party, at which you would have to have everybody around.

We met lots of girls down there and some of the classmates were married by then. We played golf, we played bridge. It was a pleasant, interesting, attractive life, and, of course, we all looked forward to getting our wings which came at the end of the course, and where we would go for subsequent duty.

When you got your wings, then you were more or less assured of your flight pay and everybody would buy a new automobile, hornswoggled into buying more insurance. But it was very pleasant.

Q: How long a period was this training?

Adm. A.: It took about nine months then. Now, it's much longer and more specialized.

They had athletic teams at the Naval Air Station, Pensacola, baseball and football teams, in those days, basketball. We met other classmates who'd be above and a few below who were going through flight training at the same time. We broadened our knowledge of people. It didn't take long before we had picked up the folklore of naval aviation and knew by name, at least, practically all the people in naval aviation as a whole, the senior officers and the junior officers and the instructors, of course. You were taken into a good fraternity as soon as you demonstrated your ability and that you were going to get your wings.

In my case, as I say, I was ordered back to the cruiser scouting squadron in the flagship of the destroyer force, which, again in retrospect, although I didn't like it as much as if I'd gone to a carrier squadron, was probably the best thing I could get, for my career.

Q: Did you have any close calls down there in Pensacola when you were training? Did you have any downs?

Adm. A.: No, I went through without any downs to speak of. I may have had one before they let me finally solo in a seaplane.

In other words, two more hours. But, no, I had no trouble in the flying.

I remember going out one day in a seaplane and the damned engine would conk out. Of course, you have to land in the wind and the wind was away from the Naval Station and, of course, the student would always have to crank up the plane. Boy, and every time we'd make a turn the engine would conk again, so we were going farther and farther away from the station. By the time we headed back, that was the worst physical workout I've ever had, I guess.

Q: What was your weight at that time?

Adm. A.: About 140.

I think we were all very impressed and became intensely loyal to naval aviation.

We had no fatal crashes of anybody that I recall in our class down there. Some people were washed out, as we would say, didn't get their wings. They were still pretty particular about qualifying people. Subsequently, I've run into loads of people who say, oh, I tried to be a naval aviator but it didn't work out, I wanted to be but I couldn't.

Q: Were any of the older officers down there when you were there? They were sending some down, like Admiral Leahy.

Adm. A.: Admiral Fitch had come down there, and Admiral Halsey had been down there, but they were just ahead of me. In my flight class, the most senior persons were two from the class of 1921 and I was 1927. The junior person was '28, class of

1928. No, we didn't have any of that particular group going through in my class. They had been down. There was some grumbling and dissatisfaction among the instructors down there, they were bringing people in senior to them, but actually it was a good thing that they brought them in, Halsey and King and Fitch.

Q: A good thing for naval aviation.

Adm. A.: Yes, a good thing for naval aviation and the navy.

One thing, of course, we had to sign - if you were going to fly on a day, you had to sign what they called the Bevo List, that you didn't have a drink the night before. In other words, they didn't want you mixing drinking with flying or too much drinking the night before, but there was a lot of drinking on weekends.

When we started in we had to live in the BOQ, then the BOQs became filled up, so after you progressed to the point where you had gotten out of primary training, they would let you go out and rent a house in town or an apartment in town. Several of us got together and rented a house in town. First we stayed at the country club, then we rented a house in town, which gave us a little bit more freedom as an officer.

I guess while we were there we took our exams from ensign to junior lieutenant. In those days, you had to take written examinations for promotion.

Q: Presumably, you studied in preparation?

Adm. A.: We had to do a lot of study in that in preparation for those exams, and that occupied some of our time, too. We took those exams but we didn't get the results until later, so I was actually promoted, I guess, in my next assignment, although I can't prove it. You spent basically three years as an ensign, then you became JG.

Q: While you were at Pensacola, did you have any cross-country flights?

Adm. A.: Cross-country flights were around to such places as Mississippi, Pascagoula, Mississippi, to Foley, Alabama. That was about the extent of it. No. I thoroughly enjoyed my time there.

Q: Were any of your classmates from the Naval Academy with you?

Adm. A.: Yes. There were more people on either side of me in my class at Pensacola - '28 below me, '26 ahead of me, '25 ahead of me, the highest was '21, because a group of my class had gone through the first class one or two ahead of me. No, not in my flight class there weren't. But I would say that we all became thoroughly appreciative of naval aviation. We were when we went down, more so when we graduated.

Q: You said a little earlier that you developed a great loyalty to naval aviation.

Adm. A.: Oh, yes.

Q: That certainly has been obvious in the history of the U.S. Navy.

Adm. A.: Yes, and I would say the fact that naval aviation was small, that you did meet a lot of the people in naval aviation, you knew the others by name, you knew your Naval Academy classmates who'd gone through, that was a stimulus to the high degree of fraternal association you had in naval aviation.

Q: It was sort of a family within a family, wasn't it?

Adm. A.: It was, very definitely.

Now, when I finished, I was assigned to the Concord, which was based up in Norfolk, but the ship was based in Charleston. The aviation unit was at the Naval Air Station, Norfolk. That was the flagship of the destroyer force of the Scouting Fleet. Admiral Sexton was Commander, Scouting Force, commander of the destroyer scouting force.

I reported in at Norfolk and immediately started flying O2U-1 seaplanes, and we were doing gunnery right at the time in seaplanes, gunnery and bombing. From there, we went on down to the ship and then went down to Guantanamo. Immediately, we built that two-plane unit up to the point where it was really the best in gunnery and bombing, fixed machine guns, free machine guns, and dive-bombing. Of any of the units around we got Es in each weapon in intense competition.

We flew down after the first of the year in seaplanes from Hampton Roads to Charleston. I remember we had to refuel at a place called Morehead City, at a commercial fueling pier. It was a cold and miserable day and we flew right off the water most of the time, low flying. We finally got in to Charleston just at dark and were hoisted aboard the ship, and then the ship got under way a day or so following to go down to Guantanamo.

Q: Talking about that procedure, how was it, a crane that picked you up at the ship?

Adm. A.: Yes, you were picked up by a crane, which would service either side as well as the ship's boats. There were two catapults, port and starboard catapults. There were four of us pilots on the ship. There was the senior aviator, I was the No. 2, then there was another lad out of the class behind me, and an enlisted pilot. Four pilots and we had about a nine-man maintenance crew. On board ship we served as regular duty officers, watch officers at sea and ashore, in port. As I mentioned to you, I would also be assigned down there to stand engineering watches. I helped out down there because I was previously qualified.

We went down to Guantanamo and they had a beach over there called Hicacal Beach and they had a little aviation camp. We would go over to Hicacal Beach very early during the day when the ship would go out for gunnery practice and we would do our aviation gunnery training and dive-bombing training down there, based from that beach, just little shacks. We got picnic lunches over there.

In those days, although we would go up to Caimanera, which was the other side of -

Q: That was quite a place, wasn't it?

Adm. A.: Yes. We'd buy our rum there, but when we came back they shifted the flagships and we were transferred from the

Concord to the Raleigh, the same type of ship, same type of duty, but we went over to the Raleigh. On the Raleigh Admiral Leahy was the -

Q: William Leahy?

Adm. A.: William D. Leahy - was the destroyer squadrons commander. He was a pretty good inspirational fellow to have on board. The captain of the ship was Captain McCandless and then a Captain Culp, I guess it was. We entered right into the ship and had a genuine participation in the life of the ship at sea. I think we were all good watch officers.

Q: And that was terribly important to be a part of the team.

Adm. A.: That's right.

We played a lot of bridge on board because there wasn't much night flying in those days, from the cruisers, certainly. Then we were transferred. They shifted the fleet from the Atlantic to the Pacific. We'd gone down to Guantanamo again and then went out to the Pacific. They held the Scouting Fleet out there in the Pacific. We -

Q: Based at San Diego?

Adm. A.: We based ashore at San Diego, at North Island. The first time we were ashore I stayed at the BOQ, then we got together with other young aviators and had a bachelor house over in San Diego. We played a lot of golf, played a lot of bridge, we did a lot of running around, all bachelors, we did a lot of flying, had a very fine gunnery and bombing record, we would embark on the ship occasionally for local ships around, fleet exercises out on the West Coast, up to San Francisco.

I remember one day we were up in San Francisco, Admiral Leahy was still the division force commander, and Ginger Rogers came on board. We saw lots of movie stars. We'd go up to Hollywood, around Los Angeles, and had a heck of a good time.

Q: Sounds like an ideal life.

Adm. A.: It was an ideal life, it really was, with a lot of professional interest, good bachelor life, a lot of fun. That lasted until 1933 when I was due for shore duty and I was then assigned to the Naval Station at Norfolk, Virginia. I turned in a car on the West Coast, got delivery of one in Detroit, then drove on down to Norfolk. I was assigned there to the experimental division at Naval Air Station, Norfolk. Captain Fitch was the commanding officer, Commander Mason was the executive officer -

Q: Charles Mason?

Adm. A.: Charles Mason, an oldtime aviator, I was assigned in this group in the so-called experimental division, which had primary responsibility for carrier-landing tests, roughwater tests, and accelerated-service tests. The main flight test was then located at Anacostia. We'd get the new planes, the experimental planes, and we'd run through these tests. We had a platform out at the corner of old Chambers Field in Norfolk with carrier arresting gear on it, we also had test arresting gear, and we'd go round and round and make one landing after another in this carrier arresting gear, proving hooks, proving the wires and the sets, and also testing the new planes that came down.

The attrition in our group there was very high because there was a number of accidents there. I remember I was sitting in an airplane -

Q: Actually of the testing pilots?

Adm. A.: That's right - I was sitting in a plane to make twelve o'clock flights, and an officer senior to me came down and said would I switch from the twelve o'clock flight to the two o'clock flight, because he wanted to play golf that afternoon. I said, sure, so he got in the plane when I went off to lunch. When I came back, the plane was missing. He'd crashed and been killed.

We had several accidents. The only accident I had at that time was when I was returning an experimental plane to Anacostia, over here, and when I came in to land one side of the landing gear didn't stay down and so it ground-looped.

The only other crash I'd had was right after I'd finished Pensacola. I hit a target and it wrapped round the propeller and caught on fire, and the steel wing, so I had to land on the beach at Lynn Haven Inlet. It was a rough day with a strong wind blowing onshore over a sloping beach, and after I'd made what I thought was a very nice landing, the landing gear on the high side of the beach cracked and the plane tipped over on its back. I rapidly got away, thinking that it might catch on fire, which it did not do. Then my chore was to get the damned airplane

Anderson #1 -45-

off the beach, have it hauled back to the Naval Air Station, and then immediately go up for another gunnery run, the same type of run I was practicing when the collision occurred.

Q: You weren't jolted by that experience?

Adm. A.: No. They, my senior officers got me in the air as rapidly as they could in order to dissipate any apprehension.

Q: As a pilot of that sort, a test pilot, was this a voluntary thing or were you simply assigned?

Adm. A.: Well, you were given the opportunity and you were happy to get it, yes, very happy to get it.

Q: These were the elite, were they not, the test pilots?

Adm. A.: Yes. They wouldn't let you go in to those units unless you had a good reputation, which I had, for gunnery and bombing and my career in cruiser aviation. I guess I had what you'd call a good service reputation.

It was a very interesting period because we had the first single-seat Grumman fighters, the first artificial horizons, and the first controllable-pitch propellers along with many interesting projects which led to the betterment of naval aviation.

Q: This was a new horizon, wasn't it?

Adm. A.: Oh, yes, greatly expanding your opportunities and interest in aviation, which was rapidly improving and taking advantage of technological developments. We maintained close liaison with NACA, over at Langley Field, the forerunner of NASA, and with the people in flight test at Anacostia.

Q: How much time did you spend at Anacostia?

Adm. A.: Very little time, but maintained very close liaison.

That year was 1933. I had become engaged to a lovely girl, Muriel Buttling from Brooklyn. She graduated from Smith College in Northampton, Massachusetts in June. We were married in St. Teresa's Church in Brooklyn which was the parish of both our families. The priest who married us was Father John M. Jacobs, S.J. who was the head master of my old prep school. My best man was my close friend John Walsh who after graduating from Holy Cross College studied law at Fordham University. That year I got married and we came down to Norfolk right after our honeymoon at the Farmington Country Club in Charlottesville, Virginia. I had previously rented an apartment in the Meadowbrook Apartments on Hampton Boulevard right opposite the country club, fifty-five dollars a month, partly furnished, five dollars a week for a maid, a good-looking automobile. We would go to dances at the country club every Saturday night played a lot of bridge, played a lot of golf. There was a lot of interesting flying, and a good social life on the station.

Captain Aubrey W. Fitch, the commanding officer, was a very distinguished officer. There was good morale on the station. We met a lot of people in Norfolk itself. Membership in the country club was cheap. It was a very good life as a married gentleman officer, you might say.

Q: But you weren't completely unaware that the Depression had set in?

NOTE: The typist did not use #47 in re-typing the MS.

I had had a real good life there as a naval aviator bachelor but the contrast in going into married life was very, very pleasant there at our Norfolk Naval Air Station. Prohibition was still in effect, but they had the bootleggers in the area who would come in and liquor was plentiful. We got a Norfolk "corn" at a reasonable price of good quality. The officers, I think, lived quite well. They had good respect from the community, good social life, interesting duty, interesting flying, good rapport with the navy as a whole, and I would say that morale was generally high in spite of the Depression.

Q: You did say something about the new type planes coming in. There were a lot of things on stream at that point.

Adm. A.: That's right. Let me give you an example of that.

One of the projects I had down there was the XF2F-1, which was the first single-seat Grumman fighter, with retractable landing gear, a biplane. I had been assigned for the accelerated service of that airplane and the first production airplane being produced, I guess it was on the order of about twenty-seven of them by Grumman.

I remember at Christmas time each one of the pilots would get a case of champagne sent down to him by Grumman, which we had no hesitance about accepting. We accepted it with appreciation. They sent it with appreciation and respect. There was nothing asked for it in any way.

Q: No permanence about it, either!

Adm. A.: No. Oh, God that would be horrible today. They would call it bribing test pilots. It was nothing of the sort. It was just that they appreciated what we were doing, putting their planes through flight tests, accelerated-service tests and always at some personal hazard.

I had this particular project and so when my tour of duty came to an end at the end of two years, in the spring of 1935, I was asked to go - the Bureau of Aeronautics thought it was a good idea to send me to the same squadron that got those first Grumman fighter planes.

Q: Because you knew them so thoroughly?

Adm. A.: I knew them thoroughly. So I went out there to VF-2, which was an enlisted pilots' fighting squadron on the Lexington. The only officers we had in the eighteen-plane squadron were the division leaders. I think there were seven officers for the eighteen-plane squadron, the rest were enlisted pilots, very carefully selected, highly competent enlisted pilots, who were beautiful pilots and chief petty officers. Every good chief petty officer pilot wanted to get in that fighting squadron. They flew from the Lexington based ashore at Coronado. I might add here that shortly before the end of my tour of duty at Norfolk we had our first child, George W. Anderson III, born on 2 April 1935. His mother and baby George went up to show him off to the two families while I drove the car - a Buick Coupe - across continent to Coronado, California. As I recall I left Norfolk on a Wednesday morning and caught the midnight ferry boat from San Diego to Coronado on Saturday night. Later Muriel and the baby son flew from New York to Los Angeles where I met them.

Q: Was King skipper of the Lexington then?

Adm. A.: Yes, Captain E. J. King was skipper of the Lexington. Andy Crinkley was the VF-2's squadron commander. Jocko Clark had been squadron commander of VF-2. Spiv Cunningham, who was later captured by the Japanese at Wake Island, was the executive officer. Real good officers, the seven. I was the maintenance officer and I flew 2 Fox 7, which was the third section of the first division of an eighteen-plane squadron.

The carrier squadron did all training at North Island at the Naval Air Station San Diego. We would embark from time to time on the Lexington for at sea periods and fleet exercises. It was a very interesting tour of duty. We did very well in gunnery although the only armament those planes had were 30-caliber machine guns. They had no bomb racks, no 50-caliber guns. The plane was fine as a flying machine but was rapidly superseded by the F-3F because it had 50-caliber guns, which were needed rather than the 30-caliber.

At the end of that tour of duty I was about to be plucked out of that squadron and sent as the landing signal officer on the Lexington when I got orders back to Norfolk to be the landing signal officer of the new carrier Yorktown. The Yorktown was commissioning and her squadrons being assembled back there. I guess I was ordered to the Yorktown because Commander C. P. Mason, who had been the executive officer at Norfolk when I was in carrier flight testing at Norfolk was assigned as the first executive officer of the Yorktown. He made his way up to

Washington and got me assigned as landing signal officer there, rather than to the Lexington, where I would have gone anyway as a landing signal officer.

So, at the end of that tour in VF-2, I remember taking my exams for promotion from junior lieutenant to lieutenant, while I was living in Coronado at 742 "c" Avenue in a nice cottage. A very pleasant life for a married person. Actually there was not too much family separation away from home. When the ship made its cruise down to Panama, my wife and first child made a trip through Panama, she was coming back to the East Coast because I had already received orders to go back to Norfolk, to the Yorktown.

King was the skipper of the Lexington.

Q: Tell me about him.

Adm. A.: Oh, he was a very, very capable captain. He used to interfere a lot with the activity of the flight deck, so to speak. There were lots of amusing stories about King and the people in the air department. They felt that King was unduly interfering with the operations of the flight deck, which he was -

Q: He didn't want to miss anything!

Adm. A.: He didn't miss a thing, but he was a very capable officer even then, but with the reputation of being a tough son of a bitch. At the same time, he did go around a lot, at Coronado, in that area, you know, in social activities, and he was quite a heavy drinker at those times. He liked the gals. But a very capable officer, there's no doubt about it.

When we got back to the Yorktown, which was scheduled for reasonably early commissioning - they were assembling the squadrons and I had the primary job of training the pilots for landing on board. Then there was a major difficulty with the engineering of the new ship, with the reduction gears. They were too noisy. And so the ships were delayed while they reworked the gears for both the Yorktown and the Enterprise, her sister ship. However, the squadrons continued being formed and being trained there at Norfolk and I worked with all of those squadrons. I also ran what they call the utility unit of the ship, which was composed of a couple of amphibian planes and some O2Us for proficiency flying for the aviators based at Norfolk waiting for the ships to be actually accepted and commissioned.

Then, when it was, we went off on a shakedown cruise, down to the Guantanamo area -

Q: How many planes did you take?

Adm. A.: We had a complement of seventy-three planes, four squadrons, a dive-bomber squadron, a torpedo squadron, and two fighter squadrons - no, two dive-bomber squadrons, a scouting squadron, VB, VT, and one fighter squadron. The group commander was Miles Browning, who had quite a reputation as a pretty able flying officer - not so good in his personal character and his marital affairs, but he was pretty good pilot and officer on duty.

We went down to Guantanamo trained up, came back, and went into post-shakedown repair. Then we took off again with the Enterprise, which had the same four types of planes, and went down and finally went over to Panama to join with the carriers from the Pacific Fleet for exercises. Admiral King was Commander, Air Force, Pacific Fleet, by then. Admiral Halsey was the commander of our division of the Yorktown and Enterprise with his flag flying in Yorktown.

Q: That was a great fleet exercise, wasn't it?

Adm. A.: That was quite an exercise in the Caribbean area. I was the landing signal officer during flight operations and stood officer of the deck watches both at sea and in port.

Q: Wasn't it a simulated attack on the canal or something of the sort?

Adm. A.: That was not the particular fleet exercise of which I'm sure you're thinking, but we operated down in the South Atlantic and I remember they had the air group out there one day, then the weather deteriorated and they had no field that they could go to. The stern of the ship was bouncing up and down fifty five or sixty feet and the poor air officer, later Admiral Sprague, "Ziggy" Sprague, was wondering how the hell we were ever going to get them back on board without a lot of crashes, but we got them all back without even blowing a tire that day.

Q: What kind of arresting gear did you have at that point?

Adm. A.: I forget the mark number of this gear, but seven wires across the deck, and of course heavy wire barriers. There were no angled decks at that time.

Q: No, no, I realize that.

Adm. A.: It was hydraulic arresting gear.

We had wonderful officers in the complement of the Yorktown on the flight deck and in the air department, most of whom survived to much more responsible and higher rank as time went on.

The Yorktown (CV-5) was 100 per cent regular officers and enlisted men in contrast with the second Yorktown (CV-10) when I was assigned to her commissioning crew and we had such a preponderance of new people in the navy, reserves and a very small percentage of regular officers and enlisted men.

When the Yorktown and Enterprise joined the fleet in 1938 the Navy was developing at that time what you might call air group tactics, combined tactics, and also the operation of several carriers in the same formation. We had some amusing experiences with that whole setup. Admiral Halsey, as I say, was our division commander and, of course, being ship's officers we had to stand officer of the deck watches at sea and in port, the aviators I mean, just the same as everybody else did. There again I found that my previous experience, having been an aviator ship's officer on a cruiser, was extremely valuable in adapting to the officer functions as distinguished from the naval aviation functions on the carrier itself.

With Admiral Halsey we came in to St. Thomas and he sent word down - I was the officer of the deck and was coming to anchor watch - that Pat Mulcahy, who was a Marine friend of his and had command of the Marine station down there in St. Thomas, would be coming aboard and for me to render him honors. Well,

Pat Mulcahy's boat came out and the coxswain held up four fingers, which indicated the level of honors, so I had four sideboys formed up and the guard of the day. Halsey came down and said, "Hell, no, two." Here was my boss, an admiral, saying "two" and the coxswain of the boat saying "four." I was looking at him and I saw these silver leaves on his uniform. Halsey said "Two, two." So I sent away two of the sideboys, chased away the guard of the day, and up came Pat Mulcahy with silver leaves on his shirt collar. I was convinced of it. But the admiral greeted him and took him up to the cabin.

So I sent the quartermaster of the watch up. I said:

"You go up there, look in the admiral's cabin, and tell me whether the visitor has gold leaves on his collars or silver."

He came back and said silver. I said, "Well, that's four sideboys. Look it up in the Regulations." Four sideboys, guard of the day. So, getting ready for the departure, they sent word down that he was leaving. I had four sideboys and the guard of the day there. Down the long ladder inside of the hangar deck with Admiral Halsey and Mulcahy coming down. Halsey looks over and waved them away. I reluctantly chased the guard of the day away, two of the sideboys away, and "Major" Mulcahy, Pat Mulcahy, went over the side.

By that time I was really confused in my own mind. The admiral's orderly came down a little while later and said:

"Will the officer of the deck call his relief and report to the admiral's cabin."

I thought, Jeez, "I've really got my neck in a noose. I went up to the admiral's cabin. I could hear the shower run, the shower shut off, Admiral Halsey stuck his head out of the shower with a towel around him and said:

"Andy, I'm sorry. I'm sorry as hell. I really fucked up your honors. I'll never do that again. I just never thought that Pat Mulcahy could be a lieutenant colonel."

Q: That was honest, anyway, wasn't it?

Adm. A.: Sure was. He was a great guy - Admiral Halsey.

Eventually, we took the Yorktown and Enterprise around to the West Coast and they picked up in the Pacific Fleet there. The squadrons went ashore on the North Island, and the ships stayed in the San Diego area. The Saratoga and Lexington were up in the Long Beach area, the San Pedro area.

About that time I got orders detaching me to go to a patrol squadron up in Seattle, which again shows the rotation of duty, which was very, very valuable.

Q: You speak of the new carriers. They were beginning in the fleet to supplant the battleship, weren't they?

Adm. A.: In our minds (those of the naval aviators) they were.

Q: And the manner in which you used them?

Adm. A.: And the manner in which we used them, and, with these people like Admiral Towers, who had command of the Saratoga at the time, Admiral King, Admiral Frederick Sherman, who later took over, they were just as impressed with the offensive capability, potential capability, of the carrier as even the younger officers were. There was getting to be more offensive armament on the airplanes themselves. They had initially 30-caliber guns, then they got up with 50-caliber guns and carrying bombs and rockets. So there was a whole increase of the offensive power of the fleet in aviation, which they had not had before. Although the capabilities had been envisaged earlier, in these attacks like on the canal and earlier exercise attacks on Pearl Harbor on a Sunday morning, when Admiral Yarnell and Admiral Towers, who was his chief of staff, Admiral Forrest Sherman, Admiral Radford, they were all on Admiral Yarnell's staff. They had a great deal of imagination and great skill in developing tactics.

So, by the time the war began, later, the capability had been envisaged and was coming along pretty well.

I remember arriving up in Seattle - we drove up, my wife and two children at that time (my daugher Mary Annette, Nan, had been born in March in 1938) - we had a pleasant drive up the coast to Seattle, reported in to a patrol squadron of P2Ys, which was scheduled to receive PBYs, as an expansion of patrol aviation. Those squadrons up in Seattle were based at Sand Point on Lake Washington and they were sent on rotation, without dependents, up to Sitka and Kodiak, and had some of the patrol functions, the scouting functions of the patrol squadrons.

There was a very elaborate schedule laid out for the re-equipment of the squadrons with PBYs, Catalinas.

I reported aboard and I remember my squadron commander, Dave Johnson told me Sand Point was the last outpost of serene aviation left in the navy. When the circus came to town, they would secure the squadron. We would do a great deal in the way of night flying, instrument flying, greatly to improve our capability in that regard, with a long way to go.

Then the war broke out in Europe and we immediately went out patrolling in the northwest Pacific. We didn't know what we were supposed to do but we were out there patrolling, anyway.

Q: What was your range of patrolling?

Adm. A.: Oh, we'd fly around three or four hundred miles, I guess. Of course, the planes could fly from Seattle to Sitka. We were waiting to get the newer PBYs, which had a greater range capability.

While I was there, the war had broken out in Europe, and in the spring of 1940 I got orders to report to the Navy Department in the Plans Division of the Bureau of Aeronautics in the key job for a younger officer there, called Programs and Allocations, to relieve Commander P. D. Stroop (later Vice Admiral) which was the key job that justified the appropriations for airplanes and allocated and assigned where they'd be bought and things of that sort.

Q: How long were you in Seattle?

Adm. A.: I was there, oh, I guess a total of about nine months. It was a short tour of duty.

Q: Did you get up to Sitka?

Adm. A.: No, I didn't because it was due to rotate after I'd left. I had moved up. I'd become executive officer of a six-plane patrol squadron.

I was ordered back to the Bureau of Aeronautics. I came back and relieved Admiral, then Commander, Stroop two weeks before the Germans went through France. In other words, a whole acceleration of the war from the U.S. point of view - the expansion of lend-lease programs, our own aviation programs expanded. We were then working on a 2,500-plane program which was to be expanded to a 3,000-plane program, and we went up to 10,000, 15,000, 25,000, really an unlimited program.

Q: That's probably a good place to stop.

Adm. A.: That's just what I was going to suggest.

Interview No. 2 with Admiral George W. Anderson, U.S. Navy
(Retired)

Place: His apartment in the Watergate Apartments, Washington, D.C.

Date: Thursday morning, 19 June 1980

Subject: Biography

By: John T. Mason, Jr.

Q: Well, Sir, it's nice to see you again this morning and to resume this fascinating story. Last time, when we broke off, you were leaving your assignment out in Seattle and you came back to Washington to go into BuAer and into the plans division. This was in April of 1940. So, will you take up the story at that point?

Adm. A.: Yes. I arrived in Washington and immediately started house-hunting. Fortunately, we were able to stay with my good friend and classmate, Don (later Admiral) Griffin, who was on duty at the Naval Air Station, Anacostia. We looked around various parts of Washington and fortunately found a brand-new house just completed in the northwest section, on Upton Street, 3634 Upton Street. It was beautifully located and actually across the street from me lived Admiral Ramsey, then Captain Ramsey, who was the head of the plans division in the Bureau of Aeronautics, for whom I was going to work. We had very attractive neighbours and I think I paid $18,500 for the house and it's worth probably

$350,000 now (1982). Unfortunately, I sold it when I was the chief of naval operations for about $45,000.

Q: You couldn't have anticipated all of these -

Adm. A.: That's right.

In any event, I reported in to the Bureau of Aeronautics to relieve Commander P. D. Stroop, a class ahead of me at the Naval Academy, a naval aviator and a very good friend, who retired as Vice Admiral Stroop. This position was called the Office of Programs and Allocations, which really worked directly for the chief of the Bureau of Aeronautics, Admiral John H. Towers, a great pioneer in naval aviation. Of course, Admiral (then Captain) Ramsey was the head of the plans division at the time. This desk had the responsibility for formulating the aircraft programs and then supervising, through the regular materiel divisions of the Bureau of Aeronautics, actual procurement. By tradition, I accompanied the chief of the bureau to the Congress in the justifying of all the papers and therefore had to appear with him regularly before the House Naval Affairs Committee, the Senate Naval Affairs Committee -

Q: Vinson and Walsh, at that time?

Adm. A.: Vinson and Walsh - and also before the Appropriations Committee of both the Senate and the House. It was a very, very busy job, but I had available, as I took over, one civilian assistant, a chap by the name of Bill Kesmodel, and one secretary. That desk sat just next to the aircraft requirements desk in the plans division, which was headed at that time by Commander A. B. Vosseller, late Vice Admiral Vosseller. They would specify the requirements in quality, depending on the types of aircraft that were being available or recommended by the engineering division of the bureau of Aeronautics, and I would formulate the number that we needed and reconcile that with the possibility of the appropriations. The cost would be given to us, including the spare parts and so forth, and we would go up eventually to get the appropriations, and then, with the approval of the chief of the bureau, we would decide the orders and they would be contracted for by the regular divisions of the Bureau of Aeronautics.

Q: What was the general attitude of the Congress at that point? They were being influenced, I imagine, by the situation in Europe—

Adm. A.: The attitude particularly of Carl Vinson and Senator Walsh was one of doing everything we could to prepare the military forces of the United States, with considerable emphasis on the navy, including naval air, and, to some extent, although we weren't involved with them much, with the air corps of the army, the army air corps. As a matter of fact, Congressman Vinson had proposed a program for training 50,000 pilots, which was a tremendous magnitude of thinking in those days.

Q: Was that in 1940?

Adm. A.: This was in 1940 when he said that's what we were going to have to have and therefore we should get ready for it.

Two weeks after I reported and relieved P. D. Stroop, the Germans went through the Low Countries and France. As a result, the whole situation and attitude of the Congress as well as the president was stimulated and great expansion in our planning took place. I've outlined in this memorandum which, fortunately, you've located and of which I might be able to find a copy later on what the status of the aviation program was at this particular time. I think it was a 2,500-plane program and was being, with a laborious amount of red tape, processed through the system to be increased to a 3,000-plane program. Shortly after that, why, sights were set higher and it was made up to a 10,000 plane program and later on it went to 15,000 and then practically unlimited. (Memorandum in Appendix)

Q: The president somewhere along the line made a very startling speech, didn't he?

Adm. A.: That was later.

Q: Oh, later?

Adm. A.: Yes. In any event, it became very apparent that we were going to have to greatly expand our naval aviation as well as the navy. The total programs at that time were being formulated, navy programs, in the Office of the Chief of Naval Operations, then Admiral Stark, and had to be considered by the General Board of the navy and then would go up to the secretary of the navy, and, of course, to the White house, where Mr. Roosevelt had a great deal of personal interest.

Q: Let me ask what role the General Board actually played in this? Was it just to give approval after examining it or what?

Adm. A.: Well, they had some very definite ideas of their own of what they should have. Now, at that time there was the question, as always, about the role of the aircraft carrier, the patrol planes, the types of airplanes that the country would need, the navy would need. There was a great deal of emphasis on what was called inshore patrol. They envisaged a large number of small aircraft to patrol our coasts. As a point of fact, in retrospect they had no real utility in the war, as it developed.

The next major development was a very secret mission which was sent over by the British with some outstanding officers of intermediate rank, fairly high, to do planning with representatives of the Joint Board, army-navy board, and Admiral Ramsey, my boss, was one of the members of that planning board. He was a captain and Kelly Turner was another one. What they did was formulate a joint plan that was ultimately called Rainbow 5, which would delineate the major objectives of the United States and Great Britain in the event that the United States became involved in the war, and it did envisage a war against Japan and the Axis powers, and, of course, the major determining decision was that the first objective was to win against the Axis powers and we would take a strategic defensive against Japan. It was not envisaged that we were going to have a Pearl Harbor to change the situation as markedly as it did, nor did it really envisage the tremendous resurgence of American public support for the military that flowed from the debacle at Pearl Harbor. But, again, we're back in 1940 when this planning was initiated and carried on into 1941.

It was very tightly held from a security basis, as you can well imagine.

Q: What a curious title, Rainbow 5.

Adm. A.: I guess this was the one that was evolved from a series of plans. They had had color plans, Orange against the Japanese, Red against others, so this was a combination of opponents and they call it Rainbow, and then I guess the fifth approximation, Rainbow 5, was ultimately adopted. This was put into effect basically but it was locked in a safe on the Sunday when Pearl Harbor occurred and they couldn't get the safe open until Monday!

This development of the program, every airplane had to be earmarked for a specific spot, and normally you would buy 50 per cent spare aircraft, replacement aircraft, and spare parts to take care of the airplanes for the first few years of their life.

Q: Real consideration was given to spare parts?

Adm. A.: Yes, it was in the appropriation, that was included in the original appropriation.

We didn't have too many planes of the type that we ultimately needed in the war under development. We had the Grumman fighters, we had the Douglas dive-bomber, we had a torpedo plane, and the principal emphasis was on patrol seaplanes, Catalinas, PBYs, and the Martin PMs, I guess they were called at that time, PBYs and PMs, the emphasis being on patrol rather than the bomber role. In any event, we had no land patrol planes and we more or less took (with great difficulty in obtaining deliveries) the same type of training planes that were being ordered by the army air corps, which was perfectly reasonable. Originally, we had done our primary training in seaplanes but it became apparent, even at that time, that primary training could better and more economically be accomplished with greater volume in land planes. We did have the naval aircraft factory producing some - they were in Philadelphia and there was a rule by political arrangement that the naval aircraft factory had to produce a certain number, percentage, of planes for the navy -

Q: They were largely flying boats, weren't they?

Adm. A.: No, they were training planes, NYs.

Also we were buying convertible land planes-seaplanes, seaplanes that were used in the cruisers and the battleships. I think they were being built by Curtiss at the time, SOCs they were called, scout-observation and "C" for Curtiss.

The air corps was in a better position. They had a wider variety of airplanes potentially available, fighters, bombers, training planes, the SNJs and basic training planes, and transport planes, the DC, and the DC-4 was under development. They had a wider range and I would say, although they hadn't had sufficient money to do what was necessary to build up a good base, they had had some pretty good thinking behind their programs.

Q: And prototypes?

Adm. A.: Prototypes, yes. We had been limited in what we had in that area. Among the planes we had was a Brewster fighter plane and, of course, the Grumman. Then we were learning lessons from the war in Europe of the need for armored seats, for self-sealing fuel tanks, and the planes we had in service did not incorporate those features at that time so it was necessary to get those adjusted.

Q: I take it that at this point there was already a fair exchange of information with the British?

Adm. A.: Yes. We had our observers over there and, as a matter of fact, we had some pilots go over and actually fly British PBYs. One of my former pilots in the patrol squadron I was in was in the British patrol plane that actually found the Bismarck, in the search for the Bismarck. That brought back an amusing story because my old squadron was flying P2Ys around from the west coast to the east coast and they were down in one of their intermediate stops in Yucatan, I think it was, or Mexico, and when a request for volunteers to go over and serve with the British came through, the squadron commander Skee Erdmann got all the boys together around a few beers and then announced to them and he said, "Of course, you're all going to volunteer, aren't you?" and they naturally did. Well, one of them was a young chap, Ensign Hall, who had just gotten married and his bride was out in Seattle and he was one of those who were selected. So he'd written back and said - he didn't tell the full story that he'd volunteered, he said that he'd been ordered over there. Then that came back through the Congress and caused a little bit of a flap because here they were ordering these people to go over to the war zone and the pacifists were very much against it. Hall finally had to admit to his bride that he was over there by being a volunteer. I don't know whether his marriage eventually hung together or not.

Q: I suppose you'd call that an adjunct of the neutrality patrol!

Adm. A.: That's right, an adjunct to the neutrality patrol.

In any event, we were getting information back on the lessons learned and, of course, one of the big lessons was that we had to have more armament, offensive armament, in all of our aircraft, as well as self-sealing tanks and armor. This required our aircraft manufacturers to redesign the planes we had and the Brewster fighter, for example, just did not measure up. As a result, we determined that we would not procure any more Brewster fighters. Well, you saw a democracy come into action with the lobbyists going forth, and loads of letters would be written to everybody up and down the line. Brewster was located in New Jersey, and all the letters came back to the same desk, which was my desk, and so they'd get the same reply although signed through different sources, different signing officers. But the labor leaders, the manufacturers, the congressmen from New Jersey, the senators from Jersey would all get the same reply. It was the right reply and we didn't hear very much more about that.

Q: Incidentally, what was the status of the aircraft industry at that point? Was it adequate to the new demands?

Adm. A.: Oh, grossly inadequate. It required a tremendous expansion but this expansion was facilitated by the lend-lease program. Also valid orders had been placed by The Netherlands, and they had a very good aircraft program in which they had envisaged getting all these new and modern planes coordinated with a pilot-training program and sending them out to the

Netherlands East Indies. We also had the various incidents that took place of trying to bail out the French, which is a little story in itself, because the French had called up President Roosevelt and he promised assistance. We were told to turn over fifty dive-bombers to the French, Curtiss dive-bombers, and to get them we had to take them from the naval reserve stations. The French were sending over to Halifax in Canada the aircraft carrier Bearn. We called up naval reserve officers and had them fly the planes up to some central point, I think it was Buffalo. There the pilots were demobilized, put on civilian suits, and continued the delivery to the Bearn. The U.S. Navy identification was eliminated in this process. This was being handled by Curtiss for us, and the air craft were delivered on board the Bearn. Unfortunately by that time it was too late and the Bearn then went down to Martinique and the planes remained down there for most of the rest of the war.

Q: Admiral Robert, yes.

Adm. A.: Then we had another case where the Greeks were in dire straits and we had some new Grumman fighters about to be delivered to us where they were badly needed. We were directed to provide those, although we badly needed them for the U.S. Navy, to the Greeks. Grumman jumped in and translated the instruction books into Greek, lettering on the panels, and internal markings of devices were all in Greek, and those planes were sent over to the western desert where, of course, the British took over after Greece had fallen to the Nazis.

A classmate of mine, later Admiral "Cliff" Cooper, was over there on duty as one of our observers with the British Navy and he got them all. He said he never saw such a finely prepared package of aircraft, everything down to all the Greek documents and so forth. Of course, the British couldn't read the Greek and they had to translate them all back. But they were delivered to the British down in Egypt I think it was.

Q: El Alamein, that area?

Adm. A.: They eventually arrived.

Apart from the program side of this desk in the Bureau of Aeronautics, which involved the actual direction of procurement of the aircraft, planning for the procurement, the allocation side reposed on this little desk in the Bureau of Aeronautics, with the assignment of all the aircraft in the navy and the naval reserve to ships and stations and squadrons that were training and about to be commissioned.

Q: That was not an easy task, was it?

Adm. A.: No, it wasn't, and I got a reserve officer to come back to active duty and assist me (Thomas W. Jones 1928 USNA). Then, with two of us there and a civilian assistant, a tremendous amount of work was focused in this particular section of the plans division in the Bureau of Aeronautics, which under present circumstances is handled by dozens of people today and supervised by all the echelons of the Department of Defense and the higher civilian echelons of the Navy Department, I suppose also, the Bureau of the Budget and the General Accounting Office.

Anderson #2 -71-

In any event, it was a tightly knit, hard-working, capable group of people we had, and we worked with a minimum of red tape, a maximum of efficiency, in handling our affiars.

Well, the next side of this period was the evolution of further planning with the British, initially under the lend-lease program and later, of course, during the war. They formed a joint aircraft committee and Admiral Towers, the chief of the Bureau of Aeronautics, was on it and General Arnold, head of the army air corps. They were the two top U.S. representatives.

Q: Who were the top British?

Adm. A.: Sir Richard Fairey, who had been sent over -

Q: Of Fairey Aircraft?

Adm. A.: Originally of Fairey Aricraft - and there were some higher-level groups that were meeting.

Q: Was Sir John Dill on the scene at that point?

Adm. A.: Sir Henry Self was over here at that time, but, in any event, the joint aircraft committee, British-U.S., and I've described this in my memorandum - (Appendix)

Q: In your report, yes, which, incidentally, we'll put as an appendix to your volume.

Adm. A.: Yes - had two major subcommittees: the allocations committee, which was to allocate not only the production and the assignment of new aircraft and inevitably for into the need to expand aircraft production, and the other side was standardization. This work was carried on and I'm sure there's quite a large history of the joint aircraft committee in the files some place.

Q: It's interesting that they were working on standardization at that point.

Adm. A.: That's right and also on the organization of the War Production Board. The exact dates here I'm not certain in my mind at this point, but there was the War Production Board and Mr. Knudsen -

Q: Of General Motors?

Adm. A.: General Motors and Ford. He'd been in the automobile industry. He was quite an individual. Well, we got into such amusing situations, not amusing but serious situations, of matching aircraft engines with air frames and there was a shortage of aircraft engines, and at one meeting Mr. Knudsen in his Danish accent would say, "Vell now, we vant to know how many airplanes you're going to build, how many bombers, how many fighters, how many other kinds of planes?" That starts them all off and he says "Now, who's going to make the engines? How many engines they going to make? The Pratt and Vhitney and Vright until there'll be an engine for every airplane." (I think whether four or single engined airplanes made no difference).

Then, of course, we had arrangements to expand the aircraft industry, which really had gotten under way before Pearl Harbor, but we reached a tremendous peak and acceleration right after Pearl Harbor, when they converted the automobile factories for engines and air frames, greatly expanding the whole production base.

Q: Did federal funds go into that?

Adm. A.: Oh, yes.

When Pearl Harbor occurred, which was, of course, in 1941, aircraft production had been greatly expanded but so were the requirements greatly expanded by that time, and we had very great difficulties meeting the needs, for example, of our training program on the one side and secondly planes for the squadrons that were being refitted or reequipped or were being organized on the other. We made the maximum use of every conceivable aircraft we had and there was tremendous competition for them. We had a good training program but we didn't have enough training planes to go around.

At Pearl Harbor, which occurred on a Sunday afternoon, as you know, I happened to be at the Redskins' football game, as many other people were, and as we came out we knew something was up. I went down to the old Navy Department building on Constitution Avenue - those buildings have been taken down and that area is now The Mall - and went in there late on Sunday afternoon. Everybody was sort of shocked, nobody knew what the whole impact of it was. Secretary Knox was going out to Pearl Harbor the next day, and Admiral Towers told me:

"You know more about what the aircraft situation is than anybody else in the navy. I want you to report to Admiral Stark in the morning, first thing, and stay with him wherever he goes all during the day, stay with him as long as you can help him."

So early the next morning, I did. I reported to Admiral Stark and the first thing I remember was a meeting in his CNO's office, and Admiral Nimitz, who was chief of the Bureau of Navigation at the time, came in, and Admiral Stark said to him, "Well, Chester, what's the news?"

Admiral Nimitz said to Admiral Stark, "Well, I'm sorry to report that Ike Kidd was lost in the Arizona and Mrs. Kidd is in Annapolis. I'd like permission to tell her."

And Admiral Stark said, "Oh, sure, Chester, go ahead."

Admiral Nimitz said, "She's a good navy girl and she'll keep her grief to herself until we can let the news out publicly," and so he did.

But, in any event, later on that morning, I accompanied Admiral Stark to the first meeting of the old "Joint Board," army and navy. It included General Marshall and Admiral Stark, General Arnold was out of town, Tooey Spaatz was pinch-hitting for him, General Gerow, in charge of army plans, and Sherman Miles I think was intelligence. On the navy side were Admiral Horne, Admiral Towers, and Admiral Kelly Turner - there may have been one other person there, and two secretaries of the board. There they discussed what the situation was, what they knew, what they didn't know and their apprehension of the situation that might occur. It was really very apparent that the outstanding individual in the room from the standpoint of calmness and judgment was General Marshall, who had his feet right on the ground. I would say also from a standpoint of good common sense was my own boss, Admiral Jack Towers, who was also a relatively unruffled individual. Of course, Admiral Stark was quite shocked by the tremendous losses we had had at Pearl Harbor, and the concern of whether further raids might be made on Alaska or even on the West Coast, and there were various reports of sightings of Japanese ships or submarines threatening our Pacific coast, and what they would do about the island positions and so forth, all the natural concerns that one would expect after a surprise attack.

After that was over, I went back and Admiral Stark thanked me for my assistance and let me go back to my own job. Normally, the role that I played in advising Admiral Stark on the aviation aspects would have been fulfilled by Commander Forrest Sherman, who was actually in the plans division of the Office of the Chief of Naval Operations, but Commander Sherman had had to make a quick trip up to Ottawa to exchange information and tidy up plans with the Canadians because before Pearl Harbor we had gone through the various stages of enforced neutrality, yet at the same time doing our best to assist the British cope with the submarine threat in the Atlantic. We had established a force, a patrol force of the Atlantic Fleet under Admiral Bristol -

Q: Mark Bristol?

Adm. A.: Mark Bristol - and he had assembled a very fine staff and what forces we had available had moved up into the Newfoundland area and were actually conducting these patrols in the western part of the Atlantic Ocean.

So there were lots of things that had to be done in coordination with the Canadians and Commander Sherman had gone up there, and I kept feeding information to the Office of the CNO almost directly. Admiral Towers had said to "cut out the red tape and deal directly as rapidly as you can. You know what the job is to be done. Do it."

Of course, we immediately were busy trying to expand our own preparations for an all-out war, and we didn't have any more resources really than we did before.

Q: You were galvanized?

Adm. A.: That's right. Admiral Towers was the first navy person to appear before the Congress after Pearl Harbor because he was scheduled to go up before the old House Naval Affairs Committee on Tuesday morning, I guess it was. So I went up with him and some of these congressmen were avid to get the information and, in some cases, throw the harpoons at the military. Some congressman said:

"Now, Admiral what do you mean about this backbone of the fleet having been sunk at Pearl Harbor."

He came back and said:

"You're in error because the backbone of the fleet is in the aircraft carriers and that was at sea."

He said to me: "Now, what do you want?' I said:

"Well, I think we need 500 patrol planes, PBYs, we need 1,000 dive-bombers, we need 1,000 fighters, and we need 100 transports, as the first thing, not pinned down to any particular billets, types, or to any particular assignments."

This was just the first cut that would give expansion in our orders and, therefore, production ultimately, and also provide replacements. It was a rough count but it was a tremendous help to getting everything going because that was fed into one of the bills that was already in process up there.

Q: It was something tangible?

Adm. A.: That's right, and we were authorized to go out and get additional assistance that we might need. I remember I said I needed another officer, and I got a young man, a Princeton graduate, and we brought him in under a program that was initiated by Admiral Towers for air intelligence officers. He could then use various people in the Bureau of Aeronautics to find out who were the outstanding young executives and potential executives that were available, and initially they came largely out of Ivy League colleges in the first cut and they had been sent up to Quonset Point to an air intelligence school. Well, this young officer I got was Oakley Thorne, who came in to me as a junior lieutenant, but he ended up as Admiral Nimitz's flag secretary. We had wonderful people and we couldn't have done the things we did without that fine group of people who came in initially, were available to us initially, right about the time of Pearl Harbor.

Q: Wasn't Gus Read involved in that?

Adm. A.: Gus Read was running that program for Admiral Towers and Admiral Radford.

Q: And Luis de Flores?

Adm. A.: Luis de Flores was instrumental there. He came down and was a great help. I remember I got Luis de Flores's private airplane for the navy - I forgot what type it was but it was a light communications type plane.

We had wonderful people there who came in and helped us carry the load. And, of course, Admiral Radford, then a captain I guess, was put in charge of the aviation training program and he had, later, Admiral Doyle, Artie Doyle, brought in to assist him in the aviation training expansion.

Q: What about the base requirements?

Adm. A.: The base requirements had been prepared before this period because we had had an expansion program that was twofold. The first one was bases in the United States and the second one was bases that we acquired in the destroyer deal, the fifty destroyers for the -

Q: In the Caribbean?

Adm. A.: For the British in the Atlantic.

But we had had the foundations laid for the building up of Jacksonville, Quonset Point, Alameda, they were coming along very well. Then, on the training program, and this went back right about to 1940, early in 1940, we had decided to expand into Texas, in the Corpus Christi area, as well as Pensacola. There was a very definite understanding made on a political line by the congressional delegation from Florida that if it became necessary later on to cut down on the bases Pensacola would be held and the Corpus Christi base area would go by the boards.

Q: Tom Connolly would not have liked that!

Adm. A.: No, but this was one of the realities of the political situation.

Another interesting sidelight in this particular period, Admiral Towers had felt very strongly and the Navy Department wanted to have WAVEs in the navy, and there was very, very strong objection from Senator Walsh. He said never would they have women in the navy again while he was the chairman of the Senate Naval Affairs Committee.

Q: The Bureau of Aeronautics had developed full plans with Joy Hancock?

Adm. A.: That's right, but Admiral Towers knew that I knew Senator Walsh, and I had known Senator Walsh because of his principal assistant, a relative of mine, so he said:

"George, I want you to be sure that you can win over Senator Walsh so that he'll no longer object to having women in the navy."

Q: That was not an easy task!

Adm. A.: Well, about once a week for a long period of time, my friend Joe McIntyre would bring Senator Walsh up to my house on Upton Street and we would sit around and drink Scotch and we'd talk about various things. I'd talk about the needs of the navy and so forth in aviation programs, and each time the main objective was to persuade him of the usefulness of the role of women in the navy. Finally, one night Senator Walsh said:

"All right, I'll withdraw my opposition on the assurance that the morals of these girls will be protected and never will anybody propose that they be sent to ships."

I reported that to Admiral Towers and we got the doggone thing through. Actually, it was the aviation side of the navy that really carried the ball in the testimony because we really had as good a case for them as any part of the navy did at that time.

Q: Men like Nimitz were opposed to them.

Adm. A.: Oh, yes, sure, and I'll never forget later on, when the first three WAVEs arrived in Honolulu when I was out there and it was -

Q: That was later on.

Adm. A.: The three ladies were Winnie Quick, Love and Billy Wild, I forget Love's first name. They were both funny names in the combination, but they came out there, I guess this was in 1944 or 1945 to prepare for WAVEs to "move forward".

During 1942 it was quite obvious that there had to be a great expansion of aviation training. No longer could they train all the European pilots in Europe, in the light of the deteriorating situation over there, and so they had what was called an Allied Training Conference in Ottawa. I was told to go up with Captain Radford, who was the representative for the navy at that conference, because I could handle the aircraft side and advise him on that aspect. There were meetings with the British, the Canadians, some French around, and, of course, the army air corps. It was a tremendous conference. I think I've got a picture of it some place.

Well, right in the middle of it I got a telephone call saying to come back to Washington, that Admiral Towers wanted me right away for something more important. I got back and he said:

"We're leaving for England. Be ready to go tomorrow morning."

Q: This was in April or May of 1942?

Adm. A.: It was - well, it was just before the Battle of Midway, after the Coral Sea but before Midway.

Hap Arnold, General Arnold, had arranged the transportation over in a Boeing Stratocruiser. It didn't go very high in the air but it was one of the few long-range transports taken over from commercial usage.

Q: It was pressurized, wasn't it?

Adm. A.: No, it wasn't pressurized to any extent.

We went over to Bolling Field and took off from there to go to Canada and Newfoundland and then on over to Prestwick. I was with Admiral Towers and Major Vandenberg, Hoyt Vandenberg, later chief of staff of the air force, was with Hap Arnold. Generals Dwight Eisenhower and Mark Clark were aboard, a British air marshal from the delegation here -

Q: Who was that? Slessor?

Adm. A.: No, this was Air Marshal Ewell, and a British naval officer, Commander Jackson, were aboard, and a few other people.

We started off and we got up to Goose Bay and I remember at the end of a runway there there was a big moose at the end of this runway. We got in there, miserable facilities, and found out that they couldn't make any progress because there weren't enough nails to do the construction work. Admiral Towers told them who to get in touch with to get an urgent shipment of nails up there.

Then we started out to fly across the Atlantic. We got, I guess, about halfway across and found out that the winds were so strong that we couldn't make it, so we had to turn around and come back. We flew back about a hundred feet off the water with a load of ice on our wings, got into Gander -

Q: What a flight and what a cargo!

Adm. A.: Yes. We had to wait for a change in the wind and for the crew to rest up, and that day, I remember, they went out and shot skeet and we played poker and bridge, and finally we got going again. That time the wind had changed all right but the driftmeter in the plane had stuck and about the time we thought we were going to see Prestwick, where we were to land, why, it became apparent that we were way off course to the north and far far east. We had to make about a 120-degree turn and eventually got back in to Prestwick. There they reported that London was fogged in, but we had to get down there because they were to meet with the prime minister the next morning, so we had to go down by train. Being the junior one in the party - I was a lieutenant commander at the time, I was entrusted with the responsibility of paying for the tea and biscuits in the morning, which was the equivalent of a pullman fare. We were given the tickets except for the cost of the tea and biscuits.

We got in and were met. Admiral Towers was the guest of the British Navy and we stayed at the Dorchester Hotel, were nicely accommodated in a suite, and he had a British naval aide, a young chap by the name of Dennison, I think it was, no Tennyson, who was related to the old poet. He had put a torpedo in the Bismarck actually, from one of the British carriers. He was assigned as an aide and he'd been given some money to take care of our expenses for the admiral and I'd been given some money to pay the expenses that we might incur over there from the U.S. side. The admiral was always taken care of, so we entertained ourselves quite properly by using each other's funds.

Another amusing sidelight on that trip was that Alan Kirk was the naval attaché in London at the time and he told me:

"Obviously, you've had some expense. You've taken care of this mixed bag of people, paying their way down to London out of your own pocket. Let me know how much it was and I'll arrange to have you reimbursed." Here was army and navy and British and a civilian or so. I went in there the next day and he said, "Here's some money. Just sign this, sign the voucher, incidental expenses pertaining to operations against the enemy. This is the only way we can do it without a lot of red tape."

Q: Was Stark over there by that time?

Adm. A.: Yes, Stark was over there at that time.

Well, during the course of this meeting, which was really

to get an amicable allocation of aircraft between the United States and the British because Marshal Slessor had been over before and he had worked out with General Arnold, principally, and also with Admiral Towers' participation, a broad allocation of aircraft which did not satisfy the desires of either the RAF or the army air corps. They were the ones principally concerned because we were in reasonably good shape for the navy, except in the case of training planes, where we had lots of problems filling our needs there.

In any event, we met at 10 Downing Street with the Prime Minister, Mr. Churchill -

Q: This was your first meeting with him?

Adm. A.: This was my first personal meeting.

Q: Yes, that's what I mean.

Adm. A.: That reminds me of an amusing situation. But, in any event, he went down the list, and he was pretty well briefed on everything, and he went down first on bombers, then he went on into fighters, then he came on down to transports, and Admiral Towers said:

"I think Lieutenant Commander Anderson can probably give you the best information on that because he knows more about it than any of us do." And I said:

"The simple problem is you say you want transports, you want bombers, you want your cake and eat it, too. There are four-engine airplanes, four engine sea planes, if you want more four-engine transports you've got to give up some four-engine bombers. They are just not enough engines to go around."

Well, it worked out all right in the general allocation and there was no final head-banging and so forth. As we got up, old Winston turned around to me and said:

"Young man, you realize I established the rank of lieutenant commander in His Majesty's navy."

We'd been in the British naval war room and they had plotted on the board there all the deployments of U.S. ships, and they had the Lexington up there on the plot. They didn't know then that the Lexington had been sunk in the Battle of the Coral Sea. They didn't have the information on that.

Q: Their intelligence was not up to date?

Adm. A.: Not on that. But we got called back. President Roosevelt wanted Arnold and Towers and Eisenhower back in Washington as soon as possible. On the way back we picked up Lord Mountbatten, who was coming over -

Q: In the same plane going back?

Adm. A.: In the same plane going back, yes. Also Averill Harriman.

The President wanted them back in Washington because the Battle of Midway was developing and he didn't know what was going to happen. Of course, no one did.

There was another major problem that the navy had because it quite rapidly appeared to me getting in this programming business and working with Commander Sherman, who was up in the war plans division of the chief of naval operations, and Commander Duncan, who was there -

Q: Wu Duncan?

Adm. A.: Wu Duncan, and Captain Sallada, who had gone in to replace Captain Ramsey as the head of plans. But to do our job in convoying and antisubmarine warfare, as you well know, the submarine threat was an increasing menace to us, losses were increasing all the time, the navy had to have land patrol planes, and this was steadily fought over by the army air corps, as a straight partyline, so to speak. Yes, we could perhaps have them if it was agreed that it was in our role to have the land planes, but only after the need for bombing aircraft had been adequately fulfilled.

Well, we eventually worked out a deal for some PV aircraft made by one of our manufacturers, Lockheed, I guess it was, for us to get some. Finally, it took Admiral King and General Marshall getting into the act. Marshall, of course, was supporting the army air corps, but it got up to the top level and I guess probably President Roosevelt had really gotten into it at one point. The principle was established that we could get the land planes, and specifically the PVs, to meet the antisubmarine requirements of the navy, which was a tremendous breakthrough.

Then, of course, we expanded that to get production of the PB4Y which was a version of the Liberator bomber B-24 converted to patrol plane use to give us longer-range patrol planes. That was the big breakthrough of getting adequate patrol aircraft suitable to the task for the U.S. Navy and it has held ever since.

Q: Let me ask you, was Admiral King satisfied with the London arrangements because it seemed to put the emphasis on supplies for Europe rather than anything for the Pacific?

Adm. A.: Well, we were always faced with the U.S. Army's view and the British view of the emphasis on Europe versus the Pacific. But we were also, I would say, pretty skillful in meeting the essential needs, you might say, what we had to have to keep going.

Now, in 1942 King had with Nimitz, Nimitz having gone out to the Pacific, had put through the operation for Guadalcanal, and inadequate preparations for the logistic support, particularly in replacement aircraft, of which there were very, very few at that stage of the game, had not been made because they had such tight security that I, the guy who was supposed to allocate aircraft was not clued in on even the existence of that prospective operation. Someone had said, "Well, they can do that afterwards," after it becomes known. Well, to put planes in a pipeline that long and arrange for their transportation, to get them and arrange for their transportation, takes about six weeks lead time, and we'd lost that. As a result, they would really have strapped down to a shortage of aircraft out there. That was the fault of our own particular system rather than the question you raised of whether there was too much emphasis on Europe to support that. That was the inadequacy of our implementation of plans in the United States.

You've got to see in any operation, that enough people are cleared on the essentials of it to make sure that you don't run into a precarious position by overemphasis on security at the expense of logistics.

Q: That was a continuing problem with the navy, wasn't it?

Adm. A.: Yes, and I think it carries forward at times today, hopefully not to the degree as bad as it was.

Q: King was so adamant on this subject.

Adm. A.: Oh, King was very adamant on security.

When you are in a war, particularly in the early phases of a war, no matter how good you think your planning is, you must be prepared for the unforeseen actions of the enemy. He has a lot of initiatives and you can depend upon it that he has some pretty bright people. This applied in my thinking at the time, particularly to the adequacy of aircraft production, not putting all your eggs in one basket. You had to have a broad enough base to take care of unforeseen developments, particularly so if the enemy would be able to destroy some of our plant facilities or engine-making facilities, where we'd be completely stymied. We had to have duplicate facilities. In our planning we tried to have alternative sources of production for the things we needed, most needed, such as fighters, torpedo planes, dive-bombers for our carriers, and patrol planes. Inevitably, this led to a point a little later on where it appeared that we might have too much potential production and, therefore, we might not be able to kill the last Japanese with the last bullet of the last plane off the production line. In other words, the cost-analysis that we'd like to have.

Q: That was McNamara's argument.

Adm. A.: Well, we also had a few but not as bad as McNamara.

In any event, we did have in our navy programs, we arranged to get Grumman and Vought fighters, the F6F and the F4U. We had two sources of Grumman fighters. We had the Grumman's own manufacturing and General Motors made Grummans, and in dive-bombers we had Douglas and we had Curtiss, for patrol planes we had Consolidated and we had Martin.

Q: North American was on the scene, too, wasn't it?

Adm. A.: North American was producing planes primarily for the army air corps and the RAF.

But this is the important thing, you've got to have enough of a base so that if production is interfered with by some condition, whether it's the enemy's action, sabotage, strikes, or whatever it may be, you're not going to have your pipeline cut off sharply without any alternative source. I find today, and I found it when I was CNO, a great lack of appreciation by people of what actually happens when you're in a war as far as production facilities and requirements are concerned. We have today nobody in a civilian or a military capacity in the army, navy or air force in the Defense Department who is presently in a responsible position who was in a position of responsibility at the time of and prior to the early phases of World War II, because they've all gone away and so many of these people have been so busy for so many years that they are completely unaware of some of the problems that you run into in those particular times, and they can be very, very difficult to solve.

I remember walking down, later on, to give a lecture at the Armed Forces Staff College and the commandant, who was walking beside me, said: "Admiral, do you realize that nobody in this audience, in the student body, was even in the Korean War, much less World War II?"

This is the situation we've got, so it's very important that, somehow or other, in our educational system, people be able to learn and profit by the lessons of such an experience as World War II or later wars. Even in our war colleges today, they're so busy talking about political affairs, elements of national power, that they don't get down to the nuts and bolts of how are you going to take care of these things.

Going back to the immediate aftermath of Pearl Harbor, which, as you know, occurred on Sunday, 7 December, at Christmas time, who arrived over here but Winston Churchill and Lord Beaverbrook. They were staying at the White House and they were going to resolve all the problems, because they were particularly apprehensive that King, Admiral King, and the Navy Department were influenced (with the indignation that the American people had) to put greater emphasis on the war in the Pacific than the war in Europe, so Churchill was very anxious to pin things down at the White House.

So he came over with Lord Beaverbrook and stayed at the White House, and President Roosevelt had Harry Hopkins up there. I guess, from what we heard, they were kind of fed up with Churchill keeping after them and changing the hours and so forth-

Q: He was a night owl, was he?

Adm. A.: The president was going up before the Congress with

a dramatic program in January, greatly to expand our aircraft production and enunciating the requirements that we had. He wanted 50,000 planes in 1942 and 100,000 planes in 1943 and this we were going to produce.

Q: That was a startling figure.

Adm. A.: This had started with what is the maximum capacity of the production facilities in the United States, and they had added in production facilities that included spare parts and everything else, and they wanted it rounded off to a round figure, which was 50,000 and 100,000, but that included the spare parts. This evolved from a New Year's Eve conversation between Roosevelt, Hopkins, Beaverbrook, and Churchill, in which they, more or less, had gotten together with Roosevelt over a good many drinks, I guess, to round out these dramatic figures. A couple of days later, these had filtered down to Admiral Towers' office and Admiral Towers sent for me, and I looked at them and said:

"My God, they've included the spare parts. It should be less." He said, "How much?" and I said, I think, 10,000 less in 1942 and 25,000 less in 1943. He said:

"Well, we'll get that word up there."

Well, what the hell did they do? They increased the numbers instead of subtracting! They increased it, but it still went in and this was the big objective that was presented to the world, I think it went round -

Q: And it was really startling!

Adm. A.: It was really startling, to all of us, too, and this was then to be implemented, you see. Fortunately, I don't think they ever got to those levels, but they spent an awful lot up there on this broad statement.

Churchill was very broad-brush and very demanding and very annoying and irritating at times. I remember on this trip over to England that I was talking about--this aide and I were entertaining each other while the admiral was off being with the high rank. In the morning I'd get up, go into his room, and say, "Admiral, what would you like for breakfast? You could have this or that," which was the same thing, and he'd say:

"Geez, you look as though you've had a hard night." I said, "I sure have."

He and General Arnold were invited to Chequers for the weekend. They went up to spend the weekend, and they were rooming together. Well, they were old, old friends, contemporaries at West Point and the Naval Academy. They were getting ready to go down to dinner and Admiral Towers was in the single bathroom tying his bow tie and Hap Arnold turned the key in the lock. Well, Admiral Towers, not to be outmaneuvered in this thing, couldn't get the door open and there was no bell to ring, so he went out of the window and down the drainpipe -

Q: In his skivvies!

Adm. A.: Well, in his black uniform and bow tie. But in any event, after dinner, a long dinner, much to drink, Churchill wanted them for the movies, and Admiral Towers told me just before the lights went out the butler brought in a table with a decanter next to the prime minister with a full decanter of brandy. After the movie was over, very early in the morning, the brandy decanter was empty and the prime minister wanted to talk some more. So, he said, we had to stay up most of the night talking.

When I met him at the train on Monday morning, I looked at him and said:

"Admiral you look as though you've had a hard weekend." He said:

"I sure as hell did!"

Oh, there were many, many incidents that were told over the period that I was in the Bureau of Aeronautics. We were gradually meeting, with difficulty, the requirements that were put on us, if we had enough warning, which was not the case in the Guadalcanal situation.

In 1943 Admiral Towers had been transferred to the Pacific in command of the Naval Air Forces Pacific and what they felt was absolutely necessary, and it was, they had to have a senior naval aviator in command of Air Force, Pacific Fleet, ashore, because you couldn't have them running around on these secret operations, Halsey or whoever they had out there trying to run the increasingly complicated logistics of the whole aviation operation in the Pacific from a carrier out at sea conducting operations. You had to have what we now know as the type commander in the Pacific ashore. He'd been sent out and Admiral John Sidney McCain had been brought back from Guadalcanal to replace him as chief of the Bureau of Aeronautics. Captain (later Admiral)

Ralph Davison had replaced Admiral Ramsey as the vice chief of the Bureau of Aeronautics, and Captain Sallada, was the head of the plans division in the Bureau of Aeronautics. Admiral McCain, having just come out of the Guadalcanal situation and never liking any desk work, anyway, used to go up to the Army and Navy Club to play pinochle.

Q: Sounds like his son!

Adm. A.: Yes - and Captain Davison, who was a little bit unstable at times and would tipple a little bit too much, would wander off, and poor old Captain Sallada was holding the fort and I had something or other urgent. I went up to Miss Bacon, the secretary, the elderly, ladylike secretary in the Bureau of Aeronautics, and said, "Where's Admiral McCain?" She said, "I don't know." I said, "Where's Captain Davison?" "I don't know."

I went in to Captain Sallada and I said:

"Captain, you're the senior one here, this is urgent, it's got to be signed."

He said, "Well, how about Admiral McCain?" I said:

"He's not here. Do you know where Captain Davison is?" He said, "No, but if I knew I'd go join him!"

Admiral McCain was invited to accompany Secretary Knox on a trip to the South pacific, to Honolulu. He was going down first to Corpus Christi, and then he got the message to join the secretary and go to Honolulu, and I was going with him down to Corpus Christi, Pensacola and Corpus Christi, and we went on out to San Francisco and got on one of the old PanAm clippers, and flew out to Honolulu. Then Secretary Knox decided he would also go down to the South Pacific and we went along there. We started out in a four-engined patrol plane, a P2Y. I think we had seven of them which had been included in the program that was formulated originally before the war. These were not very good planes and they hadn't been adequately proven at that time, but they assigned two to take the party on down and the first one, with Admiral Nimtiz in it, had to land immediately after takeoff, a rough landing and Admiral Nimitz bumped his head, I recall.

In any event, we all got going down and we went down the chain of the islands to Nouméa, where Admiral Halsey had his headquarters, and then were going on up to Espiritu Santo and Guadalcanal. As we were leaving Admiral Halsey's headquarters, McCain had been staying with him and had gone into the bathroom just before taking off and before he and Halsey joined the secretary at the plane. He left his false teeth on the bureau and Admiral Halsey picked them up, slipped them in his pocket, and walked out of the room. McCain came out to pick up his false teeth and they weren't there and the others were at the end of the line and he was huffing and puffing, yelling and looking all over the place. Halsey came in and said, "Come on, John." "Can't go, I can't go. I've lost my teeth." At that Halsey said "How do you expect to run naval aviation if you can't take care of your own teeth?" They bantered back and forth but Halsey gave McCain back his false teeth at plane side.

We went up to Espiritu Santo. Admiral Fitch was there in

his headquarters, then we flew on up to Guadalcanal. By that time the situation was reasonably improved at Henderson Field. We got a little bombing and people went off into the foxholes, but it was a worthwhile visit.

Secretary Knox had accompanying him Adlai Stevenson and Raleigh Warner, friends of his. Eventually, we flew on back to Hawaii and back to Washington.

Q: This was a look-see?

Adm. A.: This was a look-see. On that trip I picked up Herb Riley, who'd been down there - I was afraid of getting stuck in the Bureau of Aeronautics for the rest of the war because I was getting to the point of being an indispensable individual. Riley came back with me in the plane, we gave him a ride, and I persuaded Admiral McCain that he was a very suitable relief for me. We also gave a ride to Jocko Clark. Jocko was going back to take command of the Yorktown and he asked if I would like to come and be navigator of the new Yorktown. I said sure. So on that trip I was able to manipulate a relief and a prospective job at sea in a new carrier.

In the course of this whole trip, the Japanese and Tokyo Rose were aware that the secretary of the navy and Admiral Nimitz were down there, but they were always one day behind us. For example, they sent a bombing plane over to harass us one day after we'd left Canton and another island.

Q: Were they reading our codes, too?

Adm. A.: I think they were reading more of our English

rather than our codes. I don't know whether they were actually reading our codes, but they were very active in following the information they were getting.

In any event, I got back to Washington and it was agreed that Riley would come in and relieve me and that I would go as navigator of the Yorktown. The bureau had already ordered somebody else as navigator but Jocko Clark in his determined way had arranged to get his orders cancelled and see that my orders followed through. So, finally, in the spring of 1943 I was able to extricate myself from the Bureau of Aeronautics and turn it all over to Herb Riley.

Q: Let me ask you one more question about the time when you were there. When were the demands coming in for Russian planes? When did that happen?

Adm. A.: Oh, the demands were coming in. They started in the summer of 1941.

Q: Immediately after the invasion?

Adm. A.: After the invasion. The Russian requirements were just extravagant. They came in not only for planes but for all sorts of military equipment and materials. For example, they would come in and they'd want a number of PBYs that would have taken up our whole year's production. They had demands for rubber- it was just fantastic. All the way through, we had to resist the pressures that were being put on us. Most of those pressures did not affect naval aviation as directly as they did the army air corps, but we sort of supported the army air corps in trying to resist all this excess pressure. Resistance would appear in the various committees and they had a heavy supporter in Harry Hopkins at the White House.

Q: Yes, pressure came directly from the White House.

Adm. A.: That's right, from Harry Hopkins. There were some other things where pressure came through on political sides. We were told that we were to produce a transport to be made out of stainless steel by the Budd Corporation.

Q: The railroad people?

Adm. A.: The railroad people up in Jersey, including building them a plant and so forth. The plane really hadn't been properly designed. Stainless steel was a scarce commodity. There was no prospect of getting the airplane in time, and I went up and told the boss who was handling this - it was actually Cap Davison that this thing didn't make sense and shouldn't be approved. Well, a few days later I was told that this is approved and don't ask any more questions and don't raise any more fuss about it, there are other things you should take care of. And all the correspondence that had come up saying how inadequate and costly and unwise and not recommended the decision was subsequently cleaned out of the files. By the time I came back to check on it later on, the files had been completely cleaned by somebody. It was done in a political operation directed out of the White House. Those things happen.

Q: How much of your time was spent visiting airplane factories and that sort of thing?

Adm. A.: Not too much because we had very good relationships with the manufacturing people. The heads of those companies would come down and see us. I remember we were trying to conclude a contract with Consolidated which, at the time, was being run by Reuben Fleet on PBYs and the final negotiations on price, which were very, very difficult, were being conducted by Admiral Towers' own office up there, and finally he got Reuben Fleet to the point where he'd almost agreed to the final price, which was a navy price rather than his outlandish price, and finally he took a handkerchief out and said:

"Excuse me if I leave. I must compose myself."

Well, it took three days to get him back where we could pin him down and dot the "is" and cross the "ts".

These negoatiations depended upon the chief of the bureau and we didn't have to go through all these higher echelons. The responsibility was there. It was well and effectively carried out, recognizing all the unknowns and problems you have of a tremendous mobilization of a country in the early phase of a war. You just could not have run the war preparation and initial requirements of war as they existed at that time under the concept of McNamara and Brown and the present Department of Defense. The whole thing would become completely constipated very rapidly. You'd have to go back to something like what we had at the beginning of World War II.

Q: Providing you had time to do that!

Adm. A.: That's right.

Now, this jumps much farther ahead, but at the end of the war, when the so-called unification problem was raised and the establishment of a separate air force, known originally as the merger, the navy, through Forrestal, was able to take the very constructive position and incorporate certain features in the National Security "Act, in the spirit of the act, which would reflect the lessons learned from World war II. Unfortunately, as time has passed, less and less of the original intent in the background of the national Security Act has stayed. The lack of appreciation of keeping foreign policy, military policy, and economic policy in full coordination has sort of faded away. I mean people today make these commitments of the United States. For example, most recently against Iran and Afghanistan. They're totally unsupportable by the military forces that are available and inconsistent with the economic situation we have. Somehow or other, we've got to get back and reflect again on the lessons of World War II in our organization and the size and composition of our armed forces.

Q: It's a major step you're proposing!

Adm. A.: It sure is.

Q: While you were there in the bureau, had Sikorsky come forth with his invention?

Adm. A.: You mean of -?

Q: Of the helicopter.

Adm. A.: He had at that time some autogyros. The helicopter had not entered into the aircraft program at that time. We did have a big program advocated and implemented in lighter-than-air, advocated by Rosendahl and implemented in our programs, where we had quite a large number of blimps for antisubmarine warfare. We would ask for the funds but they were essentially handled, after the appropriations were made available, by the lighter-than-air section of the Bureau of Aeronautics for the facilities and the blimps and the training of their own lighter-than-air pilots.

I think, again, that it was probably a wise thing at the time to have moved on with the blimp program, but in retrospect, they were not really, to use a present term, cost-effective. They didn't really pull their weight.

Q: They were proven to be effective, though, off the coast, were they not?

Adm. A.: Well, but I don't think anywhere near to the degree that the ardent advocates had hoped for. Whether, in retrospect today, you would suggest that we have lighter-than-air blimps for that purpose is rather doubtful. Maybe with some of the developments in techniques they might have been even more useful now than they were then with sonobuoys and radar and infrared detection devices. I'm not in a position to judge that. I don't know, I haven't heard much about blimps being advocated at the present time.

Q: Well, Rosendahl, the chief exponent, has died. Going back to the autogyro, the Coast Guard sort of gloats over the fact that the navy didn't take up this option and they did.

Adm. A.: I don't recall, and I'm quite certain I would have. There was never a mention of a helicopter being in the navy program while I was in the plans division, and certainly if there had been one it would have been included in the research and development program because we would have been looking for something worthwhile that had a real promise at that stage of the game. I don't recall it.

Looking back, there was a major policy conflict between the army and navy and between naval aviation and the army air corps. This was partly due to the army's desire to expand greatly and get on with the war in Europe and not to get over-committed in the Pacific. Also, the air corps's attitude deprecating from the old Billy Mitchell days the aircraft carrier and their ambition to have a single air force which would take over all aspects of military and civilian air, which became apparent later on.

Q: Would you add also the basic land orientation of the country rather than navy orientation, which focused largely on land?

Adm. A.: Yes, I would guess so. That was a fact.

Q: That was one of George Miller's theses.

Adm. A.: I guess so, but in spite of that, we worked pretty harmoniously, at least I was able to work pretty harmoniously with my opposite numbers in the army air corps. On one occasion Grumman came down and they were developing the experimental XF6F, which was their next generation of fighters. There were two experimental planes on order - we'd order two at a time. In the wartime expansion you had to have an ace in the hole so you'd order two, and they were originally to be equipped with the Wright 1820 radial engine, but Jake Swinbul, Vice President of Grumman came down to my office and said:

"Look, George, our airplane's not going to be any good with that engine. It would be a hell of an airplane with a Pratt and Whitney 1830 engine."

Admiral Dale Harris, then a captain, had relieved Vosseller in aircraft requirements, and he came in and we talked about this situation. We agreed that we'd better try out a Pratt and Whitney in one of those aircraft, and then the question was (a) can we get the engine and (b) can we get approval to do this thing fast, because the airplane was more or less completed. I called up my friend from the army air corps, Lieutenant Colonel Langmead, and said:

"I need an 1830 engine fast. We don't have one available. Can you divert one from the production line at Pratt and Whitney?"

He said: "Sure, I'll get it on a truck right away."

So he had the engine on a truck down to Grumman that afternoon. I went in to see Admiral Towers, having talked to Swinbul of Grumman and military requirements, and I said:

"Admiral, I want to change the engine in the XF6F, on one of them, from a Wright to a Pratt and Whitney."

He said, "What does engineering think about it?" and I said, "They don't know a damned thing about it."

He said, "What does military requirements think?

"They agree."

"What does Grumman think?"

"They will make a great airplane."

"Go ahead and do it."

It took two weeks before the engineering department of the Bureau of Aeronautics knew that the engine had been changed!

Q: Were they mad at that?

Adm. A.: They were mad but they were so relieved that the airplane had developed such phenomenal performance.

We processed it properly through the chain of command to get the official change made. Then I had to go and work out in the joint aircraft committee with the army air corps to get the production engines for the plane, but at that time, when I think we had Buick coming in and making 1830 engines along the same design, and with the cooperation of my friends in the army air corps we got the engines for the F6F and it turned out to be a hell of a fine airplane. It really saved the war in the Pacific in that next phase.

Also, you spoke of North American. North American had produced an airplane for the British, an old lend-lease order, in which the army air corps was not particularly interested, but naval air from our observers in England found out that this was going to be a hell of a hot fighter. I went to my friend Eddy Langmead and said:

"You'd better get with your own operating people and get some of those aircraft, because they're better than anything you've got coming up the line."

It turned out to be the P-51 and, as a result of the U.S. Navy finding out about the airplane - and the British were not letting the army air corps know how good it was -

Q: They were just gloating over it?

Adm. A.: They were just gloating over it. The production was expanded, and the allocations were diverted so that the U.S. army air corps got the Mustang P-51, which turned out to be a superb fighter plane for them, and the other one that they were building was the P-38, which was a two-engine fighter, and we worked hand in glove in helping them get production of that, which, of course, we wouldn't use at that time.

But, I would say that our cooperation at that level and through the medium of the Joint Aircraft Committee, was very good.

Now, on another occasion the British Navy was represented here by a close friend of mine who later was a vice admiral in the British Navy - he's still active in British aircraft activities- then a Commander Richard Smeton. He was in the British Mission here in Washington and we were very good friends. I told him if the British Navy were to meet what they felt they had to have, they'd better get an order in soon for more Vought Corsairs (F4Us). We'd sent all we had to them. We had nothing left, I said:

"Well, look, you've got to make up your mind," and he said, "It takes a long, long time."

I said, "I make up the minds of the U.S. Navy, you'd better by a damned sight make up your mind here and do it, make it a fait accompli."

So, on his own initiative, reluctantly at the time, he made the decision, committed the British for this, before they'd made the commitment in London to do it.

Q: He didn't get called home?

Adm. A.: No, he didn't get called home, although he was later relieved for another reason, to go to sea, I guess, and he was replaced by another officer, Casper John, who was the son of the famous Augustus John -

Q: The sculptor.

Adm. A.: - who became the first sea lord of the British Navy at the time that I was chief of naval operations. When I go over to London next week, I hope to see him. Unfortunately, after he retired he was in the housing business and I just heard a short time ago that he had both legs amputated and is in a hospital down at Land's End Penzance. I'm going to try to drop down and see him.

We worked very closely and harmoniously with the British fleet air arm. We helped them a lot and had excellent rapport. We did a lot of their training of people down at Pensacola and I think that good relationship has held over the years. They've been under pressure off and on from the RAF. Of course, their topplanner in those days was Air Marshal Slessor, whom I knew then and later on at SHAPE. These contracts made in the early phase of the war held on for years after the war. For example, Mountbatten - I mentioned that he made this trip back from Europe in the spring of 1942 with us - and he, in his conversations with

President Roosevelt, emphasized the importance of having younger commanding officers in our own U.S. destroyers, which was picked up by Roosevelt and passed on down the line to Admiral King and implemented, and it made a great deal of difference in the aggressiveness of our own destroyers.

I mentioned having a tight little organization, which would cut down on paper work. Right at the time that Admiral King came in, we were trying to get approval of a greatly expanded aircraft program - I think it was the 3,000-plane program to the 10,000-plane program, the 10,000 or the 15,000, I forget which one it was - and so I sent my secretary around to get all the people who would have to endorse such a proposal, to get their own stationery, and we typed up the subsequent endorsements and approvals from Admiral King, the secretary of the navy, and the final approval from the White House, back to the secretary of the navy. Then I hand-carried this paper around for signature to Admiral Towers, who signed it, of course. I got up to Admiral Horne and he signed it. Then Admiral King, he was the smart one, he was the first one who looked at all pages and he looked at me and said:

"Boy, you're optimistic about getting things done fast, aren't you, young man?"

He picked up his pen and signed it Ernest J. King. I then carried it down to Mr. Knox and he signed the letter, and sent it over to the White House. When it came back, it wasn't signed on the endorsement that I had written but instead "FK, OK, FDR."

So we got the damned thing done in about an afternoon. Well, Jeeze, today with this -

Q: You couldn't do it?

Adm. A.: You couldn't do it these days. First of all, they'd have to have a study group to say whether the secretary of defense could approve the damned thing.

Q: Did you have any problem with ordnance for these planes that were being turned out so rapidly? The Norden bomb sight, that sort of thing?

Adm. A.: Well, that was the statement of requirements, which specified the military requirements of the ordnance equipment to go to in an airplane. The actual provision of that equipment was handled by the Bureau of Ordnance, initially, as I recall it, under Spike Blandy -

Q: Yes, and then George Hussey.

Adm. A.: That's right. Blandy and Hussey. In the aviation group of the Bureau of Ordnance we had some very fine naval aviators over the years who had gone to postgraduate training and subsequent assignment specializing in aviation ordnance. That was a very good program we had and they did a pretty doggone good job of meeting the ordnance requirements for our planes. There had to be at the time a big expansion in the production of bomb sights. I never got involved particularly. All of our requirements basically were met on time and I would say due to the successful efforts of the Bureau of Ordnance with the War Production Board. I think they had a similar close relationship with the U.S. Army on that.

Another area where the planning in anticipation of a war over the years had gone on very effectively in the navy, which paid off greatly in World War II, was in the training of intelligence Japanese-language programs and the communications intelligence. We had a good program. We picked young, bright officers and they would be assigned to Japanese-language training.

Q: In Colorado?

Adm. A.: Well, first I think they would go to the embassy in Japan under the tutelage of a Japanese teacher, a professor. Then they would be put out on their own completely in the Japanese hinterland, where they met no English-speaking people at all and just lived the language and learned the idioms and the expressions.

Q: An example of that is Steve Jurika.

Adm. A.: Well, particularly, I was thinking of Eddie Layton.

Q: Oh, Yes.

Adm. A.: Then they would get them back and they would be further specialized in communications intelligence, and those people really carried a tremendous load for us in World War II. Layton was brought back in as intelligence officer for Admiral Nimitz as CinCPacFlt, and very effective work he did. I don't know what's happened to him.

Q: He's still alive. I had a letter from him the other day. He lives in Monterey.

Adm. A.: You asked specifically about ordnance. We had good people in the aviation ordnance program. They were well trained and I think in many respects superior in aviation ordnance to most of the people in the army air corps. We got along very well, I think, on that aspect. I don't recall that as a serious problem we had.

Q: Just a little footnote. Did you have anything to do with Gene Wilson? Was he helpful to you in your program, he being a former flyer in the navy?

Adm. A.: Gene Wilson was with Chance Vought.

Q: And he was head of North American finally.

Adm. A.: I knew him in Chance Vought. Then there was Jake Swiebul of Grumman, Wright with Curtiss Wright. We had good relationships with the old-timers in the aviation industry, and Gene Wilson, of course, always was, and Donald Douglas, they were pretty good friends of aviation and naval aviation, have been over the years.

Interview No. 3 with Admiral George W. Anderson, U.S. Navy
(Retired)

Place: His apartment in Watergate, Washington, D.C.

Date: Friday morning, 17 October 1980

Subject: Biography

By: John T. Mason, Jr.

Q: Admiral, nice to see you looking so well after a summer abroad, especially in that favored spot in Portugal.

Adm. A.: Thank you.

Q: Last time, when we broke off you were about to leave the Bureau of Aeronautics and you were going down to Norfolk to help commission the new carrier the Yorktown, with a very famous skipper aboard.

Adm. A.: Jocko Clark.

Q: Do you want to pick up the story at that point?

Adm. A.: I think I mentioned that I had made a trip to the South Pacific with Admiral McCain and during the time that I was down there Admiral Clark, then Captain Clark, coming back on the plane asked me if I would come to the ship with him and be his executive officer.

Q: Had you known Jocko before that?

Adm. A.: Yes, because he had previously had command of Fighting Squadron 2, and before that he was in the Bureau of Aeronautics on fighter aircraft when I was testing F2F aircraft. Then he went to the squadron that had Grumman fighters and he arranged or urged that I come to that squadron, but he'd been detached by the time I got there. So I had known him not as a personal friend so much as a professional associate.

So, he asked me if I would come as executive officer of the Yorktown and I said I was too junior for that. He said:

"Well, how about coming as my navigator then?"

I said, "That would be fine. That would suit me very well."

Then, when we came back to Washington, he arranged for me to be ordered to the Yorktown as the navigating officer, and another officer whom I'd known quite well and was senior to me, was Raoul Waller, was the prospective executive officer. The bureau had ordered somebody else as navigator but Jocko, in his way, when he made up his mind he wanted something, he'd get it, and he arranged for this other officer to be transferred.

At the time the Yorktown was CV-10 and the Essex was CV-9.

Q: Wasn't there something of a race to see which one was going to be commissioned first?

Adm. A.: Oh, yes. Jocko had tremendous drive. He always wanted to be first. He was very competitive.

Q: But Wu Duncan was also?

Adm. A.: Wu Duncan was the skipper of the Essex. He was a more serene individual than Jocko was.

Then the Lexington and the Bunker Hill were also coming along.

Q: Ballentine was -

Adm. A.: Ballentine was the skipper of the Bunker Hill and Felix Stump the skipper of the Lexington.

Q: What a combination!

Adm. A.: It was drive, drive, drive all the time. Jocko really assembled a marvelous group of officers and men for the Yorktown. In contrast with the earlier Yorktown in which I served, I guess about 98 per cent of the officers and men in the new Yorktown were reserves who had been brought in during the war, in contrast with the almost complete percentage of officers and men of the regular navy in the first Yorktown.

Q: There was quite an array of talent among the reservists, wasn't there?

Adm. A.: Oh, yes. We had George Earnshaw, a baseball pitcher, we had Eddie Duchin, the piano-player, we had the fire chief, I think, from Boston, and fire marshals from Philadelphia. It was a great assembly of people. A classmate of mine, Hank Dozier, who was later lost at sea, was the air officer, and a very fine group of heads of departments and officers up and down through the ship.

Jocko had a young man by the name of Herman Rosenblatt, who was a lawyer whose brother was a very close friend and political supporter of Franklin Roosevelt from out in the midwest, and he was Jocko Clark's boy, you might say. He acted as sort of an aide and political adviser to him.

Q: Jocko picked well there!

Adm. A.: Yes.

Under this continuous drive we got the ship commissioned -

Q: Were you ahead of the others?

Adm. A.: Well, we were catching up rapdily on all the others, and we got down to the Gulf of Paria, off the northern cost of South America, for our shakedown cruise training because you couldn't train in the Atlantic with the German submarines down there.

Q: And Paria was protected by a boom?

Adm. A.: That's right, in a protected area. We did our training down there and then came back for post training, post-yard availability, and then got ready to go out to the Pacific.

Actually, the Essex and the Yorktown were coming on just about the same time.

We went through the canal which Jocko made quite an event

for everybody with a very limited margin to get through the locks.

Q: Yes. How did he make it quite an event? Festivities and so on?

Adm. A.: Oh, no, shouting and screaming. He was a very different ty of a captain, you know.

Q: Yes, I knew him.

Adm. A.: You did?

Q: Yes.

Adm. A.: We got through the canal and headed directly out to Pearl Harbor. Then, with our air group aboard - the air group was commanded by Jimmy Flatley, a very fine officer -

Q: Where did you pick them up?

Adm. A.: We'd gotten them at Norfolk and taken them around.
We did some refresher operations out of Pearl Harbor, in the Hawaiian Islands. Then, all of a sudden, we got an order to leave the air group ashore in the islands, and with the Essex we made a quick trip from Hawaii to San Francisco to load up the two ships with jeeps and combat vehicles in order that the army - these were all army vehicles - could be properly equipped for the first amphibious operation that was contemplated in the Pacific.

Q: The navy at that point was reverting to its traditional role!

Adm. A.: Of transport, that's right.

There was one very amusing incident on that trip. It wasn't amusing to me, but we came in to San Francisco following the Essex into San Francisco Harbor and there was a heavy tide running. The tide was running sort of from left to right, port to starboard, going under the bridge, and Jock who, as I say, was a different type of shiphandler from most, said:

"I'm just going to follow right along behind the Essex," and I said:

"No, Captain, we've got to get to port because of the tide being over there."

"No, no, we're going right behind the Essex, in the wake of the Essex."

Well, by the time we got to the bridge, the pillars were coming up awful close and I said:

"Captain, Captain, you've got to get left, to port. You're going to hit the bridge."

"No, I'm not. We'll follow in the wake of the Essex." Well, you could see the wake of the Essex just drifting by the pillars of the bridge. Finally, we got up there and he just had to put the rudder hard over to starboard to throw the stern of the ship away, otherwise we would have hit a pillar of that bridge. Jock would not have been an admiral nor would I have been a captain probably on that, but we missed it, anyway.

Q: Did he feel contrite?

Adm. A.: No, he just fussed around a little bit. No, he'd never get very contrite on anything at that point.

It was a very quick turn-around. I think we were there for only two days, one working day and two nights, while they were loading the ships, then we turned around and made a highspeed run right back to Honolulu and unloaded the jeeps. I must say that we profited a little bit because there was what we might call a "night requisition" for one of the jeeps which a chief petty officer smuggled down below. The inventory missed one jeep, I think. -

Q: No questions asked!

Adm. A.: No questions asked.

Q: You did make a notation, however, something about fair-haired bastards, while you were in San Francisco, Mom Chung.

Adm. A.: Oh, Mom Chung, was a Chinese doctor there and she had been very good to the navy, people who would come back, particularly the aviators, whom she called fair-haired bastards, and the submariners, whom she called fair-haired dolphins. So, when we were in there one of those nights we ran out to Mom Chung's place. She was very hospitable, gave us drinks, and so forth, and little testimonials, which were little leather wallets that had Number so and so, fair-haired bastard. She did this for every group of ships or submarine people that would come in to San Francisco. Extremely friendly and hospitable and I think all her boys or bastards or dolphins had a genuine affection for her.

Q: A great morale-builder.

Adm. A.: Oh, she was a great morale-builder, yes.

Well, we unloaded the army equipment in Honolulu and went out for a couple of other weeks of training exercises, bombing and deck operations, which went quite well.

Q: What kind of planes were in operation from your deck?

Adm. A.: We had F4Fs, SBDs, TBF Grumman torpedo planes

Q: How many planes did she carry?

Adm. A.: We were carrying seventy-two planes, I think, about seventy-two planes at that time.

Q: And a complement of how many?

Adm. A.: Oh, I guess 3,500.

Q: That was more than a wartime complement?

Adm. A.: Oh, yes, it was full wartime complement.

We got Rear Admiral Pownall as the task force commander and the first operation of any consequence we had was under his command, and it was nothing more than an air attack against Wake Island. I think this was in October.

Q: Didn't Marcus come first?

Adm. A.: No, Marcus was second, as I recall.

Q: Marcus was 1 September.

Adm. A.: Well, I guess Marcus was first and then Wake.

We had no trouble with that operation at all, there was practically no opposition there. Let's see. We had the Yorktown, the Essex and the Independence, I think, the first of the light cruisers converted to light carriers. We dropped a lot of bombs. Jocko was quite aggressive in his operations. He was saying what we ought to do was go in and shoot the place up with our guns, which we did not do at that time, and -

Q: Erase it from the map of the ocean.

Adm. A.: That's right.

We came back from that and then we prepared for the second training operation out there, which was, as you corrected me, the Wake one.

Q: Yes, and that was October 5.

Adm. A.: That's right. We went out there and Jocko was very, very upset with the admiral who was almost scared to death of operations with carriers under wartime conditions. Jocko made up his mind that he just couldn't be going to sea with that admiral any more because he said he didn't have the guts to fight a war properly, and he used his friend Rosenblatt, sent him back on a quick trip to Washington to get the word to the president to have Admiral Pownall removed and get another admiral in there who had greater fortitude in fighting the Japs, and he was successful in it.

Q: That caused quite a controversy with King and Nimitz, didn't it?

Adm. A.: That's right.

Q: They had a San Francisco session on it.

Adm. A.: Well, I don't think it was that particular thing. They probably had a San Francisco session at which that was an item that was discussed. But, definitely, I think Pownall was not the right type of a personality to be at sea in time of war. On the other hand, it's not right for the captain of a ship to be doing a political end run to get rid of his flag officer. Jocko justified it on the basis that, "Well, it was going to help win the war." Everything he did was with the idea of winning the war and, of course, enhancing the position of Jocko Clark as the premier fighter. I remember he made a turn coming into formation, and it was a very spectacular and very successful operation again but it was a hair-raising one for the admiral, who was on the flag bridge below, and Pownall came up to the bridge saying:

"Why did I ever come to the carriers." He was just shaking and said, "Don't ever do that again."

And old Jocko would say, "The yellow son of a bitch," under his breath, and that's when he made up his mind he was going to get rid of Pownall, which he did.

Q: Was Pownall a peacetime type officer, perhaps, rather than a wartime one?

Adm. A.: On, very definitely.

Q: Because he had a good reputation, didn't he?

Adm. A.: A nice, gentle, good administrator in a peacetime job, extremely pleasant to his associates. But, as I guess turns up in all phases of military forces, there are some who are good in a peacetime role and are not particularly suited to the wartime role. He was a thorough gentleman, and he was transferred back to duty in Honolulu, away from his sea command, and then he found his way back down to San Diego, I guess, but he was definitely out of the picture.

Q: Who was sent out in his stead?

Adm. A.: Admiral Mitscher came out. One of the things was that Pownall wanted to terminate any operation just as fast as he could. All the pilots were coming back to the ship and, of course, reporting up to Jocko that they needed to go in for more attacks, do more damage, but the admiral did not want to stay out there and he got away as fast as he could.

There was one other little incident that happened. We had a lad by the name of Jim Condit who either was - I think this may have been at the Marcus operation - a pilot of a torpedo plane and he went in the water, landed. I guess he probably had an anti-aircraft fragment, and he landed on the water. Jocko wanted to go in and pick him up close to the island and the admiral would not permit that. We didn't have as good rescue services then as we did later, and it was too bad he was captured. Actually, he's a member of the Yorktown Association now. He was a prisoner of war and -

Q: You did have submarines with you, didn't you, as rescue-?

Adm. A.: Oh, yes, and they worked very well. At that particular time, except for Condit, we didn't have anybody being shot down on those operations against Wake and Marcus.

Q: You referred to them as exercises. The Japanese looked at it in a different light.

Adm. A.: No, I'm talking about the exercises out of Pearl Harbor when we were planning to get ready for these initial wartime operations with the carriers.

When we got back to Honolulu from the Wake Island strike, I was informed by Admiral Towers, who was then Commander, Air Force, Pacific, that I was to come to his staff as the plans officer. I objected and Jocko objected. Jocko said that he wanted me to stay on and become his executive officer. But there were good reasons because of my previous experience in Washington, there were good reasons for him to make a change in his staff. So I reported to Honolulu, Pearl Harbor, Ford Island as the plans officer for Air Force, Pacific Fleet, under Admiral Towers. Admiral Sherman was the chief of staff at that time.

Q: Forrest Sherman?

Adm. A.: Forrest Sherman. The staff officers lived in little Quarters "1" there on Ford Island and it was work and eat and work seven days of the week. Occasionally we'd go for a swim or maybe play a little bridge, but basically it was work and eat.

During that period of time the Yorktown went out on another operation - I've got it correct. My memory was a little faulty there.

Q: The Gilbert Islands operation was coming up, Galvanic.

Adm. A.: That's right. Pownall was still in command. Montgomery had not taken over and Jocko had not yet sent his emissary to Washington to get rid of Pownall. But during that operation, the next time they went out, was the time when Jocko said really the admiral just had to go, and it was when they came back from that that he sent Rosenblatt back to Washington.

Q: Did did the other skippers react to this initiative on Jocko's part? How did Duncan react to it?

Adm. A.: I don't know.

Q: He's the more traditional type.

Adm. A.: Very definitely. I don't think Jocko would have talked to any of his contemporaries about this. It was the skipper of another carrier who was relieved summarily out there because he didn't have the qualities to be the commanding officer. That was the skipper, I guess, of the Independence, George Fairlamb. He was relieved very, very quickly when they found out that he just didn't have the stomach for that type of a war.

During this particular time when Admiral Towers was Commander, Air Force, Pacific Fleet, Admiral Sherman was the chief of staff and there was a very strong feeling in the Pacific, and this filtered back to Washington, that the war in the Pacific was not giving sufficient consideration to the offensive capabilities of the carriers and that naval aviators were not being given appropriate positions of influence and command at the higher levels.

At one of the San Francisco conferences, the King-Nimitz conferences, it was agreed that Sherman would be transferred to Admiral Nimitz's staff, Forrest Sherman. He was in turn replaced by Admiral Radford as the chief of staff at Air Force, Pacific Fleet, chief of staff to Admiral Towers, and there was a considerable discussion on the whole concept of strategy for the Pacific. This was, of course, receiving the highest level of attention between King and Nimitz. After Sherman got over there, the whole strategy was made more aggressive, the timing was advanced, and the concept of bypassing some of these islands was introduced, instead of taking one and going on to the next, they got into the bypassing strategy.

Q: This was a contribution of the air force people, was it?

Adm. A.: Admiral Towers was quite outspoken on this. I would say the influence was primarily from naval air on this.

Q: You were still in this transitional period, weren't you, with the battleship types.

Adm. A.: That's right, oh yes.

The next evolutionary step was in the winter-spring of 1944, it was agreed by King and Nimtiz that Towers would be moved over as the deputy CinCPac-CinCPOA.

Q: You mean in the spring of 1944, then?

Adm. A.: Yes, spring of '44, he would be moved over as the deputy, but neither King or Nimitz was willing to put Towers in what Towers really wanted, which was to command a task force at sea or a task fleet at sea. There was a longtime animosity between Towers and King, which apparently went back to years and years before when King came into aviation late and he heard that Towers had referred to him as a penny whistle or something like that. So this was a longstanding -

Q: It was very personal.

Adm. A.: It was very personal animosity, and King was determined he was not going to let Towers get out to sea as a combat officer. So, the compromise solution was to put Towers over at CinCPac really as the coordinator for logistics, for logistic support. He was not to be in the operational command or planning echelon, rather in logistic support.

When Towers learned that he was to go over there, he told me that I was to go over as his assistant and he also arranged for another commander, H. B. Jones, a civil engineer, to go over with me to be his assistant, and we moved over into the headquarters at Makalapa. Nimitz did not like this particularly, but Towers insisted that he wanted to run his organization the way he felt he needed to run it in order to do his job, and he did a hell of a good job in this whole thing. But Commander Jones and I were really hatchet men, you might say, because Towers insisted that we try to find out what was going wrong, and what was going wrong was usually involved with inadequacies in senior officers in the total alignment of the strategy in the Pacific, which, of course, as you know, was different from the standpoint of MacArthur on the one hand and Nimtiz and King on the other. MacArthur wanted to go right ahead to take the Philippines as fast as possible and use the entire navy to support him in that objective. That was incompatible with subsequent decisions of the Joint Chiefs of Staff or the president, President Roosevelt concurring, involved the two-pronged approach, with the central Pacific conducting its campaign in the center and MacArthur in the South Pacific.

At that time, this was in early 1944, the operations were pretty well secured in the Solomon Islands and MacArthur was in a position to start moving westward. The carriers were continuing their operations. Pownall was long gone. Admiral Mitscher had come in and Spruance was the Fifth Fleet commander. Halsey then became the Third Fleet commander when he came up from the South Pacific. He moved in with his staff in the house next door to us, Makalapa Drive. Amdiral Carney was his chief of staff. He had Harold Stassen as his flag secretary and -

Q: General factotum.

Adm. A.: That's right.

I remember one night I had turned in fairly early and I heard this noise, some girl yelling out, "There's a fire down here." Then Halsey's voice, "Throw some whiskey on it"! They were understandably relaxing back in Honolulu's civilization after having been around Espiritu Santo, Nouméa, and Guadalcanal.

Admiral Towers beefed up very strongly the staff on the

logistic side of CinCPac. He got Major General Leavey, a very wonderful and extremely able officer, in as the assistant chief of staff for logistics. That did not sit too well in the minds of some of the navy people, particularly those in the service force. On the other hand, with our assistance, General Leavey, who used to live right across the street from me in Washington, with suggestions from Jones and me, was able to assemble from the navy some of the more progressive and capable naval officers who were not just wedded to the old service force concept of the Pacific Fleet, among them Henry Eccles, who'd been sort of a major naval logistician for many, many years up around the War College. Leavey and his people did a wonderful job, but inevitably, they would come down to Admiral Towers and we would feed the word in that the problem we had out there in the Pacific was Vice Admiral Calhoun, who was a classmate and a very close, dear, personal friend of Admiral Nimitz. Admiral Calhoun was Commander, Service Force.

Q: Beans and bullets!

Adm. A.: That's right.

So, Towers finally went to Nimitz and said something had to be done, and Admiral Nimitz, in his very compassionate and friendly way, told Admiral Calhoun, "Now, things have got to be improved. I suggest you go down and see Jack Towers." We were at the other end of the Makalapa building, on the ground floor, Nimitz's office being at one side and Towers's at the other. Admiral Calhoun's Service Force officers were in the temporary buildings behind us.

Calhoun came down to Towers and said:

"Jack, what should I do? Poor Chester had told me this and I want to do what I can to help him, do the best I can."

Admiral Towers said:

"Well, I tell you what to do, Bill. You go back there and talk to Anderson and Jones and let them tell you what has to be done with the Service Force."

It was a tough situation for us.

Q: Juniors!

Adm. A.: Juniors, very junior, to tell Admiral Calhoun what he had to do in changing the Service Force to bring it into line with reality which he took very, very well. He thanked us and did his best to implement it. He had made some changes in the personnel in his own organization, and he really greatly improved it and took all of our suggestions. There were all sorts of suggestions, but usually in what you might say, "get those people off their asses and use their heads to cope with this changing situation."

That was one of the major incidents that occurred while we were there, and I think we did a pretty good job of it.

Q: The changing situation involved fueling at sea and that kind of thing?

Adm. A.: Well, really, getting the right supplies in the right places at the right time, and anticipating everything that was going to happen. Of course, we were building up through those months towards the operations in the Marianas, which were of major importance. It would be the first time the navy had to get into what we called civil affairs, which, of course, was a big thing in the European campaign, but it was certainly new to the navy.

Q: And approach a big island, Saipan and -

Adm. A.: Yes, with a lot of planning first in civil affairs. We had former Governor Vanderbilt of Rhode Island as a captain in the navy on the staff and he was charged with civil affairs. He had assembled a group of largely reserve officers, and they were running by books and checkoff lists.

Suddenly Admiral Nimtiz went out in town one day in Honolulu because he was very close to the civilian community and some of the people said there was a great crisis in Hawaii. There was absolutely no Kotex available, that the navy was taking it. So he came back to Towers and said, "Let's find out about this." We found out. We found that the civil affairs people, in anticipation of estimating the number of women there were on Guam, translating that mathematically, concluded they needed so many tons of Kotex to be put in such and such echelons and they'd tied up practically the entire supply of Kotex in the Hawaiian Islands. You can imagine the poor natives who'd never heard of it before!

Q: No, that's a sophisticated approach!

Adm. A.: Another incident came up. The original air groups who'd been operating for some six and a half months on the new carriers, and there were more carriers and more ships coming in. There was a tremendous buildup, you know. They'd come back from their various operations and were being rotated out. They'd finished their assigned tours and they'd get some shore duty and new air groups would come out, and we found out that there were no decorations and we had a very serious morale problem on it.

Q: Yes, the army was handing them out.

Adm. A.: Yes, the army was handing them out.

Adm. A.: Oh, they were handing them out - I've got some cartoons about this.

Admiral Nimitz had an assistnat chief of staff for administration by the name of Preston Mercer, and he heard that I had been checking on the decorations and the status of them. So, instead of coming to me and asking what the story was, he went right to Admiral Nimitz. Admiral Nimitz hit the ceiling, sent a marine down to get Admiral Towers and get me to appear up in his office and, we got the darndest bawling-out from Admiral Nimitz personally-

Q: That's an amazing thing.

Adm. A.: He said:

"Towers, I don't want you or any of your staff that you've brought over here having anything to do with awards and decorations," and then he added, "or public relations."

Well, Admiral Towers was pretty cool. He said:

"Admiral, I think Anderson - I know generally - but I suggest you let him explain what the situation is."

Well, of course, I was pretty concerned at being hauled up by a marine to the commander in chief's office and I said:

"Well, Admiral, I think the sum and substance of this - we were trying to find a constructive solution to the delay in action on the recommendations for awards for the navy pilots. All of these people from these carriers, none of the awards have been given to any of them."

Admiral Nimitz picked up on that and he took corrective action to get something done on that. We were forbidden to get involved in anything more concerned with awards or public relations or anything else.

Q: Did this reflect Nimitz's attitude towards public relations?

Adm. A.: No. I think it reflected more that he was sensitive to this. I think he was definitely trying to keep Admiral Towers and anybody working for him completely in the role of the logistician and not let him encroach into the area, the broader areas of responsibility, of command of operations and plans, and public relations, of course, which is essentially the responsibility of the commander in chief.

Q: What was it in Towers's personality that seemed to rub some of these men the wrong way, especially Nimitz?

Adm. A.: He rubbed a lot of people the wrong way. He had an

awful lot of common sense but, in applying it, he was somewhat supercilious and critical of other people, and that word would get around. And Towers, of course, had been fighting the battle of naval aviation for decades, you might say, and had been opposed by what he called the "battleship gang". His whole career was one of overcoming the obstacles which he felt were imposed by that type of surface naval officer on naval aviation and therefore on the improvement of the navy. It got into personality conflicts. He was very caustic in his comments on the original plans they had, conceived by Captain Steele, and this step by step, one island after another approach across the Pacific, which he said would take years.

Aside from being very constructive in his comments about getting troops - I remember Nimitz said, "We don't have any troops. Where are we going to get the troops?" He said, "Well, look at all these rear areas around the world, where the army's providing guards and detachments. If they assembled them all together from the backward areas, you could create some more divisions."

Then, of course, was the question of allocating to the Pacific more equipment that was otherwise being channeled under the basic concept of Europe and Germany first. Towers used to say they had to be more aggressive in fighting against the European area to get their share of equipment and people.

Q: That attitude was shared with King?

Adm. A.: That's right, yes, but I was just saying that he was very outspoken. He would refer to Captain Steele, for example, off the record he'd refer to him as "Boob" Steele. He always was a boob. We thought he was, too, but that's not very good for the deputy CinCPac to be referring to the plans officer on Admiral Nimitz's staff.

Another interesting thing that happened was that, in connection with determination of the strategy to be used in the Pacific to defeat Japan, the implementation of it, it was decided in Washington that President Roosevelt would come out to Hawaii and MacArthur would come up from the southwest Pacific. They'd have a conference in Honolulu and the president would be there in the capacity of commander in chief to make whatever decisions were necessary. So Mike Riley, who was the chief advance man or secret service man came out to Pearl Harbor to make arrangements for the president's visit. Of course, they wanted to get the proper automobile and accommodations for the president and everything else all lined up to be perfectly proper. There was a rest home for the aviators called the Chris Holmes Place down at Waikiki, which was a very nice place but was a little bit shabby.

When Mike Riley came out, Commander Jones was sort of the liaison with him, and they arranged to get that all refurnished and painted up, so the net result of that was after the president's visit we had a much more comfortable and nicer rest home for the aviators. The other was finding the automobile for the president. There was no suitable seven-passenger, open car that President Roosevelt liked to ride in that would provide enough room for his guests, whoever was with him, secret service protection, and a chauffeur. The closest they had - they went through the list of all the cars registered in Hawaii - was a five-passenger, open car, which was in storage and belonged to one of the notorious madams in the Honolulu area. So they went to her and she said, surely she'd be able to make her car available. So they got it out, rehabilitated it for the president's visit. Eventually, President Roosevelt heard about this and he just roared with laughter and amusement.

The visit went extremely well -

Q: It was rather brief, wasn't it?

Adm. A.: Oh, yes, very short, but it resulted in the final determination of what the objectives for the central Pacific for Admiral Nimitz's command and for MacArthur's command would be. The Navy from the Pacific command would be in support of MacArthur and he would be in support of us in principle, but Pacific support would be more for him but it would be under the naval command responsibility of Admiral Nimitz. Eventually, when the Southwest and Pacific Command got to the Philippines the amendments did not turn out too well because of Halsey's messing up around the Battle of Leyte Gulf.

In any event, that visit of the president to Honolulu and MacArthur and Nimitz getting together provided the formula for the final decision by the president of what we were going to do. I guess it was recommended to him by the Chiefs of Staff and, to some extent, it was a compromise although I really don't know whether it was a compromise or not.

Q: Did that involve also the loaning of ships to the MacArthur command for -

Adm. A.: Yes.

Q: That was a thorn in Nimitz's side eventually.

Adm. A.: Oh, yes.

Q: He couldn't get them back.

Adm. A.: Couldn't get them back, allocations of support. But, again, how in the world could they have worked out a better command under the circumstances that then prevailed of MacArthur being a national hero and Nimitz with the naval area there, obviously a naval area. They couldn't put MacArthur under the command of Nimitz, and it was inconceivable to put the entire U.S. offensive navy under MacArthur's command. I mean the two things were too great and I think the president worked out a very good compromise on it. And, as you know, it involved the central Pacific getting the Marinas, Iwo Jima, eventually planning to take the Ryukyus, and then building up towards Formosa while MacArthur was heading for the Philippines. And then, although the decision had not been made at that time, the final operation against Japan.

Admiral Towers made frequent trips to areas which, after the initial seizure of the islands in the Marshalls and then in the Marianas, in the consolidation phases, primarily to look over the base buildup and also, which was a point that he made very forcefully, of the rollup as we went forward, not to carry on these big establishments after they'd served their initial and essential purpose. The idea was to get what we had, use it, and then move forward, and that was quite successfully done, for example, in the Gilberts and the Marshalls and they reduced those and Eniwetok down to the essential minimum.

Q: That was a very complicated thing. How did you keep track of your supplies in the islands? Didn't have computers to do this.

Adm. A.: No. I don't think they had any computers at that stage of the game.

There was another factor in the Pacific at this time which was of increasing importance, and that was the role of the army air corps against Japan. They were very public-relations-oriented. They were immature in some aspects of military operations. They had to prove themselves, they wanted to prove themselves, which was an irritant to the navy and, to a lesser degree, I guess to the army. One of the strategic objectives in this move across the Pacific was to establish in the Marianas the bases for the B-29 aircraft. Well, this involved a tremendous construction and logistic effort. Towers handled from the CinCPac side that support in a very intelligent, objective manner. He saw that they got the support that they needed. He got Admiral Nimitz to approve the use of Seabees for construction of air force fields to give them the priority that they needed to get their essential supplies out, although not as much as at times they initially wanted, General Leavey with Towers were very responsible for getting the 20th Air Force properly established in the Marianas so they could operate. This, of course, was before there was any common knowledge of the use of the atomic bomb.

Q: Yes. Admiral Hoover was involved in that?

Adm. A.: John Hoover was made forward area commander. Incidentally, he had Henry Fonda on his staff, one of the reserves who came in. John Hoover was a pretty tough cookie and he did a hell of a good job. I must say that.

Then, after they got in operation, the question was to get closer to Japan and the air corps felt that they needed Iwo Jima, so the Iwo Jima operation was included, which became, as you know, a very tough operation.

Q: A bloody one, yes.

Adm. A.: Yes.

Q: Did you go to any of these San Francisco conferences?

Adm. A.: Yes. I went back to two of them, I guess it was, but I was not present when the two principals and their higher-level people were discussing major problems. I did go back to two, but purely, you might say, in the logistic field.

There was another project that fell on my shoulders, and that was what we were going to do as the carrier air groups and patrol squadrons needed replacement, after they'd flown so many missions and served long and arduous months at sea. How was this going to be handled? And so Admiral Towers and Admiral Sherman asked me to review the plans that they had for taking care of these replacements, aircraft and pilots. I did a lot of work and turned in a report on that, which tried to put it on a very reasonable basis, a sensible basis. In the terms of the carrier air groups there was too much in the way of team work involved, so you had to replace the carrier air group with a replacement air group, as such, that had been previously trained. They'd come aboard and they'd get some exercises on the ship preparatory to going on their first offfensive operation, and the old one would go back, be dissolved, remain preserved in designation and be reformed, and those people who would come back for reassignment would fertilize the experience in the training command and the new air groups that would come out.

On the other hand, in the case of the patrol-plane squadrons, for reconnaissance and search and antisubmarine warfare, there was not that degree - it wasn't necessary to replace whole squadrons or wings and then send them back as an entire group. They could be replaced more on an individual basis.

Q: That's understandable.

Adm. A.: And that was the report sent in, which rubbed some of the people back in Washington the wrong way but which was essentially adopted because, by that time, in spite of the efforts to roll up in the rear areas there was the tremendous buildup of personnel and equipment just to keep the momentum going for the combat echelons as they moved farther and farther forward. Actually, you were getting to the point where the Hawaiian Islands were getting overpopulated, you might say. So this was all a factor here in trying to keep these things reasonable and not have too much of a buildup of forces that were noncombat in the rear echelons, and I think that we were successful in this largely through the determination of Admiral Towers and the willingness of Admiral Nimitz to support Admiral Towers in the role that was assigned to him. In that regard, there is no question about it, that Nimitz supported Admiral Towers fully and recognized the good that he was doing, and I think he recognized the good that -

Q: Nimitz himself was under some pressure from Admiral King, wasn't he, to keep Towers within confines?

Adm. A.: Oh, I'm sure of that. There's no question about it. And Admiral Sherman, as brilliant as he was, didn't want Towers emerging too high, either, and McMorris certainly didn't. Also, Towers was a strong supporter of Halsey and not an enthusiastic supporter of Spruance.

Q: That was difficult for Nimitz, then?

Adm. A.: That made it difficult, yes. We had the case during the battle of the Marianas where it was clear that the Japanese were going to take some reaction. The carriers had been placed to the west of the Marianas but assigned a role in defense of the forces ashore in close proximity to the Marianas, and when we got the word of what the Japs were contemplating, Towers felt very strongly that Mitscher and the fast carriers should move farther to the westward to intercept them, with a primary objective of destroying the Japanese fleet. He suggested to Nimitz through

Sherman that Nimitz send a directive to Spruance to do that. Nimitz took the position, we'll give Spruance all the information on the situation but if I interject and tell him what and how to do it, then he'll never know - it'll be the beginning of my trying to run the tactical side of the operations of the fleets from ashore, and, he said, "I won't do that."

Actually, you recall, they had that tremendous air battle in which the carriers shot down a lot of planes -

Q: The turkey shoot.

Adm. A.: The turkey shoot - but they could not reach and destroy the Japanese fleet, as such, as would have been possible if they'd been farther to the west, and if the primary mission of the Fifth Fleet had delineated destruction of the Japanese fleet. The primary mission in that operation was to protect the forces in the Marianas.

That, of course, can always be debated. I think Nimitz probably was right in his interpretation of the matter because -

Q: Of not interfering?

Adm. A.: Of not interfering yes.

Q: That was consistent as a policy.

Adm. A.: That's right.

Q: What about those awards? Did you see an improvement in the giving of awards as a result of your -

Adm. A.: Oh, yes, there was definitely an improvement in the overall awards program, although they were very carefully screened by the Awards Board, and the army air corps and the army approach to decorations and awards was far, far more liberal than the navy and the marine corps.

Q: The navy was always reticent.

Adm. A.: Always reticent, yes. On the other hand, the navy did a good job on the submarines and was doing that very promptly for them.

Q: Was that because of Lockwood?

Adm. A.: I think that there was a greater sympathy, initially, for the submarine people than there was for the aviators.

Q: Maybe there was more ready appreciation of the dangers that were involved?

Adm. A.: Maybe so, yes. I just read a heck of a good book called Final Harbor, fiction but very realistic fiction, about the life of a submarine during World War II out there.

Admiral Nimitz made the decision to move his headquarters to Guam from Honolulu, his primary headquarters. He also made the decision that the logistics organization under Towers and Leavey would stay back at Makalapa. There were possibly other reasons as well as he and probably Admiral King didn't want Towers too much involved in frontline fighting. Towers made all the arrangements for the buildup in Guam, including Nimitz's headquarter in addition to the provision of a rapid buildup of the bases for the army air corps, the 20th Air Force, good communications back and forth -

Q: A great depot was erected there, wasn't it?

Adm. A.: Oh, yes, supply depot.

Although Admiral Towers kept the rear echelon headquarters in Honolulu, Pearl Harbor, he made frequent trips out there, to the Marianas. Jones and I would go along with him. We'd usually fill up the airplane. I think that the buildup in the Marianas went exceptionally well, not only for the army air corps and the 20th Air Force but also for the navy headquarters facilities, although he got again annoyed with Admiral Calhoun when it turned out that Admiral Calhoun was shipping out by air some apple trees to be put around Admiral Nimitz's headquarters!

Q: I trust that he'd made a study of what would grow in Guam! Apples don't do very well in that kind of climate.

Adm. A.: But, by and large, it worked out pretty well throughout 1944, which of course was a very active period in the Pacific, and on into 1945. In the early spring of 1945 I got word that I was going to be asked for to come back to Admiral King's staff in Washington to relieve Captain P. D. Stroop, whom I'd relieved before as a lieutenant commander.

Q: Yes. What job was that?

Adm. A.: It was in the plans division of CominCh headquarters in Washington.

I went in and talked to Admiral Towers about this. My class were just about getting command of the small carriers, Kaiser-class carriers, which were really being put into transport roles of moving aircraft for everybody else forward.

Interview No. 4 with Admiral George W. Anderson, Jr., U.S Navy

(Retired)

Place: His residence in the Watergate Apartments, Washington, D.C.

Date: Wednesday morning, 22 October 1980

Subject: Biography

By: John T. Mason, Jr.

Q: So we'll begin -

Adm. A.: Yes.

Admiral Towers pointed out to me that, in his opinion, the war was rapidly coming to a close and if I got command of a carrier it would certainly not be in any combat situation, but on the other hand, I would be going back to Washington where I might be very much involved in the conclusion of the war and the readjustments in the immediate postwar period. He felt that my chances were much better to wait for postwar command at sea. Also I would have a much better opportunity to get a more active aircraft carrier command than I would under the present conditions at the end of the war with the prospective demobilization.

Q: All of which certainly proved to be true, didn't it?

Adm. A.: That's right. It did prove to be true because I had command of two aircraft carriers, one an antisubmarine warfare carrier, the Mindoro, and later the largest carrier that we had then in the navy, the Franklin D. Roosevelt, but I'll speak of that later.

I think at this point I would like to go back a little bit and talk about some personal affairs. I had my home in Washington when the war broke out, in northwest Washington. I bought the house I think for $18,500, which now is worth far more.

Q: And many times more!

Adm A.: I had my wife and three children and when I was due to go to sea in 1943 conditions were still rather uncertain with regard to the outcome of the war, particularly possible damage to the United States, and I felt it would be better for my family to be away from Washington. So we selected a general location in the southwest, in Albuquerque, New Mexico, because my wife had serious sinus problems. So, when I went to sea, they moved out there. Also, I felt that someone who was coming to Washington could use our house, a friend of friends, who was a major in the army, came from California and rather than gouge them with high rent, we made our house available at one hundred dollars a month to them.

Q: That's incredible!

Adm. A.: So, they occupied our house during the time they were in Washington and my family was in Albuquerque.

At the time in 1945 when this change of duty was coming up, my wife was suffering from severe sinus and that also influenced me and I explained the situation to Admiral Towers. He said:

"That reinforces my view that it is best for you and your family that you go back to duty in Washington."

Before I was detached, Admiral Towers said, "I want you to pick your relief," and I recommended to him then Captain James S. Russell, who was a very brilliant officer and one I knew very, very well. Admiral Towers went out to get him, although Captain Russell, later Admiral Russell and my vice chief of naval operations when I was CNO, was reluctant to come to duty there.

Q: He being an activist?

Adm. A.: That's right. But he came and relieved me. I flew back, went to Albuquerque, joined my family, picked my wife and children up and started across the continent in my old automobile. We had decided that she would stop by the Barnes Hospital in St. Louis for a checkup on her physical condition and we did. We checked in and she was about to see a very famous chest surgeon, Dr. Evarts Graham, but he said that before he saw her he wanted her to see the eye, ear, nose and throat doctor at the Barnes Hospital, which she did. He was a doctor named Thomas Walsh. He looked her over and said that he felt it was necessary to have an exploratory operation on her sinus and recommended that, and we agreed.

Q: The climate in Albuquerque hadn't been beneficial, then?

Adm. A.: Absolutely not, and he said it wouldn't have in any case.

When he did this exploratory examination, I said to him, "Is there any chance that this might be a malignancy?"

"Oh," he said, "don't worry about that. Maybe one in a hundred."

Then he sent for me after the operation and said that she had a very serious malignancy in her sinuses. I said:

"Well, what do we do?" and he said:

"There are several things we could do. We could have a radical operation now. It would certainly result in a tragic deformation of her features. We could try radium."

I said, "What would you do?" and he said:

"If it was me, I would go ahead with the radical operation."

I said, "What would you do if it was your wife?"

He said, "I'd try the radium," so I said, "Well, let's do that."

Q: What a difficult decision.

Adm. A.: He then went ahead and inserted the radium and she would have to stay there for approximately two weeks. I had a date to report in in Washington, so I took the three children, very small, with me and we drove on east to Washigton. We made the trip successfully. In braiding my little girl's hair, I always had difficulty but I usually found some sympathetic ladies around who would always help out. We arrived back in Washington, in the neighborhood, and stayed to visit with my classmate and good friend later Admiral Don Griffin. Just as we drove up to their door we had a flat tire, so the trip was completed and I reported in in the next day or so, and my house on Upton Street in northwest Washington was available, and I resumed my duties at CominCh, in the plans division, in relief of then Captain P. D. Stroop.

Q: That was in June of 1945?

Adm. A.: That was in June of 1945.

Q: June 10th.

Adm. A.: I reported in -

Q: I wonder, Sir, if you'd lap back. There are one or two items on your list that we passed over. You listed kamikaze damage and you apparently wanted to say something about that, in the Pacific.

Adm. A.: In that stage of the Pacific war, particularly around the period when we were operating against Okinawa and later Iwo Jima, the Japanese introduced the tactic of the kamikaze suicide pilots. Under those circumstances, they inflicted grave damage to our ships. It was a new type of attack and it required that we had to greatly bolster up our antiair defense, both in fighter aircraft and in antiaircraft guns of all types. The carrier division commanders and the commanding officers and fleet commanders were anxious to have more fighter aircraft on board ship than we had originally, and it was fortunate that we were able to assemble additional fighter aircraft to put on the ships to meet this particular threat.

Q: Did it take us completely by surprise, the introduction of the kamikaze?

Adm. A.: I would say basically it did take us by surprise, although whether in the highly classified intelligence information that was available at that time there might have been some indications but certainly that was closely held. Generally speaking, the navy appeared to have been taken by surprise.

The important lesson of this is that, in war, you must be prepared for surprises, you must have sufficient flexibility and hopefully enough aircraft and weapons available to adjust to circumstances of this type. Also, in another sense, if the enemy has a capability by surprise to attack the sources of our production, such as a fighter plant or a bomber plant in the United States you must have sufficient depth to the industrial production capability to be able to sustain the flow of aircraft and weapons so that your whole war effort is not going to be stalled or come to a very catastrophic situation.

Fortunately for us in World War II, we were able to produce aircraft without enemy interference at our plants, either airplane plants, the engine plants or the weapon plants.

In the earlier days, in preparing for our wartime production, we could not assume that we were not going to have damage and indeed if the Germans had made such progress with the nuclear weapons with the atomic bomb, that we did later, our country could have been subjected to very serious devastation, which fortunately did not take place.

Q: And always the danger of sabotage?

Adm. A.: Well, there was a danger of sabotage, which required a lot of plant security. Fortunately, it did not assume a major real threat to us, the point being, in regard to the kamikaze, if we did not have sufficient excess fighter aircraft, replacement aircraft to put on our carriers, to increase our figher defenses.

There is always a school and there was at that time that thinks in terms of killing the last Jap with the last bullet fired by the last gun on the last airplane that would be produced and we'd come out all even in production and the end of the war.

Q: That persists in living, doesn't it?

Adm. A.: It certainly does, and it is something that we must recognize, that in our preparations for our national security we always have to have a cushion in the production in the availability of ships, airplanes, and weapons. The sad thing is that you project this lesson today with the emphasis on management, there is too much of a tendency to figure out exactly how much you're going to need by mathematical computation or by computerization without recognition of the unknowns that can take place in war or international politics.

One thing that impressed me in the early days when I was in the Bureau of Aeronautics and we were trying to provide assistance to the Soviet Union, their demands for materials, for weapons, for aircraft, for ships were, to us, fantastic, but they recognized this threat to them which was not fully appreciated in the higher levels of Washington. Also, I think we must recognize that today there is nobody military or civilian in the Washington hierarchy who had any experience of the period of industrial mobilization and military mobilization that we had to go through in World War II. And remember that in World War II we had the long period of the so-called "phony" war to help out our allies to build up our industrial production base in the United States, to make the transition from peace to war through the lend-lease program. The lead times today to mobilize our industry for new ships or airplanes into production are much longer than they were in the period immediately prior to when we got involved in World War II. Sometimes you have lead times today for the long-lead-items that are as much as four and a half years.

We were able successfully to convert automobile plants for production assembly of aircraft or for aircraft engines in a relatively short time, perhaps eighteen months. You couldn't possibly do that today. The metals themselves would be sophisticated types of metals such as titanium, and the working of titanium, the forging and so forth would take much longer and you cannot expect today to increase your production radically in probably less than two and a half to three years.

Q: And, on the other hand, the time element is much shorter today.

Adm. A.: That's right.

Q: You also listed, without any explanation, the 20th Air Force. I wondered if you wanted to say something about that.

Adm. A.: Yes, and I'll pick that up because the U.S. Army Air Corps had a very enlightened approach to waging what is known as strategic warfare. This started about the time we became involved in the war with their close liaison with the British and they had all sorts of plans to win the war by air, by strategic air, by destroying the enemy's capability of production, of destroying the will of the enemy to fight, and, ultimately, in destroying the enemy's populations. In Europe they established the 8th Air Force in Britain. It worked very closely with Bomber Command of the Royal Air Force. When we became heavily involved in the Pacific, they had a U.S. Air Force established in China and their thinking was directed toward carrying the air war directly to Japan with high-level bombers. The B-29 aircraft was coming along in production as a replacement for the B-17 and B-24, which had been used against Germany, and so their concept was to form a new air force called the 20th Air Force which would be based in the Marianas and would carry out the air attacks against Japan itself. They felt that air bombardment would be ultimately successful in winning the war against Japan and eliminating the necessity for the invasion of Japan.

The Joint Chiefs of Staff had adopted a policy to defeat Japan by sea and air blockades, by air bombardment and invasion, if necessary. I think you could put that in quote and unquote.

Q: The plans were made for it?

Adm. A.: Plans were made for it. The 20th Air Force was a highly efficient organization and they moved in to the Marianas. The operations were being directed from Washington more or less under the personal supervision of the air staff under General "Hap" Arnold.

When I went back to CominCh for duty, I inherited the responsibilities that Captain Stroop had as the navy liaison with the 20th Air Force.

Q: An interesting assignment.

Adm. A.: Also, before I left Honolulu I had strong suspicions that something was in the wind although I was not cleared for anything involving the dropping of the atomic bomb. However, I had strong suspicions that something was in the wind and that we should be alert to what was about to be coming into operation.

Q: What were the indications that you discerned?

Adm. A.: Well, that certain facilities in the Marianas were given special security, that certain target cities in Japan would be exempt from conventional bombing attacks, there was just at high level an area of anticipation. This was also immediately evident to me when I picked up my duties in Washington on the staff of CominCh in working in and following the activities of the 20th Air Force and their bombing.

Q: There's something else that you listed, and that was a series of trips made to the Marianas and to various places to Guam, Majuro. I wondered if there was anything of significance there that you wanted to recall.

Adm A.: I think there were some amusing things. I remember going out to Kwajalein one time with Admiral Towers and Commander

Jones, whom I mentioned, and the air base commander there was a Captain, later Rear Admiral, Eddie Ewen.

Q: A famous pilot.

Adm. A.: A pilot and a very great football player at the Naval Academy. He was very proud of the progress he'd made and the smartness of his organization. When he went to show us a communications post that he had there, he walked in and all the radio operators were at their desks. He called out "Attention," and they, all dressed very smartly, stood up. Admiral Towers said, "Carry on," and Ed Ewen said, "Go ahead with your work and they got down and started listening and pounding the keys, but very few of the radio sets were actually turned on!

Admiral Towers was very interested in making sure, first, that what was needed was adequately equipped and supplied and manned, and that things that were not any longer needed were rolled up so that the equipment and the personnel could be moved forward where they would be more urgently required as the war progressed. As I say, Admiral Towers was extremely dedicated, under Admiral Nimitz's direction, to the construction of the bases for the 20th Air Force in Guam and the Marianas as well as all the naval facilities because the army air corps was rather suspicious that the navy would only give it lip service. Actually, the navy, perceiving what the objective of the Marianas was in the long-range strategic role, was very dedicated to doing the very best job that it could for its sister service.

Q: That introduces an idea. The sense of integrity that military men have, which is instilled in them in their training, why doesn't that carry over into interservice relationships? Why did the air corps suspect the intentions of the navy?

Adm. A.: The army air pilots, from the days of Billy Mitchell, were not only against the navy because they looked down on the ability of ships to survive against air attack, but they were competition for funds and interests and publicity. Also they were having their own struggle attaining a position of prominence in the army itself, with the ground elements of the army and the service elements of the army. It was only at the beginning of World War II that General Arnold achieved a status of rank and position as a member of the Joint Chiefs of Staff, and I think they were assisted by the position attained by the Royal Air Force in Britain, that it was necessary for us to give the army air corps a high level and status to be able to work effectively with the British. And so the members of the Joint Chiefs of Staff did include General Arnold as well as General Marshall and Admiral King.

In the old days, the members of the Joint Board, army-navy, included an air corps officer and the chief of the Bureau of Aeronautics, Admiral Towers then, who were involved in the planning for the operations of the military and making major military decisions. But in the actual war plans evolved before the war, before we got involved in joint planning with the British, there was very little mention of aviation either of the navy or in the army. In other words, the feeling against aviation - the services were dominated by nonaviation personnel, army and navy which stimulated a resentment on the part of the aviators in the navy against the so-called black shoes, the brown shoes against the black shoes, and of the army air corps against the ground soldiers in the army. It was only by the superb performance of the naval aviators and the army air corps personnel and the recognition of the nonaviation personnel of the army and the navy that aviation, army and navy, did emerge to be of such paramount importance.

But, there was the rivalry, there was the distrust. Another factor was the way the army gave decorations and the air corps gave, oh, tremendous numbers of decorations, and the navy was very parsimonious in handing out decorations. The publicity that was given to the army air corps in relationship to naval aviation and the carrier pilots -

Q: The Battle of Midway!

Adm. A.: That's right, and it carried all along through. It was even reflected in what I as coming to next, postwar planning that was being carried on back in Washington when I reported in. Looking at the size and the composition of the prospective first postwar navy, which involved a great reduction of the relative position of naval aviation and the retention of about fifteen battleships in the postwar navy. This was something that I got very much involved in at my aviation desk in the plans divison of CominCh headquarters.

Q: There was one man about whom I thought you might want to say something, and that was Oakleigh Thorne.

Adm. A.: Oakleigh Thorne! When I was in the Bureau of Aeronautics I had a former naval officer come back to active duty, Tom Jones, one of my very close friends, but we still needed some help. So I got Lieutenant, jg, Thorne, who was of the prominent Thorne family, a Princeton graduate, a Golden Gloves boxer, a very smart, practical, very wealthy individual, to come in and work with us. He was so good that when Admiral Towers left to go to the Pacific as Commander, Air Force, Pacific Fleet, he took Oakleigh Thorne, then a lieutenant commander, along as his flag secretary, and he performed extremely well for Admiral Towers.

So, when Admiral Sherman left as chief of staff to Admiral Towers to go as assistant chief of staff at CinCPacFlt, he recommended to Admiral Nimitz that he get Oakleigh Thorne, who was then a reserve commander, to come over and be Admiral Nimitz's flag secretary. Thorne did a superb job for Admiral Nimitz, just as he had for me in a lower capacity and for Admiral Towers and did a fine job. So he started to work for me in the plans division of the Bureau of Aeronautics and ended up as flag secretary to the Commander in Chief, Pacific Fleet, Admiral Nimitz.

Q: Quite a climb wasn't it!

Adm. A.: It sure was, and well deserved because he was a very able fellow. He later died.

Q: Well, now I expect we're ready to go to Washington in June of 1945?

Adm. A.: Well, as I said, I relieved Captain Stroop and took up my duties as the aviation officer in the plans division of the Bureau of Aeronautics in the concluding phases of the war. One of my duties was liaison officer with the 20th Air Force. The other was involved in all the day-to-day affairs that would come to the plans division and included an input to the plans for postwar action.

During the time that I was there I did not take part in any of the big conferences although Captain Stroop has been to one of the conferences that they had. I forget which one.

Q: Cairo?

Adm. A.: Cairo or Yalta or something of that sort.

We also followed the developments of the war and at that time, of course, there was a plan for the invasion of Japan.

Q: Olympic?

Adm. A.: That's right, Olympic. My personal feeling was that the invasion would not be necessary because the superb operations of the submarines made the blockade of Japan increasingly close. The air bombardments, both carrier and 20th Air Force, were practically destroying the industrial capacity of Japan and the cities of Japan. They had the big fire raids on Tokyo. My feeling was and, I guess in that connection, I sort of echoed the sentiments that had been expressed to me over the months and years by Admiral Towers, that they would finally collapse without the need for invasion. Nevertheless, the planning for the invasion was going forward with the concept, of course, that the primary responsibility would be given to MacArthur with Admiral Nimitz with the full navy support in support of MacArthur, who would be the commander of chief.

There were, of course, other things going on in different parts of the world, the occupation of Germany and matters would come through the plans division, various facets of that, but I would get, being in the CominCh headquarters with the preoccupation of Admiral King towards the war against Japan, even though he was a member of the Joint Chiefs of Staff and responsible on these other acitivities worldwide, that our interest was primarily naval and concerned with the war against Japan.

The atomic bomb was dropped, the world was shocked, and that reinforced all our views that the war against Japan had been won and it was concluded very rapidly. Then the second bomb was dropped, and they threw in the towel.

There was a lot of talk but I was not involved in any of the decisions about the Russians coming into the war against Japan. I personally thought that it was not to our interest to have them come in, that they were just playing their own opportunistic game by coming in, even though there had been pressure to get them in primarily to reduce American casualties.

Q: I think that was a political decision.

Adm. A.: That's right, it was a political decision. The two things, getting the Russians to come in militarily and dropping the atomic bomb, were political in the sense that the president of the United States, President Truman at that time, wanted to minimize casualties among American personnel.

After the Japanese capitulation, the planning and the activities were essentially in the immediate readjustment problems of going from war to peace and the occupation of Japan, the surrender of Japanese forces in various parts of the Far East and southeast Asia, and the continuing problems of readjusting in Europe plus the planning for the demobilization of all our military forces, especially the navy as far as we were concerned. Here we had this magnificent military establishment and the urge was to demobilize it immediately, rather than retaining much stronger military forces and demobilizing at a more gradual level. The natural political and psychological pressure was to demobilize as fast as you could, get the boys home, regardless of what the impact of that was on our ability to continue combat operations, if necessary.

Q: Common sense didn't previal, couldn't prevail, I suppose.

Adm. A.: Common sense did not prevail, and I think one of the great problems of our whole postwar era and the emergence of the Russians was that we demobilized and left them in a position of increasing strength.

Q: Yes, they didn't demobilize.

Adm. A.: That's right, they didn't.

Q: And they had hoarded a lot of supplies from us?

Adm. A.: Oh, yes. So, through the end of 1945 there was also the desire quite evidently of the senior people of the army and the navy who had carried the load for so long, of the Marshalls and Kings and the Nimitzes, and the others to turn it over to someone else. However, President Truman prevailed on Eisenhower, about to relieve General Marshall, and for Admiral Nimitz to come back and relieve Admiral King. There was also going on the idea of unification, the "merger". The army had spent a great deal of time laying the groundwork for this. The navy had not been too much involved in it except fussing about what the army had done. Therefore, the navy was reacting, I guess, to the urge for unification and the establishment of the separate independent air force.

So, when we went from 1945 to 1946, you had the change of the leadership from Marshall to Eisenhower and King to Nimitz. Their bringing in people whom they had known best during the war and Admiral Nimitz brought Admiral Sherman back to Washington, and we got into all the struggle on unification. Secretary of the Navy Forrestal and Secretary of the Army Patterson started taking up the action on that, so when we went into 1946 you had this unification fight, you might call it, going on between the services and it got increasingly bitter because the urge was to get the army air corps and all air into one independent package. The navy was fighting for its own air and the marine corps for its survival because the army plan for unification envisaged the independent air force taking over naval air, all air, and bringing the marine corps down to the point where they would have only guards for legations and shipboard components.

Q: Like the secret service!

Adm. A.: Yes. So this going on into 1946, you could see the buildup of this so-called unification fight.

Q: And simultaneously, the demobilization?

Adm. A.: Demobilization going on, the adjustment to the size and the composition of the U.S. forces.

Q: What was the attitude in the U.S. Navy's high command towards this very rapid demobilization?

Adm. A.: I think it was more or less "it's inevitable, relax, enjoy it, and do the best you can with what you've got."

Towards the end of the summer, right after the war in Japan, I was sent to relieve Admiral, then Captain, Dennison in the Joint War Plans Committee of the Joint Chiefs of Staff, and all of these interservice problems, the major problems, were flowing into the JCS Joint Staff. I remember they had the size and the composition of the armed services, the roles and missions of the armed services, the base requirements overseas, problems of this sort, all descending at the same time on the Joint Staff, and, of course, the unification, which rapidly got taken out of the level of the staff, the Joint Staff itself, and taken up more at the levels of the secretaries, the chief of staff of the army, and the chief of naval operations.

Q: Enveloped in a cloud of emotion, too!

Adm. A.: Very much so.

I stayed over on the Joint War Plans Committee about three months, I guess it was, an office in the old Public Health Building on Constitution Avenue, when I was what I guess you might call sprung and came back to my job in CNO then. CominCh was disestablishing and CNO picked up.

Q: Nimitz never held the title of CominCh?

Adm. A.: No, he never held the title of CominCh.

I came back and there I became very much involved in the effort to preserve the traditional role of naval air and of the marine corps. Also, Admiral Sherman had come back as deputy for plans and operations, which was the key job in the office of CNO and in the Joint Chiefs of Staff, because the deputy for plans and operations always accompanied the chief - this was true for the other services as well - to the Joint Chiefs of Staff meetings, and they were to have their own meetings as so-called deputies to try to handle the problems before they came to the Chiefs.

Admiral Sherman had appointed me to be a member of the Canada-U.S. permanent joint board on defense. He appointed me also to be a member of the U.S.-Brazilian Defense Commission. This was all part of the postwar planning, trying to enhance the strength of the United States and its allies for the postwar period in the light of the emerging situation, our position, and aggressive tendencies of the Russians, which he recognized. I remember Admiral Sherman saying one time to me: "The three principal forces in the world that we have to recognize are the existence of the Russian army, the atomic bomb, and the U.S. Navy."

It was recognized certainly in the Plans Division of CNO that the postwar settlement in Europe leaving Berlin 110 miles inside the Soviet frontier was going to be a continuing problem to us. There were no peace treaties at that stage of the game. The maneuvering was going on as to how to get the Russians to agree to an acceptable peace treaty, how to prevent the rearming and re-emergence of Germany or of Japan. There's a considerable difference between Europe and the Far East because in Europe the Russians were there, in Berlin, and, as I say, it was 110 miles inside the front lines. You had the Russians, the Americans, the French, and the British, whereas in Japan you had General MacArthur in command and he was the control and did not brook very much interference by anybody else because primarily he was an American and, although he was MacArthur, he knew that the United States had won the war against Japan. He was not going to brook any interference at his level.

Q: The Russians weren't admitted, were they?

Adm. A.: No, that's right.

So, all during that period in 1946 we had these tremendously important postwar problems of trying to cope with the end of World War II, to meet the prospective ambitious actions of the Soviet Union, and to carry on this fight that was going on in the United States, and to get the readjustment of our military forces to try to regain some meausre of military strength in the U.S. services, which were completely depleted of experienced personnel because they'd all been demobilized. Because of the expansion we'd had, the regular personnel of the navy, for example, were a very, very small percentage. We had ships laid up because we didn't have qualified personnel to put them to sea.

In the summer of 1946, it was decided that Admiral Mitscher, who was the new commander in chief of the Atlantic Fleet, with his chief of staff, Commodore Arleigh Burke, would make a trip to Europe. Admiral Sherman decided that he would make the trip with them and he asked me to go along with him.

Q: Mitscher didn't like the idea that Sherman went along, did he?

Adm. A.: Not too much, no.

We went on in the plane with Admiral Mitscher, Admiral Burke, later Admiral Griffin, then a captain and a classmate of mine, who was with Admiral Mitscher, and I was with Admiral Sherman. Admiral Sherman had an aide, Admiral Mitscher had an aide, and we started off. I've gotten my papers down there, a photographic record of this trip.

We went to Iceland. I remember something that happened in Iceland because we landed at Keflavik in the DC-4 in which we were traveling and they were going over to Reykjavik. Going over there, we got into an army air corps DC-3 to make the short trip over and, coming back from Reykjavik, we were going down the runway and all of a sudden the plane stopped and the mechanic got out, went around to the tail, and found out that they had started to take off with the battens on the control surfaces, and they had Admiral Mitscher, Admiral Burke, Burke a future CNO, Admiral Sherman, a future CNO, I a future CNO.

Q: The navy brains were right there!

Adm. A.: In any event, we then went on to London and from London we —

Q: You had conferences with the sea lords?

Adm. A.: That's right — we went to Brussels and from Brussels we went over to Berlin, to Frankfort and Berlin, and saw the horrible devastation that prevailed in Germany. Then we came back to Paris and flew down to Rome — Trieste and then Rome, then to Malta. As we came in to Malta, Admiral Mitscher got sick.

Q: It was appendix, wasn't it?

Adm. A.: It was appendix. He could not continue the trip. Then we went down to Port Lyautey, ducked back to the Azores, and back to the United States.

Well, it was a very illuminating trip, and one thing that sticks out in my mind, as we were flying from Paris down — we'd been through Germany — and I was sitting back with Admiral Sherman and I remember saying:

"Admiral, it would be worth fifty billion dollars to prevent this from happening again. We've got to get Europe rehabilitated as fast as we can."

He certainly agreed, and he was a prime mover in getting going on the Truman Doctrine and the Marshall Plan. Naturally, it was at a very high level of the government, but it was very important to see that something had to be done rapidly to get western Europe back together if we were to prevent the complete deterioration of it in the chaos that was prevailing postwar and the communist threat, because in all of these countries the guerrilla forces that had assisted in throwing back the Germans the communist elements were very strongly partisan and they contributed a great deal in the common effort, but at this stage of the game the Communist Party was carying out the roles and dictates of Moscow in endeavoring to get control of these countries so that the communist influence could take over all of Europe. And, indeed, at that stage of the game, it was not too unlikely.

Another thing that developed, which had great postwar significance, we were down in Naples and, at that time, the commander of U.S. naval forces in the Mediterranean was Admiral Bernard Bieri, and he was living at a place called Villa Emma, the old villa that Lady Hamilton -

Q: Lady Hamilton.

Adm. A.: Right. His staff was all living ashore. Actually the standard of behavior and appearance was far below what we would normally expect of a seagoing U.S. Navy to have, particularly someone as meticulous as Admiral Sherman.

When we left Naples and throughout the rest of the trip, Admiral Sherman formulated the determination in his mind of a different role for the U.S. Navy in the Mediterranean than was being carried out at that time under current organization and directives. So, when he got back to Washington, he formulated the idea of establishing the Sixth Fleet and he persuaded Admiral Nimitz to release him from his duties as deputy for plans and operations, to permit him to go to the Mediterranean and take command of the Sixth Fleet, which Admiral Nimitz did reluctantly but recognized that this was a necessary thing to do over there.

And so the whole concept of the Sixth Fleet was Admiral Sherman's, with the full approval of Admiral Nimitz and the secretary of the navy. As a matter of fact, I was at a meeting in Washington and a note from Admiral Sherman was passed to me which said, "Why do we need U.S. naval forces in the Mediterranean? Hurry!" So I left and then drew up the reasons he asked for - but before I'd even had the thing typed in the smooth, Admiral Sherman called for it. I took it up to him in draft form and he said, "Oh, that's all right." I said, "Do you want me to do any more on that?" "No, don't worry about it." The next thing I knew I read about it on the front page of The New York Times, a pronouncement by Forrestal as to why we needed U.S. naval forces in the Mediterranean (exactly as presented in the penciled draft of my memorandum).

The point is that Sherman recognized the need for it, established the whole procedure of the Sixth Fleet under his personal direction, took command of it, and certainly for many, many years afterwards the role of the Sixth Fleet was exactly the same as Sherman had conceived it.

Q: And, all over this picture, wasn't there a real concern that we were on the verge of a war with Russia?

Adm. A.: Very much of a concern in this regard, very much so. We'd gone through '46, and '47 was the unification National Security Act, in which period it had finally gotten down to the conference between the Senate and the House of Representatives, of the final drafting of the National Security Act. Admiral Sherman and General Norstad had been established by I guess it was Forrestal and Patterson, with the approval of Nimitz and Eisenhower, as the go-betweens and the advisers to the Congress on the act. Of course, there were many other ramifications of this whole thing because Forrestal had brought Ferdinand Eberstadt in, there were exchanges of papers back and forth between Patterson and Forrestal, between Nimitz and Eisenhower, but when it finally came down there was a divergence between the Senate and the House.

Admiral Radford was in Washington at the time, working on the navy's position on unification and he was also looked upon as a sort of a coequal with Forrest Sherman in formulating the navy's position and advice to Nimitz and to Forrestal.

Q: He had the Pacific job simultaneously, didn't he?

Adm. A.: No. He was DCNO, Air. This was before he went to the Pacific.

I had been working with Admiral Radford and Radford and Sherman had certain divergencies of views. Radford took a stronger position against compromise, though they were both determined they wanted to salvage what they could out of naval aviation and the marine corps.

So when these conferences took place, I had been sent up to advise certain of the conferees from the House of Representatives, and Sherman and Norstad - I was a captain at the time - were advising the other conferees, particularly in the Senate. The one I was working with was Congressman Cole.

Q: Sterling Cole?

Adm. A.: Sterling Cole, and I wrote out the safeguards for naval aviation and the marine corps, which prevailed in the House of Representatives against the conferees from the Senate, although Sherman knew what I was doing all the time. It worked out very well because we got our safeguards into the legislation. Of course, that didn't stop the argument back and forth because we still had the problem of the roles and the missions of the services, and the army and the new and growing air force were adamant that they were going to try one way or another, regardless of the legislation, they were going to circumscribe the actions of naval aviation and the marine corps.

Norstad had been appointed. He was three years junior to me. He graduated from West Point three years after I graduated from the Naval Academy. He was a lieutenant general and had been made the deputy for plans and operations of the general staff of the army, as an aviator. Towers was back on the General Board of the navy, and Towers was a very close friend and confidant of Forrestal. They got along very well, and Towers told Forrestal what the navy should do to counteract the position being taken by the army air corps and the army was to recognize the importance of youth and aviation. Towers had put the bug in Forrestal's bonnet that what they should do was take me, as a captain, promote me to vice admiral, and put me in a position of plans and operations of the Navy Department. I said:

"Admiral Towers, that's absurd," and he said:

"Well, you've got to be prepared for it. First thing you know, we're going to get a call from Forrestal."

So I was having lunch at the Army and Navy Town Club one day and a telephone message came to me that Mr. Forrestal wanted to see me right away.

Q: Deep selection!

Adm. A.: So I ran right back to the Navy Department and walked in to Forrestal's office. He had Carl Hinshaw, a congressman from California there.

Q: A very potent member.

Adm. A.: That's right, Hinshaw came from the district around Los Angeles where there was tremendous emphasis on aviation and there was also a very strong Zionist Jewish movement in Los Angeles.

Well, they were sitting down and the subject was the position of the United States relative to Israel and Palestine. Forrestal was very preoccupied with this, tremendously preoccupied, and he said that he and General Marshall could not adopt a common position on Israel or Palestine in the Joint State-War-Navy

Committee without it being leaked immediately to the press and the Zionists. So they had taken a position, he said, where they would write out in longhand themselves and take whatever they recommended directly to Truman, then it only took forty-eight hours before it leaked.

Forrestal was trying to solicit some support from Carl Hinshaw for his position and not to get the United States committed to the recognition of Israel. Hinshaw said he couldn't do it. Forrestal asked why. He said:

"Because I couldn't get reelected. All my financial support comes from the Jewish people and they're completely under the domination of the Zionists. Why don't you go to one of these prominent people that you have such faith in, like Barney Baruch?"

Forrestal said:

Baruch? Of course, I've gone to Barney Baruch and Barney Baruch agrees with me personally but he told me that no Jewish person by race or religion could take a position against the Zionists because they are so ruthless and so determined that he would be portrayed as a traitor to his race and religion. Barney told me that he would do anything for this country that he possibly could except face up to the Zionists."

Well, I don't know what Forrestal said because I didn't have much chance to talk. Then Forrestal started talking to me about -

Q: Did you have some set opinions on this subject?

Adm. A.: No, I wasn't asked.

Q: You weren't even involved?

Adm. A.: No. This was a conversation between Hinshaw and Forrestal. Then he started to bring up the subject of the aviation review that was being taken in the Congress, primarily with the idea - the Congress had gotten into this with Hinshaw's full instigation -

Q: Hinshaw was foreign relations, was he, in the House?

Adm. A.: This was a special committee to preserve aviation production in the United States. After all, when the war stopped, the orders were canceled, production stopped, and our aircraft industry was just going flat on its face because we had such large quantities of World War II aircraft, far beyond our peacetime requirements, and there was genuine concern on the part of Forrestal and Hinshaw and others that we had to preserve our aircraft industry as one of the major sources of power we had in the United States. So, he was trying to mobilize public opinion to develop a national aviation program for research and development on production to preserve the U. S. aircraft industry.

Well, just then, Secretary Stuart Symington, who was the new secretary of the air force, came in to the meeting and that was the end of it. So, whatever was in Forrestal's mind about talking to me about other than this aspect of naval aviation faded away and I never heard anything more about it.

Q: It would have put you in a very difficult position.

Adm. A.: Oh, an impossible position, and I was later in a similar position when I was at SHAPE and I'll tell you about that later.

In the meantime, I was working with the Canadians -

Q: Yes, tell me more about that, will you, that special Canadian board?

Adm. A.: The permanent board of defense, Canada-United States, was set up by President Roosevelt and Mackenzie King in what was known as the Ogdensburg Agreement - Ogdensburg, New York, and the idea of it was that we were equally involved in the security of our two countries - this was, I guess, just before World War II, because if anything happened like a full collapse in Europe we would have to stand together and, after the end of World War II, there was considerable doubt as to whether we were going to be able to hold on to our close relationships with the Canadians. I might go back and say when Pearl Harbor occurred, the first thing that Forrest Sherman had to do was go up to Canada and meet with the Canadians to make sure that there was a haven for the British fleet there if it had come over to the western Atlantic.

At the end of the war there was some doubt as to whether our wartime arrangement would hold together, and it was agreed to send up a group of Americans to Ottawa, George Kennan from the State Department, Lauris Norstad, several other people, and I went up, flew up, to Ottawa. When we arrived we were brought in what I call sealed limousines directly to the American embassy residence. We were not permitted to leave the American embassy residence but we met there with senior Canadian foreign service and military officers to discuss the overall threat to the United States and Canada, potential threat and the danger, as you mentioned before, of the possibility of war with the Soviet Union. Then we were brought back in the limousines with the shades pulled down and flew back to Washington.

Q: Why this secrecy?

Adm. A.: Because that was the atmosphere, in Canada particularly. Some people were sick of war, and the Canadians particularly so.

But the permanent board on defense was chaired on the U.S. side by Mayor LaGuardia of New York, a great little fellow, and on the Canadian side by General McNaughton, who was really Mr. Army of Canada, a great man. This board would meet regularly every two months, one time in the United States some place and the next time in Canada, and the senior American military man on it was Major General Henry, a very fine, oldtime cavalry officer, very senior. The navy representative was Admiral J. Cary Jones, a rear admiral, and I was the other U.S. Navy member. Then there was an army air corps member, air force member, and the State Department. We met at various places in Canada and the United States, and the idea was to preserve the essential measure of cooperation vital to each of our two countries. I think that there were no nationalistic attitudes on the part of either the Canadian or the U.S. members, but it had to be handled quite carefully.

Later on, when we got into more involved pre-NATO

organization, they established what was called the U.S.-Canadian Military Cooperation Committee, and I was also put on as a member of that. In that we got into more detailed arrangements for planning for air defense, for antisubmarine warfare operations, training and bases, facilities, and so forth. But the importance of maintaining the Canadian-U.S. relationship was recognized on both sides as very important to each of our countries.

We also had a less dynamic U.S.-Brazilian Committee and Admiral Sherman had seen to it that I got put on that as a member, but that was not nearly as effective as the Canadian one because we were closer together.

Q: Were the Canadians also affected by very rapid demobilization?

Adm. A.: Oh, yes.

Q: Similar to ours?

Adm. A.: Yes, and also a reaction against the military up there, which made it a sensitive political issue, more sensitive, I guess, than in the United States.

Q: The Brazilians, on the other hand I suppose, were much more relaxed.

Adm. A.: Oh, yes.

Another thing developed while Admiral Sherman was deputy for plans and policy. He sent for me one day. I went up there and he said:

"Now, George, I want you to drop everything else you're

doing and make a study, a long-range study. You have access to all the intelligence, all research and development information on weapons, including the atomic weapon, and I want you to come up with a position that we in the navy should take as a long-range program for the security of the country."

Well, I got into this. I had access to everything.

Q: Quite an assignment.

Adm. A.: I had to work more or less alone. I didn't have anybody working with me as a matter of fact, did it all alone, put in hours and hours at it. I remember drawing up a long paper like this and came down to conclusions. One afternoon late I went up to Admiral Sherman's office and said:

"Admiral, I'd sort of like a little bit of guidance here. This is what I have evolved."

He picked it up, then he stopped when he'd reached the conclusions. He went back and read the whole thing very, very carefully. He said:

"George, the project is terminated. Tear the Goddamned thing up and go back to doing your regular job!"

Q: Interpret that, now.

Adm. A.: Well, the conclusion was that a conflict of one sort or another between the U.S. and the U.S.S.R. was inevitable. Secondly, that the conflict between the U.S. and the U.S.S.R. must be resolved prior to the time when the Soviet Union accumulated any quantity of nuclear weapons. Third, it was inconceivable that you could resolve a conflict in war between the Soviet Union and the United States by conventional means because they would be able to prevent us from creating and recreating in time the conventional forces poised over in Europe and on the mainland of Asia which could prevent them in time. By the time these forces were available we couldn't mobilize and project the forces that were necessary. Therefore we would have to see to it that any confrontation that took place would have to take place while we still have a preponderance, almost a monopoly, on nuclear weapons; that the time for decision as to what we were going to do would be when they first exploded a nuclear weapon; that we would determine that we had to resolve the conflict before they had accumulated a stockpile. The time for decision could be no later than the time they exploded their first weapon.

Remember, that was back in, I guess, 1947, and Sherman said: "Terminate it! Destroy it." It was the only copy and it was destroyed.

Q: It was destroyed?

Adm. A.: Oh, sure.

Q: It had its repercussion today?

Adm. A.: Well, it does, and I'll tell you something else.

Time went on and I continued the usual work there in the Plans Division of CNO, work on unification and roles and missions, the Canada-U.S. thing, the U.S.-Canada Military Cooperation Committee, occasionally the Brazilian committee. I had a lot of physical problems with my wife at the time, going up to Memorial Hospital in New York, she'd had a series of operations.

Q: The radium hadn't -?

Adm. A.: No. Shortly after she came back from St. Louis - this was back in 1945, so late in '45 I took her up to Memorial Hospital in New York and they did a radical operation on her face, and the doctors told me that she would last not more than two years. But she came back from that time and Bethesda took very good care of her. Well, she got another operation up in New York, too, for an extension of the disease. Then in October of 1947 she died and in 1948 - I forget - I wanted to get to sea. I had made arrangements to take care of the children. I'd leave them in Washington. I engaged a housekeeper or governess, you might say. Admiral Sherman had left for the sixth Fleet in Europe and I finally got agreement that I could get to sea, take command of an ASW carrier the Mindoro, in A.S.W. research and development at highest priority which was engaged (Admiral Towers was exactly right because she was one of the few ships in the navy that had the highest priority in the navy in the assignment of people) -

Q: You had a full complement?

Adm. A.: So I had a full complement and was working on the development of antisubmarine warfare tactics, operating out of the U.S. primarily. So I lined up for that. I had to go to certain schools and in the spring of 1948 I met my present wife, a lovely navy widow, Mary Lee Sample. I got detached, we got married, I went off to the various schools, commanding officers' schools and operated off the East Coast in antisubmarine warfare development work. This was our honeymoon as well. The ship, USS Mindoro was assigned to the Operational Development Force of the Atlantic Fleet.

Q: Somewhere along in there wasn't there an eighth fleet contemplated in the Atlantic?

Adm. A.: No. The Tenth Fleet was during the war. There was an eighth fleet contemplated around the time of the invasion of Europe, I guess, but I don't think they ever actually established it. Maybe they did.

So I was in command of the Mindoro involved in flying operations, good operations at sea, which proved that Admiral Towers was right because I got a good command, an interesting command. The ship was due to go to the Navy Yard in Boston for overhaul, and I got a message on board ship telling me to turn over the command to my exec and to report to Washington, to Admiral Radford, who was then the vice chief of naval operations for Admiral Denfeld for duty. I didn't know what it was about.

I got there and I was told by Admiral Radford that the Joint Chiefs of Staff had just organized, with the approval of the secretary of defense, a board for the evaluation of what would happen in the event of war between the U.S.S.R. and the United States called the Harmon Board, headed by Lieutenant General Harmon of the air force.

Q: That was sort of a continuation of that special study you made for Sherman?

Adm. A.: Well, but they didn't know anything about that.

Q: No.

Adm. A.: The senior navy member was Admiral Harry Hill - no, Admiral Tom Hill, and I was the junior one, but it just happened that I had more of the background of this whole situation than any of the other members, either army or air force or navy, had.

Q: I would think you would have.

Adm. A.: When I got into Admiral Radford's office, I said:

"Look, Admiral, here's my first command at sea and now I've got to go back to Washington."

He said: "I'll take care of it. You'll remain in command of the ship. We'll put a temporary captain on to take it from" - it was down in Cuba - "up to Boston, then your exec can take over and you can go back by the time the board is over and the ship is ready for sea."

So here I was in the anomalous position of being on duty in Washington on this board, the ship going through its navy yard up there, and time running out as far as my getting to sea was concerned. The board finally concluded its deliberations, and it's a very interesting report, the Harmon Committee report, which substantiated the position that it would be the hell of a war, that the Russians just would not fold up just because a few atomic bombs were dropped on them, and it would be a tough, tough war. Also, the fact that without the atomic bomb, you weren't going to be able to muster the U.S. forces that would make it decisive in Europe in a short period of time.

Q: And what about the general attitude of the public in the United States? Was that taken into consideration?

Adm. A.: Well, in any event, the board turned in its report, and here I was, trying to get away. So I said I was going to take the bull by the horns and one afternoon I just talked in to Admiral Denfeld's office and he said:

"Oh, George, I'm glad to see you. You did a good job on that report."

I said: "Well, Admiral I've just come in to say good-bye."

He said, "Oh, are you leaving?" I said: "Yes, Sir, I'm leaving tomorrow." He said:

"Well, good luck and thank you for everything you've done."

Then I walked down the corridor to Admiral Radford's office. He was very busy in there, so I said:

"Admiral, I just wanted to stick my nose in to say good-bye." He said:

"You're leaving?" I said:

"Yes, I've just said good-bye to Admiral Denfeld." I didn't tell him why I did this. "He said I'd done a good job." And he said:

"Yes, you did a good job. I think you're going away too soon," and I said:

"But I've said good-bye to Admiral Denfeld."

"Oh," he said, "good luck."

Anderson #4 -183-

I went back to Boston and took the Mindoro out to sea. We were going down for post-shakedown training to Guantanamo. By that time it was about the first of July and, on the way down, I got word that I was going to be ordered back to Washington. This was in 1949. I was going to be ordered back to Washington--no, wait a minute, I was going to the National War College.

Q: Oh, that was a little different.

Adm. A.: And I would be detached on the first of August. Well, we got a quota of three Naval Academy graduates, ex-midshipmen, right out of graduation who reported aboard when we went down to Guantanamo and I was going to have a month down there. I called these three youngsters in and said:

"All right, I'm going to be here one month. During this time I'm going to devote my full attention to you three young gentlemen. You're going to stand a watch in three and at the time I'm detached on the 1st of August either you will be qualified as officers of the deck or you will be at the bottom of the pile. So it's entirely up to you. If you put out and do what I say, you three will be qualified as officers of the deck and I'll give you jobs as division officers and you'll be way ahead of any of your classmates."

They were a little bit shocked. I stood up on the bridge and I gave those lads a concentrated course in learning how to be an officer of the deck. I just ran the hell out of them and the day before I was going to be relieved by a classmate of mine, Cliff Cooper, I qualified all three of them as officer of the deck.

Q: Where are they today?

Adm. A.: I don't know. One was a chap by the name of Noel, who was number one in his class. Another was Hartley, who went into aviation. I forget the third one's name. Anyway, they were real good youngsters. I turned them over to Cliff Cooper and he said they were the best officers of the deck of any of the officers he had.

So I was detached in August, came to Washington, went back to our house on Upton Street. The kids were in school here in Washington, and I reported in to the National War College.

Q: That's a good place to stop.

Adm. A.: Let me finish that thought.

Q: All right, Sir.

Adm. A.: This was the autumn of 1949, and one of the most startling things that happened, the Russians exploded their first atomic bomb.

Interview No. 5 with Admiral George W. Anderson, U.S. Navy (Retired)

Place: His apartment in the Watergate, Washington, D.C.

Date: Wednesday morning, 9 October 1980

Subject: Biography

Q: In the summer of 1949 you enrolled at the National War College in Washington. It was a very new institution at that point.

Adm. A.: Well, it was relatively new at that time. We were, I think, the third class there, and the National War College had been established as a result of World War II experience. First, of course, to give a better education to what you might consider officers of the rank of captain in the navy and colonel in the army and air force who would expect to move ahead to positions of increased responsibility and higher command not only in their services but of the National Security Agency and the Joint Staff.

Q: They were the cream of the crop, weren't they, really?

Adm. A.: At the time they were sometimes referred to as the College of Cardinals.

Q: Church and state getting mixed up, yes!

Adm. A.: At that time, the officers selected to go to the National War College were indeed at the top level of the age and rank groups that were eligible for selection, and they took priority over assignment to the service colleges, the Army War College, the Naval War College, and the new Air University. It was looked upon with a great deal of pride by those who were selected and annoyance perhaps by those who were not selected to go to the National War College.

Indeed, my class, and we assembled I guess it was at the end of August 1949, was a very fine assembly of officers from the services as well as representatives from the State Department and the CIA. Subsequently, many of these officers reached high command positions: General Wheeler, chairman of the Joint Chiefs of Staff; I was the chief of naval operations; and they, by and large, had very successful careers afterwards. Of course, in the officers there was a very small number who were definitely up to par, you might say, of the average of the class as a whole.

We were fortunate in our class in having representatives of the three British and three Canadian services, who came in and were warmly welcomed by all of us and who made marked contributions to the discussions in the class as a whole.

Q: Did they create a minor problem securitywise?

Adm. A.: No problem at all securitywise because basically we had had a pretty full exchange of information over the years of World War II with the British and the Canadians. It did occasion a considerable amount of, again perhaps, envy or jealousy on the part of the French, who were not included, and, as a result of the ramifications of separating sheep from goats, you might say. As time went on- I guess it was the following year - it was decided that there would be no foreign officers in the classes at the National War College. And, as you recall, later on they established the Interamerican Defense College. At the same time we had a small number of U.S. officers - I think one from each service - who were invited to attend the Imperial Defense College in the United Kingdom. I think that the inclusion of these foreign officers the British, and the Canadians, was a great benefit to us, a great benefit to them, and a future benefit to the countries concerned. It's unfortunate that it was terminated, in my judgment.

In any event, we assembled down there at Fort McNair. It was an ideal atmosphere in which to carry on, you might almost call it a sabbatical year. We had a fine staff at the National War College at that time. The commandant was General Bull, army, who had been with General Eisenhower in a position of plans and operations during World War II. Admiral Dyer was the senior naval officer there, George Dyer, and we had a very fine representative from the State Department, Ambassador Elbridge Durbrow, who had had previous service in Moscow and various other parts of the world and is still very active in work in the American Security Council here in Washington today and some of the other patriotic study activities that are carri on under the broad framework of the National Security Council.

I think altogether there were about one hundred people. Basically, the military were equally divided between navy-marine corps on the one side, the army and the air force on the other, the air force having become an independent service. The curriculum was a very fine one. Being located here in Washington, we had excellent lectures on the various subjects, the reading material was voluminous, there was almost no end to the amount that you could read on any particular subject. Normally, we would have one or two lectures by a prominent lecturer, sometimes a specialist in a particular subject, followed by a discussion in a seminar, and you'd take your turn getting a principal lecturer in your own service. Those groups were about twelve or fifteen. Then, in the afternoon you would have time for reading and pursuing what you had chosen as your own particular thesis to be written on during the course of the whole year.

Q: The faculty members were on loan from some of the major universities?

Adm. A.: Yes. We had a very fine civilian faculty there and one that I think the college could be very proud of, and they derived a great deal of benefit from their association with the military. Many of them had done work during World War II, and we were in a particularly advantageous period because we had so many officers of my rank, captain and equivalent colonel in the army and the air force, who had had very close association with activities at a reasonably high as well as a tactical level during World War II in all parts of the world. Our foreign service officers also were a very fine group, carefully selected. They were proud to be there and we were very happy to have them.

The particular teams or study groups that you would work with in one room would usually consist of one officer each of the army, navy and air force, one foreign service, perhaps a CIA, a representative of the treasury, and so you were pretty well matched up and you learned to appreciate what they had to contribute.

We hoped that we, in turn, gave something that they would take away from the year's association.

There were various little minor athletic activities during midday. There was a small golf course. Even though it was before the era of active jogging, some jogged. We had a rapid-reading course, and there was a certain exposure to public speaking for those who had not had much experience in public speaking, presenting five-minute discourses either in seminar or later on on the platform.

The lecturers were graded by the student body on (a) their substance and (b) their effectiveness in delivery. It was surprising that some very prominent people got high marks in one and low marks in the other. We got a chance to evaluate the type of leadership we had. I think we had all the members of the Joint Chiefs of Staff at one time or another come down and talk to us. We had General Marshall and every couple of months we'd have a night lecture which was generally, always, on an unclassified subject which the ladies, the wives, were invited to attend. It was a very pleasant social occasion and enabled them to meet their associates. I might say that at the beginning of the year there was not too much social activity, but as the year proceeded a great deal of social activity developed and, by the time we'd finished the course the following June - that was in 1950, there was a great camaraderie and great affection for the people we'd come in contact with.

I think the first dramatic event that occurred was the announcement in the autumn of 1949 that the Russians had exploded an atomic bomb. This was something that occurred before the intelligence agency of the government had anticipated they would have it. The estimate was that the Russians would have it in

1952, and here it was in the autumn of 1949 that they had it. It brought back to my mind, of course, the thinking I'd had that that was the time when the decision on where we would go in the future would have to be made via-a-vis the Russians. I think it also brought to the forefront the reality of the situation which previously had been talked so much in more hypothetical terms. This, as the year went on at the National War College, came more and more into the forefront of discussion, as to what are going to be the future relationships in the world, what was the strength of the communist bloc versus that of the free world.

Q: It was almost a watershed situation.

Adm. A.: It was a watershed situation and certainly it stimulated greatly the discussions that were taking place in almost every field of activity that we were exploring in our studies.

Q: Durbrow must have been a great help at that point?

Adm. A.: I would say so, very much so. He was quite a realist on the machinations and the objectives and the strategy and the tactics of the communists and the potential of Soviet power in the years ahead. He had no illusions whatsoever about what the Russians were.

There was another major area that came up frequently, particularly of course when we got into studies and discussions of the situation in Asia and the Pacific, and it focused on the unsettled conditions in what was then known as Indochina and the various problems that Indochina was going to pose to the United States and to the Free World in the years ahead. At that time Emperor

Bao Dai was a force there; Ho Chi Minh, of course, was the Communist leader, and there were the questions of the various sects, the French position in Indochina, and there was a lot of discussion and thought given to the deteriorating situation in Indochina. Really nobody came up with a very good solution as to how it was going to be solved, particularly in light of the fact that everybody seemed to agree that the French approach in Indochina was one of reestablishing their former colonial position. Related to that, of course, was the French position in North African, in Algeria and Morocco, where the French were endeavoring to hold on and the movements for self-determination or freedom from France were very pervasive on the part of the Africans.

We had the usual problem of looking at what was going to happen in Europe itself, NATO had not yet been organized into a military- the treaty had not even been signed and the military organization certainly had not been established, but there was a great deal of thinking going on and preliminary discussions which were to lead ultimately to the formulation of NATO and the European command and the Atlantic command.

We were studying factors of national power, instruments of national security in all the aspects, military, economic, political. Many of us had little knowledge of the true economic situation. We got a brief course in economic and financial factors of national power, which gave us just a smattering of a vast problem but it certainly stimulated every one of us to think in the years ahead of the importance of economic factors. You must recall that the

National Security Act had been adopted a couple of years before, which had as one of its purposes the coordination of political, military, and economic power in the United States, the coordination of those factors in determining national policy. Certainly it was an education to all of us, certainly the military students there, that the economy and the political factors were of very great importance and could not be ignored in making any military judgment then or in the years in the future.

One of the interesting programs in the National War College course - of course, there were many - was the selection of the thesis that you would write. You had a broad group of subjects from which you could choose individually.

Q: Who provided that group of subjects?

Adm. A.: Well, they were there as suggestions, but if you wanted to take one of your own you could submit it to your faculty adviser and he would say, "Why, sure, go ahead with that."

I happened to choose the subject of the Vatican as an anti-communistic force, which was of some interest to me at that time and has always been an interest to me. I think that the more recent developments of having Pope John Paul, the new pope from Poland, the recent riots in the workers' position and the strikes in Poland, which are taking place in, here it is 1980, show that this has been a continuing problem and a possibility of ultimately having a greater influence in breaking down the strict communist control of those people. Of course, we know how ruthless they are and when the chips are really down they do not hesitate to apply power not only against the church but against any instrument of freedom that is within the so-called iron curtain.

The second interesting feature about the National War College course was the spring trip. There were arrangements for trips that would be made, called field trips, one to Europe, one to the Pacific, one to South America, and I forget what the fourth one was. The groups were divided into these four groups. In my case, we made a trip to Europe.

Q: That's the area you chose?

Adm. A.: That's the area that I had chosen to visit. The interesting thing about it was that we flew over in an air force plane, got to London on a Sunday, and a group of us were stuck in the elevator in the headquarters at 20 Grosvenor Square, the navy's headquarters, in between floors on a Sunday afternoon. You can imagine the difficulty of getting out of the elevator or getting assistance on Sunday afternoon, but eventually we did extricate ourselves by climbing out.

We visited London and, I think, Paris, Germany, Italy, and stopped in North Africa. There we had the opportunity to meet people our own U.S. military command people, officers of the host country, ambassadors. We met people at receptions. It was an extremely valuable trip.

Q: Did you not have exposure to foreign ministries and what have you in each country?

Adm. A.: Yes, we did. They would give us briefings and were generally quite gracious in answering questions, and some of the questions posed by some of the students were rather provocative and characterized, perhaps, by a few barbs. But they were all very gracious and generous in their responses.

We came to the spring of 1950 and I guess the last part of the course was involved in studying war plans, the developing of war plans for various parts of the world of particular interest. I happened to be assigned, my group was assigned, to draw up a tentative war plan for the Atlantic command. It was an interesting operation, in which all members of our team, some six of us, participated. Then, after they were submitted, each one of the study groups was required to make a presentation on the stage of the war college to the entire student body.

Q: Covering the subject matter?

Adm. A.: Covering that particular subject matter.

Also, it was of interest, when we did have these guest lecturers, a limited number of people, subject to the capacity of the auditorium, guests, were permitted to attend and many officers came down from the Pentagon, from the services, from the State Department to listen to the lectures.

Q: Were these scheduled as off the record? I mean the speakers didn't hold anything in reserve?

Adm. A.: They spoke quite frankly, and transcripts were usually made of their talks and the questions and the responses that they made. If a student wanted to ask a question, he would question the lecturer. They might be provocative in terms of bringing out the subject matter, but they were courteously phrased. There were many controversial subjects to be considered and some of the questions did provoke quite a bit of controversy.

We were due to graduate from the war college early in June.

Q: Before you tell me about that, would you say something more about your own particular study, that paper, which interests me?

Adm. A.: The Vatican as an anti-communist -?

Q: Did you have access to the nuncio in Washington for material?

Adm. A.: No, we got most of the material from the library or would go up to the Library of Congress. We solicited, depending on our subject and mine in particular - I did a lot of reading for it. They gave a general idea of how you should prepare a study of this sort, a thesis, and I followed the generally accepted approach, did a lot of research, made, I guess, a couple of drafts of it, and concluded that the Vatican would be a continuing force against communism but with the ruthless approach of the Soviet leadership and their willingness to apply it in the satellites, it was going to be a prolonged struggle in which the Russians, the Soviet communists, would impose their will and not hesitate to use what power was necessary to keep the force under control. So it was a question of hope but no immediate prospect of altering the subjugation of the people as a result of the religious factor, in the long term -

Q: You had that trip to Europe in 1946 when the continent was in disarray and communist guerrillas were very active in western European countries. What was the attitude of the church, what was the position that it was able to maintain? Did you observe that, and did you incorporate that into your paper?

Adm. A.: Yes, to some degree. Of course, the case of Italy was a very good one, where the communist partisans from World War II emerged as a very strong communist force, with the effect of modernism, of the ramifications from their liberation, a general lowering of the control of the church of the people of Rome, and yet, there was the inherent respect for religion, the Catholic religion, among the people of Italy, even though they didn't live by all the tenets of morality and behavior that the church would strictly expect of them.

In France, of course, which had traditionally been a very strong Catholic country, and Belgium, there were divisive forces as a result of the general letdown at the end of World War II. The communists were very strong in Italy, they were active in France, in Belgium, and, of course, the continuing concern of the communists penetrating and getting increasing control in the western part of Germany.

Q: We then go to the graduation?

Adm. A.: To the graduation, which we'd all looked forward to. Everybody was interested in where they were going. I was ordered to go as the operations officer of the Sixth Fleet in the Mediterranean. I looked forward to that with a great deal of anticipation.

In any event, just before we arrived for graduation, in the auditorium for graduation, was the day the war broke out in Korea.

Q: The 25th of June.

Adm. A.: That's right, and there was practically an empty platform because many of the people who were expected to be there were not able to appear. Fortunately, General Bradley, who was making the graduation address, chairman of the Joint Chiefs of Staff, did appear, but he was obviously very preoccupied and everybody else was wondering just where we were going to end up as a result of this war in Korea.

Q: That was your second surprise?

Adm. A.: That's right, at the beginning and the end. The atomic bomb first and the Korean War second.

Q: Let me ask, you lived out in town?

Adm. A.: I lived in town.

Q: Did you have a car pool?

Adm. A.: Yes. We had an excellent arrangement for car pools. They had a big map of the environs of Washington on which everybody put their little tag with a pin, listed where they lived, and the car pools were encouraged. We had a very interesting group, I forget just who they were, from my area of northwest Washington.

Q: That was a very profitable sort of thing, wasn't it?

Adm. A.: Oh, yes. This was long before people were thinking of the energy shortage.

Q: Oh, yes, but the interchange of ideas.

Adm. A.: Oh, the ideas. We talked, and it was easy because everybody had the same general time frame. If somebody was going to be down there late, maybe he wouldn't drive in the car pool that day. It was easy parking at Fort McNair. Certainly, they didn't charge any parking fees at that stage of the game.

Q: Was the Industrial War College in being?

Adm. A.: The Industrial War College was in being. In many cases, they shared the auditorium when we had a very prominent lecturer, but they were separate institutions and there was a little bit of rivalry in golf and minor sports. We would see them up at the officers' club for lunch, but generally they went their way and we went ours. We had the supercilious attitude that we were the higher of the two colleges, and the division of the type of people who went was - they did have people who were more in the fields of supply and logistics, industrial mobilization.

Q: But their presence and their program would have a tendency, I should think, to emphasize the economic aspects of war, which was something that you were considering?

Adm. A.: That's right, and we had the benefit if they had a distinguished lecturer or visitor or some economic problem, they would have a joint lecture for the two colleges. It was a good program, an excellent program.

Well, as I say, I looked forward to the opportunity to go to sea. I felt that I was going to the very best possible position for me at that particular time. Admiral Sherman had told them where to send me because of his interest in the Sixth Fleet and his knowledge of me from my previous associations with him. I flew over, I think it was commercially, and joined the flagship of the Sixth Fleet in Villefranche. When I arrived at Nice Airport, I looked down and there was no flagship present, which was a surprise because I'd heard the schedule -

Q: What was the flagship?

Adm. A.: The flagship was the Des Moines.

Q: Cruiser.

Adm. A.: At that time we alternated three heavy cruisers, the Des Moines, the Salem, and the Newport News. They would stay for four months at a time and only the Commander, Sixth Fleet, and his staff and a few people attached to the staff were homeported over there. The rest of the ships were generally on rotation from the United States.

In any event, I arrived and I looked for the flagship and there was no flagship there, but the consul had sent a person down to meet me and inform me that I was to stay there, that the flagship would be in shortly. It had stayed at sea. There was a change in schedule because of the fact that the Korean War was on and I guess there was some little particular crisis at that moment so that they had not come into port as scheduled.

The commander of the Sixth Fleet was Vice Admiral John J. Ballentine, a naval aviator, who was successor in that job to Admiral Sherman. His chief of staff was Captain Robert Campbell and I was the third senior officer on the staff, as the operations officer. It was a very, very interesting job that I had. The Sixth Fleet was the best operating fleet we had, certainly in the Atlantic and the Mediterranean. Admiral Sherman had more or less laid down in his tour all the guidelines for the operation of the fleet and the behavior of its officers and men, the concept was; one of readiness; and, two, of maintaining respect for the United States and the U.S. Navy.

Q: You still at that point shared the Mediterranean with the Royal Navy, didn't you?

Adm. A.: The Royal Navy was down in the Mediterranean and based in Malta. Relationships were very friendly. There were joint exercises that were conducted by the Royal Navy and the U.S. Sixth Fleet. We also had exercises with the French and, to a minor degree, with the Italians and the Greeks. The Commander, Sixth Fleet, maintained excellent relationships with all of the navies around the Mediterranean and with the U.S. ambassadors, with the local authorities. The schedule of the fleet was quite well established. About 25,000 officers and men and their ships would come over for a period of about four months at a time and those four months permitted one wide circuit of the Mediterranean, and then a second, shorter circuit around the western Mediterranean, where they had the better liberty ports.

Meticulous attention was paid by the fleet commander, initially Admiral Sherman and then currently Admiral Ballentine, to the indoctrination of the commanding officers and, through them, to the crews of the ships, in their appearance and behavior as well as readiness and scheduling the fleet. Usually the fleet commander would arrange for the incoming fleet, ships, to go to an isolated anchorage where they could clean up from their passage across the Atlantic, get the ships shipshape, indoctrinate the crews as to their behavior ashore, indoctrinate the senior officers in the war plans and the training schedule. We had a very definite active program of fleet training and readiness, joint exercises as well as unilateral exercises -

Q: Did your planes use Wheelus?

Adm. A.: We had available Wheelus Field in North Africa - well, at that time, most of the airfields around the Mediterranean were available to us, in North Africa and in the islands such as they were before the development of the NATO facilities. But they were still airfields where, if we had a plane that was in distress, we could send a plane ashore and send help to him.

I reported aboard. My family was coming over through the Mediterranean by an army transport, the Private Johnson, which arrived after I did.

Q: Where were they to be located?

Adm. A.: They were going to be located in Villefranche, on the French Riviera, where all the dependents of the officers who were homeported there lived, on the French economy. We didn't have quarters. We found our own accommodations. We passed them down from a predecessor to the relief. Some of them had very nice villas on Cap Ferrat, others had minor apartments, depending on the size of their families and the way they decided to live during that particular tour of duty. As I say, my new wife came over with my two younger children in an army transport. I was permitted by the fleet commander to fly down to meet them in Naples and accompany them back to France.

I met them and we drove up to Rome, then flew on to the French Riviera, Nice. An incident, sad at the time, occurred because the last night we were in Naples, I had apparently gone out and had some shellfish and by the time I got to Rome it hit me and I had what they called the Mediterranean Miseries. But it gave me a very good lesson, never to assume that any individual was intoxicated on alcohol because I must have looked, certainly at the airport as if I had had too much alcohol, when it was rather something that had occurred anatomically from the diet.

In any event, we got up and we found a small apartment at Beaulieu-sur-mer, which is just next to Villefranche. We had bought a little Hillman Minx automobile for my wife and we lived on the French economy. We had the two children, my daughter, who was ten or eleven years old, and my youngest son, who was later in the navy and was killed, was about seven years old. We sent them to a French boarding school, actually it was a girls' school in Cannes, with Pam the daughter of the chief of staff, Admiral Campbell. They would go down to Cannes for the week and come back to Villefranche on weekends. It was a school in French and difficult for them to start with, and also they didn't have all the frills that they would have in an American school, but I think all three of them profited from it. The school was Cours Maintenon run by three generations of French ladies, a mother, a daughter, and her mother, the grandmother. It was a suitable experience.

We eventually got some allowance from our government to offset the cost of the school, but as I say, we lived on the French economy. There were no PXs or commissaries or schools or dispensaries for us. When the flagship would come back into port, which would be about every six weeks, perhaps, the dependents, the wives, would come out to the flagship and they would get some most urgently needed supplies that they obtained from ships' stores. They would buy them, and that would supplement what they could buy on the French economy.

Life was very, very pleasant over there, and many of the ladies who followed the flagship on visits to other ports-

Q: This being essential because of the social aspect?

Adm. A.: That's right. It was very helpful socially.

Q: Mrs. Ballentine did a lot of that, didn't she?

Adm. A.: The wife of the Sixth Fleet commander was authorized to fly in a navy aircraft to go from one port to another when it was in interest of the Navy for her to do so. It reminded me very much - there's a book I have up there on the book shelf called <u>Memories of a Rear Admiral</u> at the turn of the century, Admiral Franklin.

His wife, on various tours of duty in the Mediterranean, of course these were in the days long before they had airplanes and modern transportation, but the pattern of life was very, very similar, although we had more modern conveniences in moving from one place to another. But even in those days when U.S. ships in the Mediterranean were few, they were still homeported in Villefranche, and the wife of the fleet commander and some of the staff officers' wives would follow the ships from one port to another, sometimes by coach or by railroad car, whereas our girls usually flew by airplane or drove their own cars, if it was close. Many times they would drive from France down to Italy in their own cars and meet the ships when they came in to port. It was a very pleasant side of it because there were very pleasant social activities when the ships came in. The people in the host countries and the host cities were very cooperative and fairly hospitable, I would say. We would have a program on board ship. From my standpoint of plans and operations, we would have our work all finished by the time we got into port. The orders for the next operation, for anything of significance, were all accomplished so we had a minimum amount of paper work in port, which was appreciated not only by the officers concerned but by their wives.

I had a very tight, small staff organization, the whole organization necessarily had to be small because it had to be accommodated in the cabins that were available in the flagship, the cruiser. So the staff was small, we had very capable people, they worked hard, they did a very, very good job, and the wives appreciated the positions their husbands had and the fact that when they came into port they were able to participate - see their families and participate in the social activities.

Sometimes we would play golf. The admiral would perhaps go hunting. We did a great deal of sightseeing. For us, it was really our first time around in Europe, so the sightseeing was avid. My wife is very interested in that type of leisure, and it was a very interesting tour of duty.

We visited all the ports in the Mediterranean, Naples, the Italian ports, went over to Greece and as far as Istanbul. I remember we were in to Beirut. In Beirut the visit of the Sixth Fleet flagship was warmly welcomed by the cosmopolitan community there. There were a lot of American oil people there and the American College in Beirut. The ladies always arranged for a canteen for the sailors, which was greatly appreciated, more so than the USO canteens that were established in various places, because in the USO they did not permit them to have beer, whereas the privately arranged canteens did have beer for the enlisted men.

Q: How about the ports of the new country of Israel? Did you go there?

Adm. A.: We did not visit Israel because there was always the apparent hostility of the Arabs to Israel, which brings up an interesting little anecdote. I was in Beirut for the first visit and there was a reception held by, perhaps, the American Chamber of Commerce or some similar organization, and they had people from the local community as well as the international community there. A British general was attached to the United Nations mission for the assistance of the Palestinian refugees.

His name was General Collins and that evening, when he'd had a little bit too much to drink I was talking with him, he said:

"Captain, you are getting the bad feelings for your country about your position on the Palestinian refugees, but, after all, we British should really share it because in order to get the support of the American Jews to get the United States into World War I, we had to promise the Jews a home in the Middle East, the Balfour Agreement." But the condition of the refugees in that area was absolutely deplorable. The first time I went there, we had a U.S. representative who'd been sent down to look after the refugees in the Beirut area. He was a typical bureaucrat and said, "We're getting the feel of this problem and we will solve it."

Some years later when I went back on another visit - I think I was in command of the Roosevelt at that time - he was still there and he said, "We're now in the implementation stage," but nothing was better. As a matter of fact, on my first visit there I ran into some Franciscan missionaries who were working with a papal mission to look after the refugees, and they told me and showed me the most deplorable situation that prevailed and pointed out that this was a hopeless situation for these poor people and one that would certainly be exploited by the communists and by the various anarchistic groups in the years ahead. And what has taken place certainly justifies what they told me at that particular time, which was initially in 1950 and in subsequent visits when I went there in 1952, 1958, and 1959.

Q: Those people had been forced to evacuate their lands?

Adm. A.: They had been pushed out of their lands that they had by the Jews in Israel, particularly the Zionist element of the Israelis.

I was fascinated with my duty.

Q: You have a note on the French Foreign Legion, too.

Adm. A.: That's right. We visited at that time the ports in North Africa. They were open to the Sixth Fleet. We were warmly welcomed by the French who were down there. We went in to Algiers. At that time, my brother-in-law, Admiral Switzer, was in command of a carrier division in the Sixth Fleet and he was in Algiers at the same time we were. The consul general had a very nice party and he and his wife thought it would be nice if they could have some of the enlisted men at the party, instead of just a party for the officers. So the enlisted men went over and they had a very nice time, but when the party was over, my brother-in-law got a call saying in distress from the consul general that his wife was so upset because anything that was small had been taken as souvenirs. So he had what they called a conscience party and recovered most of the souvenirs, which were sent back to the distressed Mrs. Locket, the wife of Consul General Locket.

After we visited Algiers, we went down the coast to Oran, to the old French naval base at Mers-el-Kebir. We came alongside a very nice pier, which was a little bit unusual in the Mediterranean because normally we anchored out or moored at a buoy, but this time we were alongside the pier. We had looked forward to this because the admiral had been invited to go down to the French Foreign Legion base for an inspection and a luncheon at Sidi-bel-Abbes. My wife and the wife of the chief of staff, Mrs. Campbell, were following the fleet at that particular time and they were invited to go along, the two of them. Mrs. Ballentine was not present on that particular visit. It was a very great experience for them and they were very much impressed with the greeting they received, the luncheon that they attended, the opportunity actually to see the principal base of the French Foreign Legion in North Africa. The French Foreign Legion at that time was composed of large numbers of former German soldiers whom the French had actively recruited. It was a very fit and capable fighting force. Unfortunately, I was not able to make that particular trip down to Sidi-bel-Abbes because at that time we had a planning conference and we had to develop some contingency plans and work with the staffs of some army and air force people who had arrived to do coordinated planning with us. I'm sorry I missed because I never did get a chance later to visit Sidi-bel-Abbes and the French Foreign Legion.

Q: CinCNelm came down at one point, too.

Adm. A.: That's right. The CinCNelm planners had arrived down. I think they were involved in that particular planning conference.

Q: Admiral Conolly himself came, did he not?

Adm. A.: That brings up another interesting thing that happened on that particular tour of duty. Actually before we went to North Africa we had been in Cyrpus and Admiral Conolly came down from his headquarters in Grosvenor Square in London and flew his flag in the Columbus, a heavy cruiser, which was his flagship based up in northern Europe. We had the usual calls that had to be made by the senior officer present, Admiral Conolly being senior to Vice Admiral Ballentine had the responsibility of making calls in Cyprus. He started out in the morning. The distances were considerably great, so he used a helicopter, and on the return from his morning calls, the engine failed in the helicopter and it dunked him in the water. Fortunately, the landing was not too severe, except that in scrambling out of the plane his flag lieutenant, who was with him, put his foot in the admiral's face, which was a little bit embarrassing. The admiral was dressed up in the full-dress white uniform, complete with sword. He got in the water and, of course, he discarded his blouse and sword, an impediment to swimming, before he was actually rescued. But he was rescued and there was no damage. When he got back aboard, he had calls scheduled for the afternoon and he realized he had another white uniform, of course, he could always pick up a sword and belt, and he had a second hat but he didn't have any four-star epaulettes, shoulder marks. So they started looking around to see if anybody had any four-star shoulder marks. The ship's store didn't have any. After all, there wasn't much volume of sales for four-star insignia. But this word got around and over in one of the ships a junior officer of the deck said, "I have some four-star shoulder marks." The captain said, "You do?" He said, "Yes." "Would you make them available to Admiral Connoly?

"Why certainly I would."

And so he sent down and came up with a pair of shoulder marks with four stars on them, all wrapped up in a little plastic case. They were being sent over to the admiral and the question was asked, "How did you happen to have four-star shoulder marks?" He said:

"Well, you see, in June when I graduated from the academy, my girl came down to pin on my shoulder marks and she pinned these on with a note that said 'You may be an ensign in the navy, but you're a four-star admiral to me," which is an anecdote I've told on several occasions.

Q: It's a cute one, too!

Adm. A.: Let me go back. Did I tell you the story in 1946 when with Admiral Sherman, Admiral Mitscher, and Commodore Burke, at that time, and the admirals left their suite at the Claridge?

Q: No, you did not tell me that and you promised to tell me. It relates to 1946?

Adm. A.: This relates to the 1946 trip when we were in London. Admiral Mitscher, Admiral Sherman, and Commodore Burke had been invited to spend the weekend with the British Navy at Dartmouth and some trips around. They left early on a Saturday morning and were due to come back on a Monday morning, but rather than move all their baggage they suggested that their flag lieutenants take care of their things in their suite at the Claridge, the most prominent hotel in London. So the flag lieutenants were very anxious to take care of the admirals' suite and in the course of the weekend they got together with a couple of young London "Popsies" and, unexpectedly, the admirals returned Sunday afternoon when the two flag lieutenants were gladly taking care of the admirals' suites and bedrooms, in London. They came in unexpectedly and

Admiral Sherman described the situation: "Imagine the admirals returning to their suites in Claridges and finding the flag lieutenant rolling their wenches in the admirals' beds! A very interesting and amusing experience.

Q: Yes. I imagine they got called down for that.

Adm. A.: Yes but by absolute silence on the part of the admirals.

I mentioned this anecdote about Admiral Conolly, but we traveled around the Mediterranean, carried on our exercises, and in December of 1950 we were due to go to Naples to spend Christmas in port, which Admiral Ballentine liked to do because he could get the ships inside, tied up at buoys, and didn't have the problems of boating at the anchorages, which could be rough in the month of December.

Q: Did he rent the Villa Niki also?

Adm. A.: No, no, he did not have Villa Niki. Villa Niki was not available to the commander of the Sixth Fleet. As a matter of fact, at that time I don't believe we had Villa Niki, the navy no longer had Villa Emma. Villa Niki had not yet been acquired. Villa Niki was a later residence for the Allied Commander Southern Europe whose headquarters were establsihed in Naples.

In any event, we were due to go to Sicily and then go to Naples for Christmas and, as I said, my brother-on-law, Admiral Switzer, was in command of the carriers. He was due to be in there and we decided to bring my wife, my two small children, and my stepdaughter down to Naples for Christmas, and my sister-in-law was there. We had all the presents for the children in the flagship. Everything was set up for Christmas in Naples. But, I got permission, instead of making the visit to Sicily, to take a little bit of leave and we went down by bus to Florence and then to Rome. On a Sunday morning in Rome, I got a telephone call, right after I'd returned from St. Peter's where I had had an audience with the pope. I had borrowed a uniform from my classmate and friend then Captain, later Admiral, Tom Neblett, to wear for this audience. I had no uniform with me and I got this telephone call from Sicily, which said:

"Captain, if there's anything we can do to help you out, just let me know."

I said, "What do you mean?" He said, "Don't you know?" I said, "No, what?"

He said, "Well, there's a message coming in to you at the embassy, so if there's anything we can do to help you out, just let us know. The admiral wants you to know that he'd do anything for you."

So I went over to the embassy and there was the message. This was the 18th of December of 1950, a Sunday, and the message said: "From CNO to Commander, Sixth Fleet. Direct Captain George W. Anderson your staff detached immediately, proceed Brussels, Belgium, to arrive if possible 18 December. In any event no later than 19 December. On arrival report to Admiral Jerauld Wright for further assignment to General Alfred M. Gruenther. For your information, Captain Anderson will be assigned to the staff of the Supreme Allied Commander, Europe, when appointed. A suitable relief will be supplied in due course. Attention is directed to the classified nature of Captain Anderson's prospective duty."

There it was, a Sunday in Rome, the afternoon of the 18th of December when I was supposed to report in, in any event no later than the 19th in Brussels, Belgium. All I had was dirty clothes, no uniforms, practically no money, children on the way down to Naples, toys and everything to Naples, and, here I had to make my way to Brussels. The war in Korea was at a critical stage!

Well, I rapidly did some rescheduling. I got an airplane to Paris, then to Brussels, and I arranged for my wife to stop the children from going down to Naples and hold them in Villefranche, on the Riviera. My older daughter, who was driving our car, would go on down to Naples, as planned. My wife would reverse course. Eventually, I arrived in Brussels just in time for the Brussels meeting when it was announced that General Eisenhower was appointed Supreme Allied Commander, Europe. I reported first to Admiral Wright, then to General Gruenther.

Q: What was Gruenther's position?

Adm. A.: Gruenther was prospective chief of staff to General Eisenhower. He had been on duty in the Department of the Army and gone over to Brussels for the final decision of appointing an American as the Supreme Allied Commander, and it was understood that General Eisenhower would take the job.

Q: Admiral Wright was CinCEur?

Adm. A.: No. Admiral Wright was on duty in Washington and he'd been over there, too. He'd been in the naval planning group in Washington.

General Gruenther had an air force plane available to him, a C-47, and I rode with him over to Paris and went to the old Hotel Astoria, which was to be the initial headquarters for General Eisenhower when he came over to Europe in January to assume the duties of Supreme Allied Commander. General Gruenther said:

"You get the headquarters ready. There'll be lots of people in. They'll be coming in from all over. General Eisenhower will be over in January and I'll be back in January. Do what you can and money is no object.

Fortunately, a lot of very good army officers started to arrive and people were coming in from all over, people who would be the nucleus of the staff. The Hotel Astoria gradually took form and we managed the difficulty of refurbishing it over the Christmas holiday season in Paris in 1950. Nevertheless the work was accomplished, it was furnished. The army gave full cooperation. They just moved everything in to Paris to set up the headquarters, people and vehicles and furniture, and there was plenty of money. There was plenty of money. The army always seemed to be able to get plenty of money for something like that.

In the meantime, I had to rearrange my whole family problem. The people on the flagship were very nice. They attended to all my baggage and arranged to send it to me. The flagship then moved over to Naples from Sicily. We stopped the children and had the toys sent back. The family went back to Beaulieu in France. Fortunately, I was able to get away for a few days to go down over Christmas and made arrangements that as soon as my regular orders came through we would move my wife up to Paris and go house-hunting, while we would be in Paris.

Q: Another family item that perhaps you want to mention is the death of your father?

Adm. A.: That was when I was operations officer of the Sixth Fleet. It was on 20 August 1950. I had gotten word from my brother-in-law, who was asked to tell me, that my father had died. Admiral Ballentine was very considerate. He said that, of course, I could go back, but at that time it was a very active period, with the war going on in Korea and not knowing what was going to happen in other parts of the world.

Q: And you didn't have jet planes.

Adm. A.: We didn't have jet planes, and so, very reluctantly, I had to send word back that I could not come back. Fortunately, my oldest son was in the United States and he was, I guess, sixteen at the time and he represented me with my aunt, who was the sole surviving member of the family, for that funeral.

I might also go back to that time when we were with the Sixth Fleet. There was a need for reinforcing the naval forces in the Pacific, off Korea, and they were drawing off from the Sixth Fleet to get ships and airplanes and send them out in anticipation of the amphibious operations that were contemplated, when they turned the tide in the Pacific at Korea.

I remember also that when I first reported on board at the end of June, when the flagship came in to port, we stayed there for the 4th of July and for the French celebration of their national holiday, the 14th of July. They had a parade in France and our marine contingent from the ship - we had a small amphibious battalion embarked afloat while on the Riviera. They had a French parade, in which our marines took part. There was a fine-looking, young marine officer who had command of the marine detachment on the flagship. He was in that parade and, later, when they were scraping together all the marines they could get to send out to Korea, he went and he was a casualty and was killed in one of the first operation out there.

Again, I'm reverting to the time we had in the Sixth Fleet. There was the apprehension of how the war in Korea might expand, which put great emphasis on the readiness and the flexibility of the navy, including the Sixth Fleet in the Mediterranean, remote as it was from Korea. We had to switch ships out there. The Leyte was one of our carriers, that went through the Suez Canal, I believe, and went out to the Pacific that way. The largest carriers we had at that time were the Midway, the Coral Sea, and the FDR. The Essex-class carriers could go through the Suez Canal. We had lots of ships that we had to send and we had to adopt quite a program of austerity in our own operations to make the most of what we could in the Mediterranean.

Also, at the time that I recieved these orders to Paris, in December of 1950, there was a great uncertainty as to what was going to happen in the world because the Chinese had just come into the war in Korea and nobody knew what was going to happen, whether that war would be expanded or whether it would extend on over to Europe.

In any event, we come back to the point where we were getting the SHAPE headquarters organized. As I said, there was an assembly of the finest officers, U.S. officers, principally army officers, who came in. I was the senior U.S. naval officer there. I was in the plans group. The staff was being organized under General Gruenther's direction, when he came back over. Actually, in his first trip over in January, General Eisenhower did not spend very much time in Paris or at the headquarters because he made visits to all of the NATO countries, his first visit around his prospective supreme command. Then he went back to the United States while he was disengaging from Columbia University and preparing to come back over and take up his duties. In that period of time, we started receiving allied officers, British, French, Italian, no Greeks or Turks at that time, no Germans, of course, but Belgians and Dutch.

We organized the plans division, of which I was the senior American, but the head of the plans division, the assistant chief of staff for plans, was a French air force general by the name of General Pierre Bodet. He was a French aviator, a very pleasant, very polite man who had nowhere near the professional competence of most of our U.S. Air Force or the Canadian lieutenant colonels who were working for him. Over him was a British air vice marshal, Ted Huddleston, a very capable not only planner but operational officer with a great deal of experience and a very fine reputation in the RAF.

Then, at the top, of course, we had General Eisenhower, who had Field Marshal Montgomery as his deputy, a British air chief marshal, Saunders, as air deputy, and Admiral Lemonnier, a French admiral of fine reputation and very pleasant. They were at the higher echelon, and then the chief of staff, General Gruenther, and assistants to the chief of staff, Major General Courtland Schuyler, who was an outstanding officer in the army, a planner in the army, and we had people like Genral Goodpaster, then a lieutenant colonel, I believe, Lieutenant Colonel Starbird, Bob Wood, who was the staff secretary, Bill Knowlton, later superintendent of West Point and now a retired four-star army general. These were the outstanding people of the army and the air force and, I guess, as far as the navy was concerned, they felt that I was at that time.

Q: Had you had connection with General Eisenhower before?

Adm. A.: No, never before, except I had made a trip over to Europe with him when I went over with Admiral Towers and General Arnold and he was on the plane with us. I played bridge with him on that particular trip. In fact, in 1942 -

Q: That's a big incentive!

Adm. A.: As a matter of fact, I was the only winner. I played three rubbers around and three rubbers back. We played poker and the junior officers won. Why, I don't know. Maybe the senior officers were all preoccupied with more important things.

But, no, basically, I had not known General Eisenhower, except that Admiral Sherman had given me a great big buildup. He said, "Well, I'll send you the finest officer in the navy."

Anderson #5 -219-

and so Gruenther and Eisenhower were very cordial to me and I had a degree of access to them that very few other people did, even though I was under the echelon of allied and U.S. -

Q: Of the heavy brass!

Adm. A.: That's right.

We had to develop a command organization that gave due consideration to military requirements as well as the political sensitivities of the nations that were involved. Working with me in preparing the command studies, which would then go up through the chief of staff to General Eisenhower, I had outstanding officers of the U.S. Army, the U.S. Air Force, and British and some Italian people, and some fine Canadians. The heavy work had to be done by the U.S. officers.

General Eisenhower was anxious to keep his staff small. He was anxious to minimize American participation and encourage the allied participation, but to get the work done in time required that we had to rely on the U.S. officers. This did not always meet the particular formats and procedures that Field Marshal Montgomery liked to see followed.

Q: What kind of voice did he have in this whole thing?

Adm. A.: Well, Eisenhower had told him "to forge the weapons," in Eisenhower's language, and Montgomery interpreted that as putting him in charge of everything!

I might mention that one of the officers who arrived first from the U.S. Army over there was, in logistics, General Leavey, who had been on the staff in Hawaii during the war. He was an old friend of mine and I had very good rapport with him.

In any event, I was able to operate at a level that exceeded my rank and the particular position that I had in the staff. As a matter of fact, General Eisenhower tried to get me promoted to rear admiral there. General Gruenther very nicely recommended the promotion, and there was an exchage of correspondence between Eisenhower and Sherman. Being aware of it, I wrote to Admiral Sherman and said I was greatly relieved that they did not succeed because the problems over there that I was involved in were not going to be solved by substituting stripes for stars, stars for stripes, on an officer's sleeve. They were involved in great sensitivities on the part of the allies, particularly the British, and the jealousies of the French.

Coming back to the command organization, General Eisenhower envisaged the command to be him as the supreme commander and he would exercise command in central Europe. On one flank he would have the British Navy under the command of a British admiral and on the other flank, the southern flank, he would have the U.S. Sixth Fleet under the command of a U.S. admiral. The British did not like the idea of having the southern flank under a U.S. admiral. Admiral Lord Louis Mountbatten was down there in Malta in command of the small British Fleet, but he had been a Supreme Commander in Southeast Asia in World War II.

Q: It wasn't only French sensitivity, it was British, too?

Adm. A.: Oh, very great British sensitivity and, when you come right down to it, a certain justifiable sensitivity of Mountbatten's position. After all, a member of the royal family, a supreme commander during World War II in Southeast Asia, you simply could not put him under the command of Admiral Carney, who was being brought down from London. Initially, Admiral Carney was moved down as Commander in Chief, Southern Europe, but he retained his duties as Commander, CinCNelm, in London, which extended beyond the NATO area command. He moved into Naples temporarily in the Adirondack, I think, as his flagship and eventually got his headquarters ashore, provided by the Italian government and the residence at Villa Niki. But you couldn't conceivably affront the British sensitivities by putting Mountbatten as subordinate to Admiral Carney, in the light of Mountbatten's prestigious position and wartime experience.

This posed a very serious problem. Eisenhower recognized that what he was getting was not the ideal command relationship, from a theoretical point of view or from a U.S. national point of view. So he said, "We will make this initial step. Carney will be the Commander in Chief, Southern Europe. He will have the U.S. Sixth Fleet as his striking force, southern Europe as a part of that command. Mountbatten will be the Commander in Chief, Mediterranean, which will be essentially the British Navy, such support as the U.S. Navy can give, and then the local commands, the French, the Italians, and, later, the Greek and Turkish navies. Then, he said, "later on it can be sorted out."

In the north a lot of people didn't like the idea of a British naval officer being the Commander in Chief, Allied Forces, Northern Europe, and the British did not want to pull their naval forces out of the Mediterranean and concentrate them in the North sea up there. In any event, Eisenhower's view prevailed and he had Admiral Sir Patrick Brind, Royal Navy, as initial Commander in Chief, North, with his headquarters in Oslo.

In the center, central Europe, Eisenhower said we'd have to give the Commander in Chief, Land Forces, Central Europe, to Marshal Juin, French, with his headquarters at Fontainebleau.

Q: He made the billet for the French?

Adm. A.: Made the billet for the French. Also it was General Norstad who became Commander in Chief, Air Forces, Central Europe. He had his headquarters in Germany but established close liaison at Fontainebleau.

It was an expedient solution, obviously of temporary duration, but it was one that Eisenhower perceived as one that could work and he said, "After all, we've got to build this thing up. We've got to build up the forces, we've got to build up the logistics base." Then, as time went on U.S. Army forces in Europe were being expanded. We built up, at least initially temporarily under Eisenhower's testimony to the Congress from the one and a half U.S. army divisions that he had inherited from the old occupation forces in Germany to a force of six divisions until such time as we could get the Germans rearmed. That brought in an entirely new and complicating situation.

Q: Yes. Well, he certainly was the man for that job. I mean with his experience.

Adm. A.: No question. He and Gruenther were the men for the job.

The irritants were Montgomery, who managed to irritate everyone, internally and externally. And the problems of getting the French to accept a German rearmament.

Q: Yes. How did you approach that?

Adm. A.: That was handled principally through the planning groups outside and by General Eisenhower using the best influence he could. He would get conferences going on what type of German organization there should be, particularly the army. They were thinking of the army and the air force at that time. It was interesting. The Germans provided some very, very fine people, who were extremely well informed. They'd done a lot of thinking on their own and they could produce answers at the drop of a hat, indicating that they'd given a lot of study to this problem.

Q: Did they realize the delicacy?

Adm. A.: Oh, they realized the delicacy of the whole situation. It took a long, long time to get that thing going forward. There was also the problem of the accession of Greece and Turkey to NATO and their incorporation in the southern European command.

Q: Was there objection to that?

Adm. A.: There was all sorts of objection on the command organization, again on the part of the British. They simply did not want to have a U.S. naval officer commanding the group and the air forces of Greece and Turkey in southeastern Europe, and this took a long, long time to iron out, but eventually it prevailed.

During this period, I found myself in a paradoxical situation, where I was writing letters for General Eisenhower's signature back to the U.S. Chiefs of Staff, then writing a reply back from Admiral Sherman, chief of naval operations, back to General Eisenhower in reply to the letter I'd originally composed for General Eisenhower.

Q: It was good that you knew Sherman so well.

Adm. A.: It was very fortunate, yes. At one point, Admiral Duncan sent a courier over. I'd written a letter back and he had received it and was so suspicious that somebody had tampered with that letter that he sent a courier over to show me the envelope and ask if it was in this condition when it was mailed, and the answer was "No." But Admiral Duncan was sufficiently apprehensive of the situation, he felt somebody between SHAPE and delivery in the Pentagon had opened that letter, between the time it was mailed in the secure mailroom at SHAPE and delivered in the Pentagon.

Q: They were very clumsy about it.

Adm. A.: It had been sent back by courier but it had to go through the U.S. State Department in Washington. Where it was opened, who got it I don't know. In any event, it showed the problems of security that existed over there. Actually, there were no particular ramifications of the thing, as far as I was concerned.

Q: We had a good man in Germany, did we not; did he help you people in SHAPE, Conant?

Adm. A.: I didn't come in contact with him at that time because dealings with all the higher-level people were handled by Eisenhower and Gruenther. Of course, they were having serious problems in France over relationships with de Gaulle and, of course, with the British on every sort of thing.

Then we had the problems of getting the proper logistics facilities and lines of communication set up for the support of the forces that were being built up under the stimulation of Eisenhower and the somewhat reluctance of the British and of the Dutch, the Belgians, and the Italian government to build up the forces. The Italians had been quite cooperative throughout the whole formulative period there, both to Admiral Carney in Italy and to General Eisenhower at SHAPE, and they had some very fine people, certainly cooperative.

Working under General Gruenther as the chief of staff was difficult, because he was a very demanding taskmaster.

Q: Was he as brilliant as purported to be?

Adm. A.: Very bright, very pleasant, but very tough and demanding in the service given to the headquarters by all staff officers. We lived in a little apartment in Paris eventually, a ground floor apartment, and my little boy I brought up and put in a French school outside of Paris, Ecole de Montreal, which had been a German air defense command during the German occupation. My daughter I left in school in Cannes. My wife used to go to the American Protestant cathedral. She left to go to an eleven o'clock service and I was going a little bit later to Mass at St. Joseph's church and, after she left, I was due to pick her up at the cathedral, the telephone rang and it was General Gruenther, who said, "Get out to Orly right away. I want you to go to Rome."

So I had to wrap up everything, toothbrush and so forth, get a uniform and go to Rome and she was waiting for me to pick her up outside the church.

Q: Did he give you some indication of why he wanted you to do this?

Adm. A.: No, he said, "I'll send the papers along." So I went out there and actually General Eisenhower was going to Rome, he and General Gruenther.

Another time, on practically no notice at all, I had to go to Portugal with General Eisenhower and General Gruenther. Being from the plans division, while they were very allied in their approach to thing, they recognized that when they had to get something done they had to rely on the U.S. officers, and this was sometimes embarrassing to them.

Q: I suppose it was understood by the foreign officers?

Adm. A.: Oh, they accepted it. The British, I think, were a little bit vexed. The British deprecated the French and the Italians and later the Greeks and the Turks on any staff work, so they were glad to have U.S. officers do it. But we had fine British officers and had very good rapport.

Actually, the headquarters was officially established, commissioned, I think in April of 1951, and then a search went to get a permanent headquarters. General Eisenhower wanted it outside of Paris, in the suburbs of but not in Paris. The search went on for a headquarters, a site for it, and they built a headquarters outside. The following year it was completed and we all moved from the Astoria Hotel out there to the new headquarters.

Q: At Versailles, was this?

Adm. A.: It was near Versailles.

There were many conferences going on because they had the NATO Council, which was established in Paris, the Standing Group on the military side was back in Washington, the representatives of the U.S. and British chiefs of staff, and the French, then there was a military committee that met about twice a year. They were the chiefs of staff designate, members of the chiefs of staff of all the NATO countries. And they had all sorts of logistics facilities planning groups. So there were a great many conferences on a great variety of subjects, ranging from German rearmament to bases to build up the support facilities, standardization of equipment, the buildup of the air defenses of Europe. Everything had to be done from scratch.

Q: What was the time schedule for all this? Did you have one set?

Adm. A.: Oh, yes, a time schedule was set for everything, except that the time schedules were never met, mainly because of the political differences.

As I say, we found an apartment in Paris and established a pleasant life there. There were good social relationships with our allied colleagues. Paris was an interesting place to be. The ladies like it. We had good arrangements for the children in French schools. As soon as the army got into the situation, they established a commissary and a PX and an officers' club at SHAPE. A good standard of living abroad came up to army standards and we all benefited from that.

General Eisenhower insisted that similar arrangements be made for the allied staff officers, and the British NAAFI, Navy, Army, Air Force Institute, contributed the way our PX system did, and it became a very cohesive headquarters. Genral Gruenther insisted that all the U.S. officers would study French and that the allied officers would all study English, take classes, so much time each day.

Q: That was a wise provision.

Adm. A.: Oh, yes. He had great wisdom, and so did General Eisenhower, in the whole thing.

It was initially agreed that among Field Marshal Montgomery's duties would be included a yearly conference, which led to "SHAPE-X". Field Marshal Montgomery ran that for the supreme commander, and he plunged into this with great enthusiasm. Eisenhower used his best efforts to solicit and obtain the full support of all the NATO countries, and the attendance - well, the first SHAPE-X included the chiefs of staff, the principal military commanders, not only internal allied command, Europe, but allied command, Atlantic, and the individual national staffs. These were very well attended, well conducted meetings, usually three days, and very pleasant social arrangements set up, and they became a tradition that carried on when the headquarters was subsequently moved to Belgium after the departure from France.

Q: What was the theme of SHAPE-X? Did it differ from year to year?

Adm. A.: They would differ from year to year, posing a potential threat situation, a combat situation, the reactions to it, a scenario appropriate to what they were trying to develop. Of course, the lines of supply and support, the combat forces, the deployment of forces, and, of course, German rearmament.

I went through all of 1951 and in 1952 it was apparent that my usefulness had been accomplished.

Q: All these studies had been prepared?

Adm. A.: Most of these studies had been prepared, and I was anxious to get to sea and get command of an aircraft carrier.

Oh, a very sad and interesting situation. Admiral Sherman had come over on a visit to Spain and then he came to Paris to visit General Eisenhower. Then he was going to London and then to Italy to visit Admiral Carney, then return to the United States. When he came to Paris, I accompanied him on his visit to General Eisenhower, with Gruenther, and Eisenhower was very anxious to have Sherman stay and take a little breather, as Ike said, and go over to Berchtesgaden and Garmisch. Sherman said he appreciated it but he had urgent tasks to perform. He had to go to Naples to straighten things out with Admiral Carney because, at that time, Carney was under attack by the British and a carry on from British sensitivity to Carney's efforts to try to get the whole of the Mediterranean as well as southern Europe under his command.

Q: Was Mountbatten still there?

Adm. A.: Mountbatten was still there, yes, and a jealousy which prevailed and the reaction on the part of the British to Carney's actions. Sherman, sensitive to Eisenhower's view, where Eisenhower said, "Well, the first thing you've got to do is get rid of Carney's dual-hat job in London and the CinCNelm job and let him concentrate on the principal job that he's got down here."

Sherman felt that he had to go to Naples and therefore he declined Eisenhower's visit to Germany with him. He said he had to go to London for one day, to visit in London, then he was going to Naples and go to Washington as he had to report on the situation in Spain, his negotiations with Franco. Well, he made a short visit to London. Ike sent us down to the Tour d'Argent, told me to go down to the Tour d'Argent and take Admiral and Mrs. Sherman to dinner. Then he left and went to London, spent one night in London, and went to Naples, and that's the night he died. I had to go in and report to Eisenhower the next morning that Sherman had died. He said, "Yes, I know it. Why the hell didn't that happen to one of us old fuds instead of somebody like Forrest who had so much to offer to his country in the years ahead?" Eisenhower fully recognized the ability of Forrest Sherman, the support that Sherman was giving to the whole NATO exercise and the establishment of SHAPE and its buildup. It just showed how distressed and how human Eisenhower was about the loss of Forrest Sherman.

At the same time, Ike realized that there was going to be a lot of competition as to who was going to relieve Sherman as CNO. He also knew that Carney was very ambitious to relieve Sherman. He telephoned Carney, having known that Carney was doing a lot of telephonic politicking to get the job of CNO. He told Carney in very unmistakable terms, "All right, you can go back for the funeral, if you want to, but you come back here regardless of what happens. If you're going to turn over your command, you turn it over in an orderly way."

Actually, Admiral Fechteler became the new CNO.

This brings up another problem that was going on concurrently. It was not a SHAPE responsibility but we were in on the fringes of it, and that was the establishment and the scope of the Atlantic command.

Q: IberLant?

Adm. A.: The Atlantic command, which included IberLant and it included discussion of what was known as the Channel Command, around the British Isles. The concept of the Atlantic Command had been basically approved, which was certainly a logical solution, necessary most important to the logistic support of the Allied Command, Europe, in the event of a war. But there were all these political considerations, the British in particular, the sensitivities of the Dutch, the Belgians, and the French, and then the Iberian sector of that command, who was to command that. The desires of the American navy to get the command tied up where we had the principal forces, Atlantic Fleet, U.S. naval forces. So this was a rather prolonged discussion that went on and SHAPE inevitably got involved in it. But the Atlantic Command was established and the Channel Command was established under a British officer under a Channel committee of French, British, Belgian, and Dutch.

Q: What about the Norwegians?

Adm. A.: The Norwegians were part of the allied Northern European command and SHAPE.

These matters took up a great deal of time, a great deal of negotiation, a lot of irritations, and ultimately came up with the solution which, as in the case of southern Europe and the Mediterranean, eventually, after I left and after General Eisenhower left, fell into a very logical place. Some took years to finally become accomplished, showing the difficulty of working out allied command arrangements in peacetime in a way that would be proper in the event of war. But eventually, even though it took a long period of time, just as German rearmament did, it all worked out successfully and I think NATO, largely due to the initial efforts of General Eisenhower and the wisdom and brilliance of General Gruenther as the initial people in command at SHAPE, a very sound organization was built up and endured over the years, in spite of all the difficulties involved.

Q: They were sanguine that it would work and that it would be a defense for western Europe?

Adm. A.: And essential.

There were many related problems that came into this thing. The question of the resurgence of a German navy, and there the

British were just as sensitive as the French were to the rearmament of Germany in terms of a land force and an air force, yet they knew they had to have it. And then the scope of the activity of the German navy, would it be restricted just to the Baltic or the southern part of the North Sea.

Q: Minesweepers.

Adm. A.: That's right, or should they have submarines. The restrictions that were put on in the final negotiations to get German rearmament. Eventually these things were worked out. The Germans had very, very smart people, as I mentioned before, available in this whole situation.

Well, in the spring of 1952 it was quite evident that General Eisenhower was going to leave about the 1st of July because the pressure was coming on him to run for president. In any event there was great pressure.

Q: Henry Cabot Lodge got into that situation.

Adm. A.: Oh, they all did. Everybody was coming over. Marx, the toy manufacturer, Jewish groups, all sorts of Republicans and Democrats. Everybody was pressuring General Eisenhower to come over and run for president.

At the same time, Admiral Fechteler, who had taken over as CNO, wrote a note to General Eisenhower and said that George Anderson is a good man, his sea duty had been interrupted and he would like to make George Anderson available, to take command of the Franklin D. Roosevelt aircraft carrier in July. I'd been in that, too, in a sub rosa way of getting it laid on, and Ike said, "Well, I'm going to be going, Anderson can go and Gruenther said, "Damn it, get out of here."

Q: Did you have as much influence with Fechteler as you did with Forrest Sherman?

Adm. A.: I had very fine relations with Admiral Fechteler, and if trouble would arise I'd communicate back. Wu Duncan was deputy vice chief to Fechteler. I had wonderful support and I tried to give them as much support as possible under the circumstances.

In any event, I knew that I was going to get command of the FDR, I knew I would be detached on the 1st of July 1952, I knew that Eisenhower was going to leave at that time, and so I arranged for my family to stay over in the southern European area, on the French Riviera, and I went back to the United States to get the FDR and bring her back over to Europe where she was going to be part of the Sixth Fleet.

On 15 May 1952 my wife went down and rented a house in Cannes and she moved down. I got two weeks' leave in the latter part of May, then I had to go back to SHAPE. So we arranged for a two-week swap of our house on the Riviera for an apartment that General Persons, who was a special assistant to Eisenhower, had up in Paris, so we got the exchange. My wife came up and we moved into their apartment and they moved down by car to go to our villa on the Riviera. They took the cats along. Mrs. Anderson was there when they arrived and she said it was something because every time they'd open windows the cats would howl. It was a warm day and they had to keep the windows closed to keep the cats quiet, sweating and perspiring all the way from Paris down to the Riviera.

So, we exchanged for two weeks, then I was detached and went on back to the United States, which I guess is probably a good place to break.

Q: There is a very intruiging note you have. I don't know whether it refers to the switching of the villa and the apartment - tick-tock-tack, tit for tat.

Adm. A.: Oh, yes. As I say, I was a graduate of the National War College and I'd been over there, and General Gruenther sent me back to Washington on some business for SHAPE and while I was there they heard at the National War College that I was in town and they asked me if I could come down and give what they called a spot lecture at the National War College.

I sent a message back to SHAPE, to General Gruenther, and said I'd been asked to give a lecture at the National War College and I would if it was acceptable to him. He said yes, fine, but don't encroach on the subject matter to be given by Air Chief Marshal Saunders in a principal talk a few weeks later. I think it was two weeks later.

Q: You should not preempt what he was going to say.

Adm. A.: I went out to Ft McNair to the National War College and I was the second lecturer that morning. The first lecturer was the first sea lord of the Royal Navy, Admiral Sir Roderick MacGregor, who was accompanied by my friend, Peter Gretton, who'd been a classmate of mine in the war college. He was a captain in the Royal Navy at that time. I knew that Peter was going to have Sir

Roderick give a very good talk at the war college, so I went down and listened to the lecture and I thought, my goodness gracious, he's pulled out all the stops and I'm under this restraint not to talk about anything substantive that Air Chief Marshal Saunders, RAF, would. So I said to hell with my instructions, and I went on and I gave everything that I possibly could, inside and out. I ended up by talking on the command situation, which was above. I explained all the difficulties involved in this. I said, "It reminds me very much of a limerick I once heard:

There was a young lady named Pratt

Who had triplets, Tick, Tock and Tat.

It was fun conceiving them but awful hard feeding them

Because there was no tit for tat."

It was an apropos limerick because here they were all these command relationships, and I was talking particularly about the naval relationships in the Med and northern Europe. Ike had the idea of a British admiral and the British navy up in the North but there was no British navy to support it. In fact, all he had were the Norwegians and the Danes and a British Commander in Chief.

The experience at SHAPE was tremendously interesting, very challenging, very frustrating at times, and very satisfying when one looked back at the long-range achievements. Every year I go to the annual dinner of the SHAPE Alumni Association, which is held here at Bolling Field. I go next week, I believe, attended by many people who are surviving from the original group and subsequent replacements who served in SHAPE. The attendance from Eisenhower, Gruenther, Lemnitzer, Norstad, Schuyler, and all the others is most faithful. We all get back once a year for a reunion here. The SHAPE Alumni Association also had an annual dinner in Belgium and they get most of the Europeans who served in SHAPE to attend.

Q: Did you attend that this summer?

Adm. A.: I've never attended the one in Brussels, no, simply because I've always been too busy otherwise and involved to get to that one. But they have one there and one here. And so foreigners, British or French, who may be SHAPE alumni and are on duty in Washington come just as well, and we get Canadians down. It's a very fine reunion that we have. Certainly, the concept of an allied command as a deterrent to aggression in Europe and as a facility to cope with a threat and a war, if it develops is very valid, essential to the security of all the nations of NATO and the peace of the world, and I think it has functioned extremely successfully ever since it was organized. But due principally to what General Eisenhower and General Gruenther put in initially, the initial input and the spirit in which it evolved-

Q: And you can take pride in the role you played.

Adm. A.: Oh, well, a little bit, yes. It was fun.

Interview No. 6 with Admiral George W. Anderson, Jr., U.S. Navy
(Retired)

Place: His apartment in the Watergate, Washington, D.C.

Date: Wednesday morning, 5 November 1980

Subject: Biography

By: John T. Mason, Jr.

Q: Sir, today we're beginning with your command of the FDR. This was in the year 1952. You had been at SHAPE with General Eisenhower as senior U.S. officer in plans and operations. You are giving this up now and taking over command of a major carrier.

Adm. A.: Well, I felt very fortunate naturally in getting command of a big carrier. This was a billet that I felt I was qualified to assume with a degree of confidence, having had experience in aircraft carriers, in VF-2 squadron on the old LEXINGTON, as landing signal officer of the old YORKTOWN, and as navigator on the new YORKTOWN during the war and followed the operation and the development of carriers and the introduction of the new aircraft.

Q: Command of the MINDORO had been -

Adm. A.: My command of the MINDORO also was a very fortunate preparation for this.

I left Paris and went to the Riviera to join my family, where I spent a couple of weeks enjoying the sunshine and the pleasant life there. Then I took off and joined the FDR at Guantanamo Bay in Cuba, where the ship was undergoing refresher training in the training command preparatory to joining the fleet after an overhaul. My predecessor in the FDR was my good friend Captain Fitzhugh Lee, and he turned over to me a fine ship that was undergoing active and aggressive training at Guantanamo.

Q: And, I suppose, equipped with the newest planes and all that sort of thing?

Adm. A.: Yes. They had new planes, but, of course, the FDR had not been converted into an angled-deck carrier at that time.

The training operation down in Guantanamo was strenuous, primarily to improve all departments of the ship with emphasis on damage control, safety precautions, firefighting, and things of this sort, which the training command detachment down there was eminently qualified to do. It diverted our attention somewhat from what we always considered the prime responsibility of an aircraft carrier, that is to operate the aircraft, but it did give us the time to emphasize with good supervision the types of shipboard activities that are very important to a big carrier and you just don't have the opportunity to supervise in detail in the priorities of attention of fleet operations. But there was a fine program down there. Afterwards we came back to Hampton Roads -

Q: You mention Admiral Tommy Robbins in your notes.

Adm. A.: Rear Admiral Thomas H. Robbins, the class of '20, was a very brilliant officer. He was the commander of Carrier Division 2, I believe it was, of which the FDR was one of the ships. He was a different type of naval officer than most others in spite of his great brilliance. He was not a real flying aviator, you might say, but more involved in the intellectual side of naval operations as a whole. He served during the war on the staff at Admiral King's headquarters, and when I was in the Bureau of Aeronautics and he was so conscious of security that at the time of Guadalcanal the word never got down to the people who were actually responsible for the resupply of aircraft and weapons out there that a serious situation developed in Guadalcanal as a result of that deficiency. We were operating at that time on a shoestring. Nevertheless, he was basically a good friend of mine.

We came up to Hampton Roads and knew that we were about to take part in a major NATO exercise in northern Europe. We steamed with elements of the Second Fleet from Hampton Roads in August, I believe it was, conducted operations en route through the North Sea area. Unfortunately, while we were en route, we had a major failure of our catapult, one of our catapults. Obviously we could not operate at effectiveness with a downed catapult, and so it was arranged for us to proceed as rapidly as possible to the Clyde in Scotland, where we had people flown over from the naval shipyard at Portsmouth, Virginia, to try to put the catapult back into full operation and full commission. The prospects in the minds of certain people were rather dim, but with a very aggressive effort up in the Clyde we succeeded and were able to make our schedule on time.

Q: You were in there seeing there was an aggressive effort?

Adm. A.: That's right. I was down there by a catapult practically morning, noon, and night of every day. But they did a good job and we surprised people by being ready to go to sea and participate in the exercise.

Q: How many U.S. carriers were involved in this exercise?

Adm. A.: There were two carriers. I forget just which the other one was.

Q: Augmented by a British carrier?

Adm. A.: Yes, there was a British carrier up there. I don't have an active recollection of that NATO exercise, which was in the summer of 1952. You might be able to get a report of that exercise out of the files some place.

Q: I imagine this was one of the early NATO exercises?

Adm. A.: Yes, one of the early major naval exercises up there. The weather was rather bad and in that part of the world rather unpredictable, except frequently it was predicted to be bad. We operated close to the Arctic Circle - I guess we did go across the Arctic Circle and then down the Norwegian coast.

Q: You didn't call at Murmansk, however?

Adm. A.: No, neither did we after completion of the exercise take the carrier in to one of the Norwegian ports or the Danish ports for recreation because the schedule of the FDR was so tight that on the conclusion of this exercise we had just time for a brief stop in the south of England at Plymouth and then we went right on down to the Mediterranean to join the Sixth Fleet for our deployment there.

Q: Let me ask about communications during this operation. Were they impaired?

Adm. A.: Communications left something to be desired at that time, particularly in the northern area. But also, I would say, the greatest problem we had was the rapid change of the weather conditions, which kept a strain on us all the time because we wanted to make a good showing in the operation, in the NATO operation, and yet we had to be conscious of the safety of our pilots so that we didn't lose any pilots or planes. In my recollection, we did not lose a plane or a pilot during that operation.

Coming back towards the English Channel, however, I did have a rather hair-raising experience. We were in formation, as the guide of the formation, cruising at night across the lower part of the North Sea towards the Channel. I was in my emergency cabin up on deck and the officer of the deck called me and said there was a light approaching from the port side. I looked out there and, sure enough, when I got to the bridge and put my glasses on it, there was a light headed right on a collision course for us. We had the obligation under the rules of the road of maintaining course and speed, but as this ship kept coming in right on a steady collision course bearing, I became pretty apprehensive of the situation. Suddenly I realized there were loads of destroyers in the screen and this merchantman had come through, passed them, and he thought this was just another destroyer. So I told the officer of the deck to go to the signal bridge and turn on a searchlight on the stern of the ship, just so he would see what it was and how big it was.

Well, he kept coming on and suddenly I got to the point of extremis where you have to take action. I rapped the rudder hard left to move the stern of the ship out and this fellow almost disappeared under the port elevator and went slipping down the port side of the ship, and we did a jog and missed him. But it was a close call. It was some small German merchant vessel.

Q: Were the U.S. people generally pleased with the cooperation of the other navies in this operation?

Adm. A.: Yes, the cooperation was good, I did not attend the critique which I believe was held in Oslo. The admiral flew in for that.

Q: Who was that?

Adm. A.: Admiral Robbins. I almost forget who the fleet commander was but it was Admiral Felix Stump, who had the Second Fleet at that time.

In any event, it was a good exercise. We learned a lot, and it certainly assisted me as commanding officer of the ship, in getting the ship ready for further operations in the Mediterranean.

We went in to Plymouth, where the British were very simpatico with us, very hospitable. The crew enjoyed the opportunity of liberty although we were in there only three short days before we took off for the Mediterranean.

During this time, my wife and two smaller children were staying down in Cannes in the villa that we had down there, and we had decided that they would remain there as long as the ship was deployed in the Mediterranean with the Sixth Fleet, after which we would return to Norfolk, which was our home port at that time.

We got down to the Sixth Fleet and I was certainly very happy to be in that fine fleet in a good environment, and I think it was Admiral Cassidy who was the Sixth Fleet commander at that time. We went right into the usual operations with the fleet, including a cruise out to the eastern Mediterranean, operating on the normal fleet schedule. There was no international crisis in process at the time in the Middle East or the Mediterranean.

Q: In some other part of the world!

Adm. A.: Yes. We went in to Beirut, found in Beirut the same fine, hospitable group of Americans, very friendly to the fleet. They had set up the canteen ashore, as they did on all visits of the Sixth Fleet, and the people in Beirut entertained us. The crews enjoyed the shopping, the opportunity to do sightseeing around in the environs of Beirut.

I remember one afternoon we were invited to a supper party at the home of one of the Aramco officers. I think he was the president of Aramco, the tapline. I was going and I took ashore with me the operations officer of the fleet on Admiral Robbins's staff, Commander Winters, and we landed at the flag officers' landing at the St. George Hotel in Beirut and there, up on the terrace was Admiral Robbins drinking his usual fill of very dry martinis. Commander Winters went up to the admiral and said:

"We're going out to this particular party. I know you're invited."

And the admiral said, very superciliously, "But they're commercial people. No, I can't go to that." He had this very European accent. Winters said:

"Well, then I will express your regrets to the hostess." And the admiral said:

"I forbid you to express my regrets to any hostess. They're just commercial people."

But, in any event, we had a good visit in there. We stopped afterwards I guess it was in Rhodes. At that time it was impractical to have my wife try to follow the ship, as she did later and had done on my previous duty over there. We, of course, were in to Greek ports, Rhodes. I don't recall going in to Cyrpus on that particular trip.

Q: Alexandria?

Adm. A.: Oh, no, no, we never went in to Alexandria.

Q: At this point did we have a policy of two carriers in the Med, one in the west and one in the east?

Adm. A.: There were two carriers in the Med, yes. If there was any tension in the Med, they would always try to leave one carrier in the eastern Med. Frequently, there were two, but they normally tried to keep one carrier in the eastern Mediterranean.

I had a fine air group. They performed exceptionally well. I had excellent officers on the ship.

Q: You mentioned your exec.

Adm. A.: My first exec was Commander Turner Caldwell, later Vice Admiral Turner Caldwell, and I remember giving him his final fitness report before he was detached by saying the ship was so many thousand tons, so many officers and men, so many aircraft, steamed so many thousand miles, and conducted so many landings, visiting foreign ports, and Commander Caldwell was my executive officer and was not known as a "son of a bitch". That was the narrative report I gave him.

He was replaced by Commander Eddie Outlaw, a very fine, very aggressive officer, who decided he would be a different type of executive officer on an aircraft carrier. He intended to fly with the air group. He was a very fine pilot. And I said:

"Well, I think you'd better learn your shipboard duties first," and one of the first chores I gave him was to handle the ship during a replenishment. I went into the emergency cabin after I'd made the approach to the tanker and left him to handle it. It was kind of a rough day and he had a little difficulty doing that, but I think it made a Christian of him and made a better exec.

The chaplain in the ship was later the chief of chaplains, Captain Rotridge, a very tall, good-looking man. He was later chaplain at the Naval Academy and he was being relieved. His relief arrived aboard, Father Joe Canty, also a Catholic chaplain. I remember welcoming Father Canty and saying I didn't ask for him, I didn't know whether he was sent on board as a matter of routine to clean up the mess that Father Rotridge left or whether he thought it would be an easy chore just stepping into Father Rotridge's shoes. This was the one opportunity, I wanted him to know, that I had looked forward to for so long, that I was going to be the obdurate old pastor and he the young curate. I had the four-volume book called the Companion to the Summa of St. Thomas Aquinas, which was written by the chaplain of the YORKTOWN during the war, who was a great Dominican theologian who later died, Father Farrell. I had them shifted up to my emergency cabin and I looked through one of them on the spur of the moment and, having picked a particular subject, I would call to the marine orderly:

"Orderly, call the holy father to come up to the bridge."

Chaplain Canty would come huffing and puffing up the ladders to the bridge and I'd say:

"Father, I was just sitting here thinking," and I'd ask him some complex question about the Holy Ghost or something similar! I had a lot of fun and he enjoyed it but did lose some excess fat climbing up to the bridge.

Q: Was he able to cope?

Adm. A.: He'd usually say, "I have to think that one over."

We had fine officers, excellent officers, a fine air group, and I was very pleased with them. One operation did not turn out so well. Admiral Cassidy, when we were in the eastern Mediterranean, had arranged to have a fly-over on the ship over Amman, Jordan. It was to take place at a certain time, the air group was launched, and they came back. The air group commander, later admiral, Roy Swanson, came up to the bridge right away and I asked him, "How did that turn out? How did the fly-over go?"

"Oh," he said, "fine."

Well, about that time messages started coming out to the ship, "Where is the fly-over?"

I checked with Swanson and said, "Are you sure you flew over?

"Yes, indeed."

"What time? Precisely what time?"

Eventually, Admiral Cassidy got back to the flagship and started to check up. The planes had not flown over Amman. They'd flown over some other town out there and the magnificent demonstration that Admiral Cassidy had looked to put on to demonstrate the Sixth Fleet's readiness fell flat on its face. We checked on through and found out they had flown over what was marked on the chart as Amman, but there was an error in the charts that they had used. So it didn't go over too well.

We stopped in various ports - oh, I did have the opportunity - Admiral Cassidy very nicely scheduled the FDR to visit right next to Cannes on the French Riviera, for an in-port visit before I returned home, which was a big thrill for me because the family was there and friends were there and it was a very nice visit.

Of course, the officers and the crew always loved to visit the French Riviera. French ports in those days were sort of frosting on the cake for their cruise in the Mediterranean because frequently they had to go into the poorer liberty ports in North Africa or the eastern Mediterranean.

We came back -

Q: Before you do that, would you comment on some of the elements that made this obviously a happy ship? How did you contribute to this? What is your philosophy?

Adm. A.: Well, the first thing is to make everybody realize that what they're doing is - each individual is vitally important to the whole ship and its operation. Secondly, to make them realize that the aircraft carrier existed primarily for the operation of th air group. That was the major weapon of the ship, the air group. Third, to let the officers and men know that the commanding officer was vitally interested in everything that they wre doing, was aware of what they were doing, was interested in making things as pleasant for them as was possible, with full realization of the fact that the success of our aircraft carriers was not on the basis of a forty-hour week, far from it. Indeed they were twenty-four-hour days, seven days a week. Indeed, the aircraft carrier, particularly since the increase of night operations, involved the work of the flight-deck crews and the handling crews practically almost twenty-four hours a day, seven days a week.

One other thing that was of interest happened at that time. We were making a visit to La Spezia, in Italy, where the Italian naval academy is located. This happened in 1952, December 7th, which was a Sunday morning, and I just felt that there was such a relaxed attitude on board that I told the admiral on Saturday night not to be surprised, but I was going to have general quarters sounded at eight o'clock on Sunday morning, which I did, and you never saw people bounce out of their bunks in parts of the ship so fast to get to general quarters. Then I got on the general announcing system and explained why I had done it, because over in the Sixth Fleet, on a ship of the navy in full commission, they have to be alert at any particular time for some unexpected event, and this was just part of my effort to make them realize how important it was that they be ready at any time. It was the anniversary of the Japanese attack on Pearl Harbor early Sunday morning in 1941.

The two major points that I made in command of the FDR, which I later carried on in all my tours of duty, particularly in the Sixth Fleet, were readiness and respect. We had to maintain our readiness within our capabilities for any eventuality, day or night. Secondly, we had to demonstrate to anybody who was around respect for the United States, the U.S. Navy, and, in particualr, the Sixth Fleet. I used to point out to them - and I talked to them regularly over the loudspeaker in the ship - that, they had to consider themselves in the same general status as the New York Yankees in baseball or Notre Dame in football, that they were the best and they had to maintain that standard of operations and appearance and behavior, to live up to their reputation of being the best in the navy and of any in the world.

Q: This pertained to shore leave as well?

Adm. A.: Oh, yes, very definitely, although my responsibility on shore leave, at that time, was more limited than it was later, when I had command of the Sixth Fleet. But we insisted that the officers and men were in appropriate attire, that their uniforms were right, their insignia bright, their shoes were shined. This was in accordance with the standard that had originally been set, established by Admiral Sherman when he set up the Sixth Fleet as an operating fleet in the Mediterranean.

Q: You might comment also at this time on the role of the chaplain. You emphasize the chaplain.

Adm. A.: I always emphasized the role of the chaplain. Fortunately, we had two on the aircraft carrier, a Catholic and a Protestant. In my talks I would say that they should live by the best moral standards they had learned in their church or their synagogue, at their school, or at their mother's knee, or by the observation of some friend who made a particular impression on them. I'll get into more of that when I had command of the Sixth Fleet.

There was a continuing program of trying to solicit from the men that they were representatives of the United States, of the U.S. Navy, and that they had an individual role to play in that, and, as I said later in many talks to them, don't spend their money on "pals and prostitutes" but to take advantage of the opportunity they had to travel around and see some people in other parts of the world, to recognize how fortunate we were in the United States in contrast with the countries that had grown up from more ancient civilizations. They had an opportunity to see things and learn from them and from it to profit in their own lives in the years ahead. I think it was a very well worthwhile program. As I say, while I carried it out in the FDR, I was able to do much more when I was commander of the Sixth Fleet.

We were due to leave the Mediterranean to get the FDR back to its home port for Christmas, which was Norfolk, because the ship had been away a couple of Christmas periods in the immediately preceding years. So we left the Mediterranean, checking out at the Straits of Gibraltar and made a brief stop in Gibraltar. One of the things that had been customary or frequently occasioned in the past when ships would stop in to Gibraltar, the officers in particular and the men on occasion would stop into the big liquor stores there. One was Socony and Speed. They'd fill up their suitcases and bring packages back to have cheap liquor when they got back home. They weren't drinking it aboard ship.

Q: Was that a free port?

Adm. A.: Well, it was quite cheap there. We had had word and I knew that this was a problem to the navy with the U.S. customs and we never knew when we would get a customs inspection when the sailors left the ship when they got home or the officers left the ships. So I cautioned them all on how silly it was, particularly the officers, to take the chance of jeopardizing a naval career, the future that they had for the few dollars that they might save by buying a bottle, two bottles or three bottles of whisky or gin. Just to think and balance out what they were actually saving.

I think the message got across pretty well. I went ashore that afternoon, one afternoon, in Gibraltar, walked down the street, and most of the officers had really taken my caution to heart, except I found out that the two chaplains, the Catholic and the Protestant, were each with a suitcase standing outside Socony and Speed! I used to, as the saying runs, haze the chaplains quite a bit, so I rubbed their noses in that quite often.

Q: They felt they were immune from it!

Adm. A.: Yes, that's right, sacramental wine!

We made a fast passage across the Atlantic to get home on schedule and I'll never forget bringing the ship in to Pier 5, I guess it was, at Norfolk on, I think, the 19th of December after she'd been away, first, to go up on NATO exercises and then to the Mediterranean and the Sixth Fleet. The pressure that was involve with all the dependents on the pier, the wives and the children and the girls, all dressed up. The girls had their hair all fixed up, wearing good-looking clothes, and the enthusiasm that there was in arriving back on board.

One other thing that I did on the FDR was to use the band to its maximum effectiveness. You recall in the campaign of President Roosevelt's election, they had a theme song of "Happy Days are Here Again." Well, we would play that then as frequently as possible, and also another, one, "Columbia, the Gem of the Ocean." They're both sort of inspirational, and were among the various other items that I had used to stimulate the morale and enthusiasm of the crew.

We went in to Norfolk. My wife and children had come back from the Mediterranean, and we had a place at Virginia Beach. We stayed there. The ship had to go into the Navy Yard at Portsmouth for some work. Then, when we came out of the Navy Yard in the spring, we went into various other exercises up and down the coast, finally ending up in Mayport, which was to be the new home port of the FDR, Mayport having been developed and made available as a major carrier operating port complementing Norfolk.

Q: Jacksonville?

Adm. A.: In the Jacksonville area. That, I think, has proved a very fine arrangement. Now, of course, Mayport is used for the homeporting of destroyers and other ships that operate generally with the carriers. Mayport, the Jacksonville area, is a fine fleet operating facility, particularly for carrier aviation, good training facilities, bombing ranges, and so forth for the air groups. They have made some organizational changes, where the fighters are now moved up to Oceana and the other types of planes are down in the Jacksonville area. Basically, when they come to embark on board ship there, the ship is alongside a pier in Mayport, it's easy to get the planes on board, regardless of what the weather might be, and it's not too far away to get out to good operating areas.

Q: It didn't provide, however, any experience in cold waters and bad weather conditions such as Newport, did it?

Adm. A.: That's right, but that's a problem the navy has solved to some degree by having cruises go up off Newfoundland and in the North Atlantic during winter months, which are pretty tough operating cruises. I had one - I don't know whether I had one on the FDR or not. I did have a rather challenging experience in the FDR because I kept pretty close touch with the pilots and the air groups and the younger active flying officers. It was generally recognized that the navy had an Achilles' heel in the relatively low offensive and defensive capabilities by their aircraft at night. Therefore, it was necessary greatly to increase our capabilities to operate at night with our carrier aircraft. We had to stretch the art, you might say, not only so that we could land and take off but so that we could control the aircraft in the air and still maintain our standards of safety.

This was after we got back to the East Coast from the Mediterranean and, at my suggestion, we got the Commander, Air Forces, Atlantic fleet, who was then Admiral Ballentine, to agree that they would assemble most of the night pilots and we would conduct some concentrated night operations off the Virginia Capes. I had an operation officer given to me as the officer conducting the exercise, and I was very happy because at that time my carrier division commander, Admiral Robbins, was not going to be on board. But just as we got ready to leave for the operation, Admiral Robbins arrived back on board.

Q: Why didn't you want him on board?

Adm. A.: Because he was too timid. He was very timid, and he did not perceive as we did the necessity that we had to accept certain hazards in order greatly to enhance our night-operating capability.

Well, we went out. We had carefully selected pilots, they were good pilots, and we had a schedule of operations, but the admiral kept cautioning me all the time, they were too dangerous, too hazardous, and I kept saying:

"Well, Admiral, we've just got to press ahead with this. We've got to accept it."

Finally, on the third or fourth night, he was saying:

"You've got too many airplanes scheduled." I said,

"Now, Admiral, I'm the officer conducting this exercise. I recognize that you're the senior officer present. Do you order me, in your capacity as senior officer present, to reduce the flight schedules?

"Well," he said, "I wouldn't order you, but I think it's very, very advisable."

I said: "You're saying that as senior officer present?

He said yes and I said:

"Well, as officer conducting the exercise I'm terminating the exercise and returning to port."

Well, that upset him very much because this word had gotten all through the ready rooms of the pilots, that the admiral didn't have any guts, and wasn't going to pursue these operations the way the pilots felt they should and that the captain of the ship felt they should.

Well, of course, before we started back in to port, early in the morning, we had the airplanes fly off to their bases at Oceana, the Virginia Beach area and by the time the ship came in and got alongside the pier, the word had gotten all around through the air force, Atlantic Fleet, and up to the Commander in Chief, headquarters, Atlantic Fleet, of what had happened. I just told the boys:

"Now, just keept quiet. Don't make any issue."

Well, you can't keep a bunch of young pilots quiet. That was the last time that Admiral Robbins was aboard while I was aboard the FDR. He was sent up on some temporary duty in the Newport area because it was recognized that he was not the type of officer whose forte was being in command of a carrier division. I guess that's the last time he was at sea in a command position.

Q: What were some of the dangerous situations that he objected to, worried about?

Adm. A.: He worried that we'd have too many planes in the air, that if you had a crash on deck - and admittedly this was in the days before we had the angled deck - the flight deck would be tied up and perhaps we'd lose pilots, they wouldn't be able to get back to port, to their fields ashore. We did have one plane go in the water. I must say that that particular time I did more fast praying on the bridge that we'd pick this fellow up. His name was Wit Wright, and fortunately we were able to pick him up.

It was a period of time when the navy had no alternative, in my opinion, except to press ahead with night operations, nor that in later years we could meet our responsibilities. Now, night operations are routine. They're better than they were because of better instrumentation, better radar control, better communication more experience on the part of the pilots and flight-deck crews.

Q: We'd had some considerable experience in night operations in the Pacific in World War II?

Adm. A.: Yes, and then in peacetime it sort of fell off again. There was no alternative. They navy had to do that. If the navy could not operate at night, both offensively and defensively, with a considerable measure of success and effectiveness, the navy could not justify the high appropriations that were necessary for aircraft carriers and their air groups. I think we have done that, we'd done very well over the years.

I was told I was to be detached in, I guess, July of 1953 and would report to the plans division of the Office of the CNO.

Q: You were relieved by Admiral Thach, were you not?

Adm. A.: I was relieved by then Captain, later Admiral, Jimmy Thach, a classmate of mine. Thach had had a marvelous career in the navy. He was an experienced naval aviator, fighter pilot, he'd been on the staff of Admiral McCain, I guess it was, and he took over the ship, which was in good shape. I turned the ship over to him in the Portsmouth Navy Yard, and I remember the last cruise that I had on the ship, the last time under way, we were going from the naval base up to Portsmouth. Of course, they always had pilots available but I decided that I would keep what I call the conn and let the pilots just advise me rather than turning the ship over to the control of the pilots. This was, I guess, the first time any commanding officer of a large carrier had ever done that on that particular journey. The pilots didn't particularly like the idea, but I took the ship up and actually brought the ship up along to the pier in the Navy Yard at Portsmouth through the rather tortuous channel with just the normal group of ship-handling.

My concern in that regard stemmed from an experience I had when I had command of the MINDORO going out of Bermuda. They had a pilot there on board who had the conn, as we call it, and he missed a buoy. Visibility was not too good and I was apprehensive and I took the command away from him and did a very sharp turn to avoid running onto a reef.

Another experience I had when I had command of the FDR, when we were operating off the East Coast out of Norfolk, after having returned from the Mediterranean, which is interesting. I found that about 55 per cent of the officers and men came from the New York-New Jersey-New England area, and yet, when we were back on the East Coast, the whole urge of scheduling was to keep the ship as close to its home port which, in our case, was Norfolk. And so I asked to have them schedule a visit to New York, and Commander, Air Forces, Atlantic Fleet, Admiral Ballentine, who knew me pretty well, said:

"What do you want to do? All these married people want to stay at home in the Norfolk area."

I said, "Well, Admiral, I'll tell you what I'm going to do. I'm going to make it as attractive as possible for them to have their wives follow the ship to New York, and also those who can't afford to do that I will give them leave, both officers and men, to not make that particular visit, they can stay with their families.

He said all right. So, I told the heads of departments in particular that I hoped that they would have their wives come up to New York for the visit. I would arrange to make it as attractive as possible, which I did through friends and Navy League people and through the Grumman Aircraft Company up in Long Island to entertain them while they were there, get to a Broadway show and to a good dinner, at, I think, the 21 Club, and for the sailors we had all sorts of entertainment, tickets to theaters and to baseball games and so forth.

We didn't have the air group aboard when we went up but we'd gotten a few airplanes because we were going to be tied up at Pier 86, which is at the foot of 46th Street on Westside Drive. Among the airplanes I had, I had a Grumman jet fighter and I put it right up in the bow of the ship, looking right down on Westside Drive, so everybody in an automobile coming up and down that drive could look out and see the aircraft carrier with the Grumman fighter right up in the bow. As I told Grumman, "That's your quid pro quo for entertaining the officers and their wives while we're in port!"

It was a very successful visit, but again we come back to the question of morale. You've got to think in terms of the officers and men, what can you do within the parameters that prevail as scheduled to make life in the navy fun and pleasant and enjoyable for them. I always tried to do that, whether it be in the western Pacific, in the Far East, in the Mediterranean, or up and down the East Coast.

Another thing I did, recognizing that a lot of these enlisted men, particularly the enlisted men, were going off on weekends and driving in relatively poor automobiles or bumming rides, would go up to the New York area, the Philadelphia area, the Washington area, and, moving on their own, would frequently be over leave when they were due back on board ship on Monday morning. So what we did was charter buses through our own ship's service organization on board. We arranged these buses to be right at the pier to go to New York, for example, on a Friday, we would give the boys who were going on those buses early liberty so that they could get an early start, going up, and we got a reduced price for them on the buses because the ship's service chartered the bus and then they bought their tickets from the ship's service. This was a great convenience for them. Also we would let the bus leave up there at the latest possible time to be back at the ship on Monday morning. If there were any holdups due to traffic, we eliminated all the question of having individuals come up before captain's mast, taking the time, determining why they were late, and suspicions why they were late. If the bus was late, we knew it was late and we knew why they were late, and we had no more problems of this sort. We greatly reduced the number of automobile accidents, which was a serious problem in the Atlantic Fleet at that time. I think, also, that had been picked up by other activities and commands around the Norfolk area, but again, it was just something that could be done where the rewards and the returns were so valuable to the ship and the navy as a whole, in contrast to what it cost in the way of additional facilities or time or effort to accomplish it.

As I say, Thach relieved me and I came up to Washington with the understanding that I was going to report to OP-60 as OP-60B.

Q: A very plush outfit, OP-60!

Adm. A.: Oh, yes, it was quite an outfit. We were fortunate. We were able to get back into our house on Upton Street. It was a timely arrangement for me to come back to shore duty in the Washington area with the youngsters, to get them properly placed in schools, and it worked out very well, except that I'd been there about two weeks when it was announced that Admiral Radford was coming in as chairman of the Joint Chiefs of Staff, coming in from the Pacific.

Q: This was the new president?

Adm. A.: This was the new president. And he sent his aide, then Commander, later Admiral, Means Johnston to see me and say that the admiral was asking for me as his principal assistant in the office of the chairman of the Joint Chiefs of Staff. I said I did not think that was a good idea, that he shouldn't have another naval officer, naval aviator, as his principal assistant -

Q: What did that mean, chief of staff to him?

Adm. A.: It was sort of a chief of staff but not called the chief of staff. It would be better if he had someone from the air force or the army. Further, I felt that I could do more good for the navy in my present billet in the plans division of the Chief of Naval Operations.

Q: Who was OP-60 at that time, Dennison?

Adm. A.: I guess it was Arleigh Burke, but I'll have to check on that.

In any event, I told whoever it was, I guess it was Arleigh who was leaving -

Q: He was relieved by Dennison.

Adm. A.: Was he relieved by Dennison? Then it was Dennison, I guess. I wanted to stay there, I didn't want to go down to the JCS but I promptly told him that my fate had already been decided and that I was going to go down and do the best I could.

I reported to Admiral Radford -

Q: This was in July of 1953?

Adm. A.: That's right - and he said that the president had directed the new Joint Chiefs of Staff, the good new chiefs in contrast with the "bad old chiefs," that they were to go around on some familiarization visits and that he wanted me to accompany him, which I did. We went out to Albuquerque and Los Alamos and several other places.

Q: Getting a refresher course?

Adm. A.: A refresher course and indoctrination course in nuclear weapons.

I might backtrack. After General Eisenhower was elected as president and Admiral Fechteler was the chief of naval operations, he called me at one time - and this was when I had command of the FDR and was back on the East Coast, I guess, it was when I was back at Christmastime - and he said that he was nominating me to be the naval aide to President Eisenhower. I wanted to stay at sea in command of the FDR. Shortly thereafter, I got a message from one of President Eisenhower's aides, whom I'd known in SHAPE, Colonel Pete Carroll, who said that the president had told him to telephone me that I'd been nominated to be his naval aide but he was not going to accept me because he felt that I could be more useful some place else.

Well, when I went down to report to Admiral Radford as his principal assistant, I got another oral message from the president, through his aide, which was to the effect, "You see what I meant."

Q: Ned Beach got the job, didn't he?

Adm. A.: Ned Beach got the job. My relations with Beach were fine, with the president were fine, but I kept arm's length away from the White House in that situation, although they knew that I was down working with Admiral Radford.

Q: Much broader scope where they put you?

Adm. A.: Oh, yes, and much wider horizons as far as I was concerned.

Q: Just what was your job, it was chief of staff, actually, wasn't it?

Adm. A.: Yes, but not - I would handle all sorts of special projects. I was looking over all the problems that came in.

He had a superb staff. I was the senior officer, called the principal staff officer, and I had an office, not next to him, but right in the same suite. He had an air force officer, Colonel Watson, who sat right outside his door and was really in control of who came in and who came out. He had Colonel Hutchins, army, one of the finest officers I've ever known in any service, later a lieutenant general and chief of staff of the Pacific Command. He was really his speechwriter. Then he had Means Johnston as his senior naval aide and liaison with the Congress, and he had two personal aides, a Major Dwyer, a great big marine, a wonderful chap -

Q: Ross Dwyer?

Adm. A.: Ross Dwyer, who was later a lieutenant general in the Marine Corps. He was one aide and he had an air force major, a pilot, as the other personal aide.

Among other things, I sort of oversaw that the various staff officers worked harmoniously together, and yet they had specific jobs to do and the other people on the staff were available to be of assistance to them at their request. But they had their own jobs and responsibilities to the admiral. So there was not a lot of internal staff paper work, you might say.

We also had a group of three officers, army, navy, and air force, called the Chairman's Staff Group, who handled for him most of his Joint Chiefs of Staff papers to develop the admiral's position in regard to Joint Staff papers. But they would usually send their reports, either they would give them orally or, if they were written, they would come through me, and from me to the admiral or usually, if we had to discuss these problems with the admiral after I'd looked at them, the three of them together would be there. There was no navy domination of that staff by the admiral. He was not playing a parochial naval position. He took strong positions on a wide variety of subjects that came up before the Joint Chiefs, before the country, at that stage of the game, the termination of hostilities in Korea, the Far East, the offshore islands of Taiwan, the developing problems that went on for the two years I was there of Indochina, matters related to NATO. He relied very heavily on me in regard to NATO operations because he knew that I'd had that what you might call experience or expertise in NATO.

He never took any action that was specifically and unilaterally in favor of the navy, where the other chiefs could accuse him of being parochial. That prevailed all the way through his tour of duty down there in the Joint Chiefs.

Q: You might comment about the status of the Joint Chiefs under that particular president, his attitude toward their function.

Adm. A.: President Eisenhower had a very definite attitude on the role of the Joint Chiefs of Staff. He said then and he said on many occasions since that the Joint Chiefs of Staff represented the greatest talent of the military service if the Joint Chiefs of Staff stuck together and looked at things, not from a uni-service, but from a multi-service point of view in the interests of the security of the United States, then nobody would veto their recommendations. They had to be above suspicion in advocating what was best for the security of the United States. He said that the services had many officers qualified to run their service affairs and he expected the Joint Chiefs of Staff, while they were the heads of their services to devote their transcending consideration and time to their duties as members of the Joint Chiefs of Staff, rather than of their individual services.

The Chiefs at that time were - the chairman was Admiral Radford, the chief of naval operations was Admiral Carney, the chief of staff of the air force was General Nate Twining, the chief of staff of the army was Mat Ridgway, the Commandant of the Marine Corps General Lemuel Shepherd. Before they were sworn in in July, or

I guess it was about the 1st of August, the president directed the new chiefs to get together and formulate their recommendations basically as to the size and composition of the armed forces and what they had to do. They were to do this on their own and it was called the New Look. The chiefs prepared an agreed paper, reluctantly in some respects on the part of the chief of staff of the army, but nevertheless it was a unanimous paper submitted to the president by way of the secretary of defense, Charlie Wilson, former head of General Motors.

Wilson had as his deputy secretary of defense Roger Keyes. The relationships between Admiral Radford and the secretary of defense and the deputy secretary of defense was close, harmonious, with mutual respect, and excellent personal relationships.

Q: Keyes was something of a personality wasn't he?

Adm. A.: Keyes was a little difficult in many ways. He had practical no experience in the military. He thought the color of a telephone would provide security, and they had a problem making him stop talking on classified matters over unclassified telephones. He took basically a sort of a hostile view, you might say, of the senior military officers, but not of Admiral Radford. Admiral Radford handled Keyes very well. Admiral Radford met regularly and frequently and alone with President Eisenhower. He had an appointment every Monday morning, I think it was around eleven o'clock, and after his appointment the secretary of defense would meet the president alone. Admiral Radford would leave. So the president maintained his relationships with the chiefs of staff through Admiral Radford and he functioned, you might say, truly as a commander in chief with the chiefs of staff although he, too, had good relationships with the secretary of defense.

The trouble came after the new chiefs had been sworn in and, in our opinion, the chief of staff of the army became captured by the army general staff, that is, Ridgway, and the agreements that had been made in respect to the so-called New Look in regard to the broad strategy of the United States and the composition of the military, that he'd agreed to, he began to disavow. As a result, Admiral Radford was caused a great deal of concern. He was very personally concerned about this. Also, he was concerned in regard to Admiral Carney because Admiral Carney used to like to go fishing and hunting, he liked to be away from the office and didn't like to attend the Joint Chiefs of Staff meetings personally as frequently as Admiral Radford felt the president expected and he, Radford, expected. Also he felt that Admiral Carney would frequently come down to the Joint Chiefs of Staff without being fully prepared for the subject matters to be discussed, and then Admiral Carney would spend a great deal of time talking on extraneous matters and delaying the considerations of the Joint Chiefs of Staff.

So he had two problems, one with Ridgway, who was basically disavowing what was trying to be done, and with getting Admiral Carney to devote his principal attention to the work of the chiefs, which he, Radford, and the president and Secretary of Defense Wilson expected to be paid to it.

Q: Who was Carney's vice chief?

Adm. A.: I forget right now.

There was a great deal of attention focused on the Far East and the Pacific. Admiral Radford was, I guess, as well informed on the situation in the Far East and the Pacific as any officer of any one of the services, from his previous experience as CinCPac, his travels out there throughout his tour of duty, his interest and his talent made him exceptionally well qualified. The people in the countries around the Pacific, the Japanese perhaps less than the Chinese Nationalists, but the Filipinos, the Australians, New Zealanders knew him and trusted him. They recognized him as being a very great military statesman, you might say.

Q: Steve Jurika contributed a lot to his knowledge.

Adm. A.: I think so, yes.

Q: You've read Radford's book have you?

Adm. A.: Yes, it's too bad that this book when Admiral Radford wrote it was curtained in time so that he couldn't cover in the detail all that he would like to have had on some of these other matters pertaining to the offshore islands. He just ran out of time and he jumped to the Vietnamese experience.

There's another thing about Admiral Radford. Not having children he always took advantage of the Christmas period to make his travels. He would plan to make long trips over the Christmas-New Year period and get back to Washington just in time before he had to go through the beginnings of the annual exercise of appearing before the committ of the Congress. He had up-to-date, firsthand knowledge when he would go up to make his first appearance.

He'd done this in the Pacific. He'd make these trips around, the Far East at the holiday period.

Q: Did he take Mrs. Radford with him?

Adm. A.   Mrs. Radford traveled with him on all of these trips. She had permission to travel and she did. They were very, very close. She knew the people. And he says in his book, "We were a great team." They were. Now, this doesn't mean that she'd go to the offshore islands but she'd go to Taiwan or she'd go to Indochina. She might not visit every place while there, but she was there and she knew the Far East as well as he did, and he knew it thoroughly.

At that stage of the game, they still had the two commands in the Pacific. There was the old Far East Command, MacArthur's old command, which Ridgway had had, and General Lemnitzer had gone out to relieve Ridgway. Even though that had not been in his area of responsibility as CinCPac, he knew it very well, he made frequent visits there, he maintained close contact with General Ridgway and with General Taylor, while he was around, and he visited Korea, he knew the Koreans, even though it was outside of his territory of responsibility.

I remember the first long trip he made over a Christmas period and I had to indoctrinate his own personal aides as to what they should do on a trip, how to meet their responsibilities, which were included on a trip of this sort, the personal finances, the handling of messages, reports back to Washington, and knowing that we could get in touch with him at any particular time, how to conduct themselves. I remember telling them that they had to be very careful in their drinking, accept what they would be offered, and not quarrel with their hosts or show any improper behavior.

I remember on the first trip they were up in Taiwan and the Chinese host asked them what they wanted to drink. They said they wanted bourbon and ginger ale, I think it was. The ginger ale bottle was brought in. It appeared to be full, but actually it was kerosene or cooking oil, but these two sat down and particularly Ross Dwyer sat down all evening sipping this bourbon and kerosene! But they were very good, they learned a lot, and I guess were indoctrinated.

Previous to that, we had made a trip over to Europe, where we visited around in Germany and the principal parts of NATO -

Q: Was that when you went to SHAPE-X?

Adm. A.: No, SHAPE-X was the following year. But on that particular trip we did visit Germany, the army command, we visited London. That was the first trip. I went on the first trip with the admiral, and the second trip, which was at Christmas, the admiral very kindly said:

"George, you don't need to come. You stay home with your family and keep the store down here. Keep me informed of what's going on."

That was when they went off with the two personal aides. I think they went up to Baguio at Christmastime.

Q: That was a nice place to be.

Adm. A.: Yes.

Q: You have a note here on the offshore islands and Admiral Kirkpatrick.

Adm. A.: Yes, I started to talk about the Chairman's Staff Group. Charlie Kirkpatrick, then a captain, was the navy member of the Chairman's Staff Group, and a colonel in the army who had been with me at SHAPE, Colonel Rosson, was also a member. I forget who the air force member was. They were a very competent, capable group. At this stage of the game, this was in 1952 and carried on to 1953 and 1954, the Chinese communists and the Nationalist Chinese were conducting almost continuing operations over the so-called offshore islands of Quemoy and Matsu, which were garrisoned by the Chinese Nationalists and were close to the Chinese coast.

Q: Only a couple of miles off the coast.

Adm. A.: Oh, yes, about two miles off the coast. The communist Chinese had been contesting them, and the question was raised about the number of resources that were involved in the Chinese Nationalists being able to defend them, whether they could in fact defend them against a major attack. There was frequent shelling back and forth. The United States had taken the position that it would support the defense of Formosa and the Pescadores. But there was no specific mention of whether the U.S. Seventh Fleet would be used in the defense of the offshore islands. This was kept vague, and Admiral Radford liked to have it kept sort of vague and not too specified as to what the United States would do.

Nevertheless, we did have what was then called the Formosa patrol Force out there, Task Force 72 of the Seventh Fleet, of land planes, seaplanes, U.S. destroyers working in the closest possible cooperation with the Chinese navy, also running patrols up and down the coast, watching all the shipping that the

Chinese communists were using.

Q: Did the JCS have any control over intelligence-gathering, too?

Adm. A.: Later, when I had command of Task Force 72, there was a V-Q squadron out there, which was also in Task Force 72 and was an electronic surveillance unit. The JCS, through the J-2, who was then Admiral Layton, who had been the intelligence officer for Admiral Nimitz during the war, a Japanese-language student - he was the JCS J-2. He was a very fine intelligence officer and kept Admiral Radford very closely informed.

They also had in the JCS what was called the Joint Strategic Survey Committee, of which Admiral Boone at that time was the navy member, General Fox was the army member, and I think there was a General Ritchie from the air force. These would operate with a very small staff, more or less individually, and sort of inherited the responsibilities that had originally been vested in the World War II Joint Strategic Survey Committee, composed of Russell Willson, General Emrick, and I forget who the other member was during World War II. It was a very high-level committee working as a team coping with serious strategic problems of a broad-gauged nature, not concern particularly with a specific operation or a special war plan, but things of a broad nature. The Joint Strategic Survey Committee did indeed get involved with the roles that the United States would have to play, the positions that the Joint Chiefs of Staff would have to take on some of these very important problems, which involved at that time, the Pacific.

It's unfortunate to my mind that later on that committee was eliminated. I think we could well have one now. But, admittedly, it depended upon having people of extraordinary individual intellectual capacity and talent, rather than a large staff, which would support them and do the staff work and then they would review it, which is the normal way that the Strategic Plans Division of the Logistics Division would function.

Admiral Robbins was later a member of the Joint Strategic Survey Committee. He was well suited for that type of work, just as Admiral Boone was.

There was always the possibility that at some point the Chinese communists might try to launch an invasion of the offshore islands, and the role that the United States would take in relation to that type of invasion, particularly if the Chinese Nationalists really became in peril. These were matters that the chairman's staff group had to handle more on a day-to-day basis, as distinct from the longer-range approach taken by the Joint Strategic Survey Committee.

Captain Kirkpatrick, the navy member, was quite an aggressive individual and I always used to have to tease him by saying when he turned in a paper, "This is Kirkpatrick's plan for killing communists." But it was a very effective group.

Later on, Colonel Rosson, the army member of that group, was sent out to Vietnam, Indochina, to maintain close liaison with the French through General Bodet, who was the deputy out there in the French command and had been our previous mutual boss at SHAPE. At that time Rosson had moved on to the Army War College and, through Admiral Radford's action and my suggestion, Rosson was sent out there to see what he could do with General Bodet because of his previous association.

Q: What was the concern of the JCS in a general sense about Indochina?

Adm. A.: Grave concern about what the situation was going to be in Indochina, grave concern of the JCS of the US being overextended in Indochina, grave concern that the French would not do the things that were necessary to prevent the loss of Indochina to the communists, grave concern that the French would not do the things that would enable what U.S. assistance was being provided and they were asking for to be used effectively, grave concern that the French operation out there in Indochina was purely to regain the status quo ante of the French, maintaining another colonial power.

So, throughout that period of time, not only did we have continued vigilance and interest of the Joint Chiefs of Staff, particularly by Admiral Radford, in what was happening between Taiwan and communist China over the offshore islands. But the whole scope of developments in Indochina, the French actions there and the demands of the French for assistance - they kept burgeoning their statement of requirements, which would go from spare parts to airplanes and -

Q: And participation?

Adm. A.: Oh, yes, participation but absolutely under French control.
The French had a military mission in Washington handled by the French member of the NATO Standing Group, General Valbeg, and he would come and visit with Admiral Radford in his office very,

very frequently, processing these requests from the French. Radford took a very strong position with Valbeg and, later, General Ely took his place. The French themselves had to take certain actions that would enable U.S. assistance to be effective.

There was, of course, later on, the question of the United States coming to the assistance of the French at Dienbien Phu. This came to a head in 1954, when it looked as though the French were in a very precarious position at Dienbien Phu, which had been established as an outpost. Admiral Radford doubted, and I think the army at that time doubted, the ability of the French to hold Dienbien Phu. Admiral Radford felt that they had to put far more of an effort in maintaining effective logistic communications with the French garrison at Dienbien Phu than the French were willing to provide. The perimeter around it was being squeezed in all the time. The French really got themselves into an untenable position, which, with the casualties and the prolongation, and the publicity on it, causing a deterioration of French morale at home, in accordance with the later strategy that the communists used against the United States when we got into the Vietnamese War.

Q: There were great similarities, weren't there?

Adm. A.: Oh, I think so.

Admiral Radford was a consistently strong supporter of NATO, but he believed that our allies in NATO should provide the bulk of the forces for defending Western Europe in contrast to that of the United States. I think that Admiral Radford was influenced very much by my own thinking on NATO.

Q: That was one of the paramount reasons why you were there, wasn't it?

Adm. A.: Yes, I guess it was. That the allies should provide the types of forces, which they were capable of providing, particularly the bulk of the ground forces, the local air-defense forces, the tactical air forces, the local naval forces, which they should have been capable of providing with the rearmament of Germany. And the United States should provide the types of forces that the allies were not capable of doing, specifically, anything involving nuclear warfare, the combat naval forces such as the Sixth Fleet or the Second Fleet, if the Second Fleet had to be deployed over to Europe. The United States, Canada, and Great Britain should provide the transatlantic antisubmarine forces and German naval forces should concentrate primarily on the Baltic and the northern flank of Europe. On the other hand, the airborne forces, which the United States was capable of providing, should be available to NATO, and the heavy armored forces that we would have to provide.

The concept was an allied collectively balanced force for the defense of Western Europe and of the lines of communication across the Atlantic, and the strategic forces that would be used for offensive operations against the Soviet Union itself. Of course, there were many, many problems involved in the composition and the size and the standardization of NATO forces, the rearmament of Germany. They were of continuing concern and they're still of concern to the Joint Chiefs of Staff even today, in 1980.

His other view was that you could not concentrate solely on NATO, that the United States in particular had to consider its role in the Far East and the western Pacific. In that he resented the efforts of the French and the British, trying to get in positions of control of any operations in the western Pacific and the Far East. Any concept of a combined chiefs of staff that would run the show both for Europe and the Far East. He recognized the role that Australia and New Zealand and the British in regard to Hong Kong and the French in regard to Indochina would have in a conflict in the Pacific, but that they would control the operation and determine the strategy was almost anathema to Admiral Radford and the Joint Chiefs of Staff as well.

Q: SEATO had not yet come into being?

Adm. A.: No, and this comes up I guess in 1954, when the president became concerned, first, about the Chinese position relative to the offshore islands. There were people in the United States who felt that under no circumstances should the United States assist the Chinese in defending the offshore islands, in contrast to our commitment toward Formosa and the Pescadores. On the other hand, the Chinese Nationalists took the position that the defense of the offshore islands was related to the defense of Taiwan, and the Pescadores.

In the spring of 1954 - no, 1955 it was - the president arranged to send Admiral Radford and the assistant secretary of state for Far Eastern affairs, Walter Robertson, a very distinguished, dedicated capable American in the State Department out to meet with Chiang Kai-shek to try to persuade Chiang Kai-shek to abandon the offshore islands in return for which the United States would assist the Chinese in maintaining a blockade of the China coast opposite Formosa and the Pescadores.

We flew out in a special plane. I went with Admiral Radford. We met out there with Chiang Kai-shek and his principal people, and it was a very, very difficult experience for both Admiral Radford and for Walter Robertson. I don't know whether the report of that visit has ever been declassified or not. It probably is available and is one that we should look up. It was an embarrassing position for Admiral Radford and Walter Robertson because both of them knew intimately Chiang Kai-shek, Madame Chiang, and all of their principal advisers. Chiang emphasized how much they appreciated the friendship and understanding of Admiral Radford and Walter Robertson, but he said to them:

"You cannot sincerely believe that the United States would live up to such a commitment. We trust you, in the good faith of you making this proposal at the direction of your government, but you cannot believe that as time goes on your government could resist the pressure of your European allies to sustain such a commitment."

Q: Quite a realist, he was.

Adm. A.: He was very much of a realist and he read exactly what Admiral Radford and Walter Robertson had talked about on the way out and on the way back.

And so, at this final key conference, General Chiang got up and excused himself, went out into the garden and prayed, then came back in and said:

"I just want to tell you that I have prayerfully concluded that I cannot accept such a proposal because I do not have the faith in your government to sustain it."

I think I'd better stop there and then next time we'll pick up the question of the origin of SEATO, which followed the Dienbien Phu situation in 1954, I think it was.

Q: All right.

Interview No. 7 with Admiral George W. Anderson, Jr., U.S. Navy
(Retired)

Place: His residence in the Watergate Apartments, Washington, D.C.

Date: Wednesday morning, 20 November 1980

Subject: Biography

By: John T. Mason, Jr.

Q: Last time, Admiral, you concluded your remarks with an account of your trip to Formosa with Admiral Radford and Walter Robertson of the State Department, a special conference that was set up with General Chiang, and you related the events surrounding it. I wanted to ask, did Madame Chiang play any role in the discussions?

Adm. A.: Yes, Madame Chiang was present the entire period that the admiral and Walter Robertson were having the discussions with Chiang, and the Chinese recorder was later the ambassador to the United States, Ambassador Shen.

Q: Because she was so prominent in the activities of the government.

Adm. A.: Yes. She was present but she did not do any significant amount of talking, as I recall it.

Q: Then the other question I wanted to ask was what was the real basis for this request. It seems rather spectacular.

Adm. A.: It was felt at the higher levels of the government that if we could persuade the Chinese Nationalists to evacuate the offshore islands it would reduce the possibility of hostilities there and avoid the likelihood that the U.S. would be drawn in to support them over the defense of the offshore islands, as distinguished from Taiwan and the Pescadores.

Q: It would remove the irritant, then?

Adm. A.: That's right.

Q: Logical enough!

Now, the next subject you said you wanted to discuss was SEATO, the origins of SEATO, because this is the time when it was formed.

Adm. A.: At the time of the fall of Dien Bien Phu, the question was how could measures be taken to provide greater security for the entire Southeast Asia area and to preclude the prospect of a domino theory where the communists would cause one place to fall after another. There was also, under General Eisenhower's leadership, a basic decision that the United States was not going to go in alone and defend the area; there had to be an allied effort. And so, after discussions in Geneva, I guess it was, Mr. Dulles had worked out the arrangement to get a treaty such at SEATO, comparable but not identical with NATO, for the defense of that area, involving collective action. But the commitments to collective action as evolved were, of course, less than those of NATO. Involved were the United States, France, Great Britain, Australia, New

Zealand, Thailand, Pakistan, because Pakistan was very close there, having at that time East Pakistan. The treaty was evolved and worked out and it was agreed that they would have regular meetings at the political level, there would be military consultations but there would be no allied command structure in peacetime such as was established for NATO.

Q: Were the Philippines involved in it?

Adm. A.: The Philippines were involved, yes.

In our discussions I with Admiral Radford felt - at least I expressed my view to Admiral Radford - that you could not isolate Southeast Asia from other events in Asia as a whole, particularly the situation of Korea, Japan, and Taiwan. After all, during World War II the Japanese had their so-called co-prosperity sphere as an objective which really meant melding together the industrial capacity of Japan with the resources and markets of Southeast Asia and, of course, control of the coast of China. I felt that the Soviet objective was similar to that of Japan's earlier one, to create an East Asia co-prosperity sphere on communist lines, and that the important thing was to preclude the communists getting both control of Japan as well - of the industrial area of Japan - as well as the general resource area of Southeast Asia.

Also, if you were going to make this effective, I felt that we had to include it, in this arrangement, those two nations that really had some forces, which included Korea and Taiwan, that they were more important than trying to get Pakistan in, and furthermore we had inherent in the organization as it was established the veto power of Great Britain and of France, which would be a more homogeneous organization. Without Britain and France if we had also included in it Korea and Taiwan. But of course this was a fait accompli and there were reasons, valid reasons, for the U.S. point of view, where we had presumably greater freedom of action dealing bilaterally with Korea, even though we had the United Nations' command structure for Korea and the U.S. dealing bilaterally with Taiwan.

Well, SEATO then was about to include the so-called Associated States in an indirect association, not as full members but sort of associates. As events proved, it never really worked out to full effectiveness, certainly not in the way that NATO did. It didn't prevent, deter aggression out there. It did not provide the means to cope with a war there, as it evolved in later years, and we still had in the interim period all the handicaps of the French position in Indochina. I think Admiral Radford describes this pretty well in his memoirs.

Q: CinCPac, who happened to be Admiral Stump, had a major role to play, didn't he?

Adm. A.: Yes. CinCPac, through Admiral Radford's earlier efforts, was designated as the U. S. representative for the military side of SEATO, very logically he should have that role.

They also had the ANZUS arrangement -

Q: Did that come into being simultaneously?

Adm. A.: That had come in earlier. ANZUS originated much earlier than SEATO. CinCPac always had a very active role in SEATO and, of course, he had a very active role in the subsequent events in the war in Vietnam, even though they did establish a local commander there in Indochina, MACV.

Q: What about the military exercises that were organized on a periodic basis?

Adm. A.: Well, they had planning exercises for contingencies, and then they had certain SEATO exercises. They were on a relatively modest scale because, after all, most of the countries down there did not have the types of forces that you could involve in minor naval exercises, training exercises, but they didn't amount to too much, in my opinion.

Q: Do you want to express some reflections on SEATO, its effectiveness, and the organization at that time?

Adm. A.: I don't think SEATO was truly effective at all. Of course, this is in retrospect, but it did not fulfill its entire objective of stopping the communist advance. After all, we had the long war in Indochina and we had the withdrawal of the United States, and the communists had taken over Cambodia. On the other hand, we have not seen, at least we have not yet seen, other countries like Thailand and Malaya and Singapore fall under communist domination. So, perhaps SEATO did have some deterrent effect and enabled countries to get together hopefully to oppose terrorism and subversive actions. There was a lot of study along that line. But it wasn't really a very effective organization.

Q: Now you have in your notes mention of Admiral Radford as chairman of the JCS, and I thought perhaps at this point you wanted to make comment on that.

Adm. A.: I think we were talking about when I arrived. Admiral Radford became the chairman of the Joint Chiefs of Staff and I was ordered to go as his principal staff assistant. I had known Admiral Radford, I had the greatest respect for him and still have the greatest respect for him. He was a very dedicated American, a far-seeing American, definitely on the conservative side. He was, I would say, a military statesman. He had a keen awareness of political-military affairs, the necessity to keep the major factors of national policy in coordination at the military, political, and economic, and the psychological to a great degree. He was a man of very firm, strong character, great determination, and a very fine individual with whom to work and work under. He came in with definitely fixed ideas. I would say that he was very sympathetic to the views of the administration, particularly General Eisenhower and Secretary Dulles. He established promptly a very fine, firm, harmonious rapport with Secretary Wilson and Roger Keyes, who was the deputy. He assembled the Joint Chiefs of Staff in an effort to have them rise above what you might call service parochialism and looking at the situation primarily from the U.S. point of view, and I think we outlined in my previous interview the problems of setting up the "new look." The new look was basically to get an effective U.S. force that could cope with the requirements, that was able to perceive them, within the economic capabilities of the United States and to support U.S. foreign policy as it could be envisaged.

This meant, of course, that you had to reduce the number of people in each of the armed services, and hopefully get the allies, as I always use the term, to pull their weight in the boat -

Q: A difficult thing to do!

Adm. A.: Very difficult - and let the United States concentrate on those contributions that we were particularly capable of making and that our allies were not.

Admiral Radford was very, very conscious and the best-informed member of the Joint Chiefs of Staff on the broad problems of the Far East and of Asia, and he felt that we were overly preoccupied with Western Europe and NATO at the expense of the situation in the Far East. After all, the United States was a world power. We face both the Atlantic and the Pacific; that we looked, in terms of future security, both to Europe and to Asia, threats both in Europe and in Asia, and, of course, in the Middle East. But many of his colleagues, particularly the army, I would say continued to be overly preoccupied with Europe.

Admiral Radford felt that the army was generally extravagant in its claims for appropriations, large numbers of men, and they really didn't hoist aboard the necessity for increasing the flexibili of all the U.S. forces that would recognize the role of naval and air power, that they had a mentality wedded primarily to the battle- fields of western Europe. And so, during his tenure, he had continuo difficulties with the army and its demands for funds and people and weapons and equipment.

On the other hand, Admiral Radford got along extremely well with the air force. I would say that his rapport with General Twining, who was chief of staff of the air force, and his successor was extremely good, better perhaps than the relationships between the navy and the air force either before or since in many ways.

Q: How did he view the president's thesis that the problem should be decided within the Joint Chiefs and then passed on to him?

Adm. A.: Admiral Radford had a fine relationship with the president. Every Monday morning, certainly in the early days of the Eisenhower administration, before his heart attack, Admiral Radford would meet alone with the president of the United States. It was the relationship of a commander in chief the President, with his principal chief of staff, you might say, and also Admiral Radford would take other members of his chief of staff along with him on appropriate occasions. This is an arrangement that I hope President Reagan would reinstitute.

Q: Incidentally an arrangement you suggested a couple of weeks ago.

Adm. A.: That's right. After all, the role of the president as commander in chief is a unique role and should, in my opinion, be on a military basis, the commander in chief, the president, being the senior military officer in the country, even though it isn't exactly the same as General Eisenhower's was, but the commander in chief to his principal military chief of staff and in our case the Joint Chiefs of Staff.

I would say that Admiral Radford got along very well with President Eisenhower and loyally tried to carry out President Eisenhower's wishes. On the other hand, he tried to persuade President Eisenhower of the importance of developments in the Far East. I think all of the entire period of Admiral Radford's occupation of the position as chairman of the Joint Chiefs of Staff while

President Eisenhower was the president he succeeded a great deal, certainly in subsequent arrangements of consolidating the command structure, elimination of the old Far East Command, bringing the component commanders of the new Pacific command together in the Hawaiian area, army, navy, and air force, and eventually the separation of CinCPacFleet from the identity of the individual as CinCPacFleet and CinCPac.

All these arrangements worked out harmoniously, in my opinion, between the chairman and the president of the United States. I think President Eisenhower had great faith in Admiral Radford and he knew that Admiral Radford was trying to get the service chiefs to fulfill their role as members of the Joint Chiefs of Staff as the president believed necessary and wanted.

Q: Admiral Burke has been telling me from time to time about Eisenhower's feeling that lots of problems should not be presented to him for a decision, they should be settled on the Joint Chiefs level.

Adm. A.: That's right, and General Eisenhower, I think, was very disappointed that particularly his own service, the army, was frequently the recalcitrant member of the Joint Chiefs of Staff.

Q: And this was General Taylor?

Adm. A.: Initially, General Ridgway and secondly General Taylor.

Q: How did Admiral Radford view this much-publicized policy, (the more sound-and-fury perhaps), of massive retaliation?

Adm. A.: I was always shocked to find there was so much emphasis on the term "massive retaliation," rather than the evolution of all the studies and the plans. It was rather that we in the United States would react to a threat in an area in a way that would give the United States its best advantage. That we didn't know we'd have to accept a defensive position where the enemy might attack. We might find some areas where we could respond more effectively.

Certainly, I never felt that Admiral Radford wanted to advocate the use of nuclear weapons. On the other hand, he would never have the hesitancy of utilizing nuclear weapons if it involved the ultimate security of the United States.

Q: There's a notation in your book, right after Radford as chairman, I assume this is a footnote perhaps, "the Belgian gun-dealer."

Adm. A.: Oh! One afternoon Admiral Radford was in his office and I had an important paper to get to him, so I went up to my friend Colonel Watson, who was the man outside his office, and I said:

"I've got to get the admiral to sign this." And he said, "Somebody's in there."

"Who is it?" I asked. He said:

"Well, it's a man from Brussels taking measurements for him about a shot gun." And I said:

"Well, I think I'll go in. I've got to get this thing signed."

So I went into his office and there was this representative of a very fine gun-manufacturer in Brussels and he was taking measurements of Admiral Radford's arm and his height and so forth. I sat down there and watched and was amused, and I said:

"Admiral, he hasn't taken the most important measurement." He said, "What do you mean?" I said:

"The measurement of your fireplace."

I don't think Admiral Radford ever used the shot gun, but this was the thing he was going to do because Admiral Carney was a great hunter and I think Admiral Radford was trying to keep up with the Joneses.

Q: Well, that was amusing.

Adm. A.: There's another amusing one. About the time the navy selection board was about to convene, one of the officers on the Joint Staff was in the zone for selection. Admiral Radford sent for me, gave me a paper, and said:

"Here, George, I'd like you to take care of this," and this was a recommendation for selection, a very strong recommendation, of this captain to the rank of rear admiral, initiated by the commandant of the marine corps, endorsed by the chief of staff of the air force, signed by the chief of naval operations and the chief of staff of the army, and it was for Admiral Radford's signature to the head of the selection board, strongly recommending that this officer be selected for flag rank. He gave it to me and said, "Put an endorsement on it." I looked at it and said:

"Admiral, I can't do that. That's not right. This is an end run of the worst sort."

He said, "Well, I understand how you feel. I'll take care of it."

Shortly thereafter Colonel Watson came in and said:

"Look what I've got. The admiral wants me to put an endorsement on this for this fellow to be selected for flag rank. If I put the endorsement on that I think he should have, the guy would never get selected. What shall I do?"

I said, "Give it back to the admiral."

He took it back to the admiral and he told the admiral, "If I write the endorsement, the guy won't get selected."

The admiral said, "OK, you fellows I'll take care of it myself."

So he signed an endorsement. General Watson brought it in and showed it to me whereupon I got the names of all the officers of the army, air force, navy and marines who were coming up for selection about the same period of time and we had a recommendation prepared for Admiral Radford - I think there were about half a dozen of them - in exactly the same wording, recommending that they be selected. Admiral Radford signed every one and said:

"Well, you guys put me in my place."

That's an example of how he was. I remember out at CinCPac one time, ComAirPac when he was the chief of staff had a message written up - I forget what it was, about some fighter plane or something of the sort, and he told me to write up this message to be sent in and I said:

"Admiral, I don't agree with that. I don't think that's the right thing to do."

He said, "All right, don't worry about it, I'll write it up myself."

He'd never make you commit yourself to something that you did not believe in, against your own principles. He'd take the responsibility himself.

It was a great disappointment to Admiral Radford that he was not able to get our allies in NATO to build up their ground forces to those levels so that we, the United States, could reduce the size of our ground forces in Europe and bring those extra forces that might be withdrawn from Europe back to the United States and constitute a ready reserve.

If you went back to the original testimony of General Eisenhower, back in 1950 I guess it was, when we went from the one and three-quarters divisions of the U.S. troops in Europe and went up to six divisions in Europe, General Eisenhower testified to the Congress that this was a temporary augmentation of U.S. force in Europe, temporary until we could get the allies to create their own ground force strength, at which time the United States would be able to withdraw at least part of them. But that was never accepted by the army as a whole, the army general staff as a whole, and we still have the equivalent of six divisions and the demands to get more U.S. forces to go over there in rapid deployment and so forth.

I also remember going up to the first major joint exercise, war-game exercise, that we held and which General Eisenhower attended and all the civilian officials located out of Washington and the Joint Chiefs of Staff and the principal members of the Joint Staff relocated up to the emergency headquarters. They followed the scenario and General Eisenhower was hearing the report - I guess this was the second day of the exercise, the scenario, and the secretary of the army, John Hamer I guess it was, came in and said, "Well unfortunately, we've not been able to ship out from the New York port the forces we were supposed to deploy on Europe on D-Day." General Eisenhower turned around and said:

"Look anybody who thinks that under these circumstances we're going to send more troops over to Europe ought to have his head examined," or words to that effect. He said, "We'll need all those troops around here to pick up the pieces and clean up here in the United States."

Well, you should have seen the looks on the faces of the army general officers because this was the great thing they were going to do. We'd get attacked here in the United States and we were going to send ground forces over to Europe, and this was not in accordance with General Eisenhower's analysis of the situation at all.

Q: But from the European point of view, their reluctance has been apparent. It is largely economic or "big brother can do it"?

Adm. A.: I think it's a combination. I think probably more economic. After all, if you look back over the history of Europe over the years the principal countries have maintained armed forces of tremendous size for years, much larger than they've had in most recent times, since NATO. But economic conditions have been indeed changed. I personally believe that if the European countries could organize more to capitalize on very rapid mobilization, such as Switzerland or Israel in particular have done, marrying together manpower carefully categorized by skills into a reserve, marry that into a data processing, data computers, so that they have a close track on personnel, that you could have a much more rapid mobilization, and then have a routine two weeks training per year and so forth. Chancellor Schmidt mentioned on TV on Sunday that Germany still maintains conscription. Every man in Germany has to come up and serve in the armed forces, while we don't do this. I think that those countries in Europe could indeed have larger forces available D plus two days, three days, than they are maintaining today.

Now, of course, if you have that kind of a system and you call these people up and the threat is maintained for a long period of time, then you've got real vulnerabilities on the economies of the countries. But, of course, that's still far less than being faced with being overrun by the Russians.

Q: Yes. At least one and maybe more of the NATO countries, the small ones, have unionized military forces. Is that a deterrent?

Adm. A.: Oh, I think it's a horrible thing and I hope we'll never have that in the United States. But, essentially, what the United States should provide is those forces for contributions to NATO and a firm commitment which our NATO allies cannot provide, the big strategic forces, the high-seas combatant naval forces, the large submarine forces, the air mobile forces. Unless the allies provide the types of forces which are on the ground for local air defense, local naval forces, minesweeping, minelaying forces, and capitalize on what they can do in conjunction with the geography of Europe and, together, I think that it would be a much more manageable and effective deterrent than we have, although one must say that NATO, as it's been going, even with all the difficulties we've had, has succeeded as a deterrent at least in western Europe. It hasn't stopped the Soviets from going into Afghanistan or Czechoslovakia or Hungary or places like that, but as a deterrent in western Europe it has succeeded.

Q: Somewhere along here you attended, I assume, with Admiral Radford, a special SHAPE-X meeting that you made note of. You were also planning to go to the Mideast, but that was cancelled- that aspect of the trip.

Adm. A.: We left to go to the SHAPE-X -

Q: Was this in '54?

Adm. A.: This was in '54, the year that Dien Bien Phu was under great attack.

We went over to the SHAPE-X in Paris with plans then to go on down to the Middle East. In the meantime, the whole situation relative to the U.S. involvement in Indochina, the precarious situation of Dien Bien Phu, its expected fall, what was going to be done about Indochina rose to be of transcending consideration. It was decided by Admiral Radford that he would cancel his trip to the Middle East and proceed to London to meet there with Prime Minister Churchill, to outline to him the U.S. military views on the situation. He had met in Paris with such members of the French and the British chiefs of staff - let's see. I guess Mr. Dulles was over there at the same time, and so it was decided that we would proceed on a Monday morning over to London, instead of going to the Middle East.

We met in London, we were met there by the U.S. ambassador, Ambassador Aldrich, and that afternoon we - I was with Admiral Radford - met with the British chiefs of staff and discussed the general situation in Indochina and what could be done about it. Then that evening we were invited to go out to Chequers to have dinner with Prime Minister Churchill. We had dinner with Prime Minister Churchill, his secretary - I forget the name of his secretary - Admiral Radford and I. We sat down at the table at eight o'clock and got up at about midnight, went directly to the airplane and flew back to the United States. During the course of flying back to the United States, I wrote out the report of this conversation, and it was a very, very interesting, fascinating, conversation that lasted from eight o'clock until twelve o'clock at the dinner table. The prime minister was very articulate. He had a good memory at that time and he was in a very unusual frame of mind. Let me give a particular example of this.

He stated that he always knew how to cope with any problem that came up in the world, that he was well qualified by his study of history and his experience to cope with any problem.

Q: Quite a claim!

Adm. A.: That's right - he said until this "thing" came along, the "thing" being nuclear weapons, the big-bang weapons. He said he shared responsibility for that because he had helped the United States getting organized to build the atomic bomb and in its subsequent developments. Now he was approaching the stage where very shortly he would have to render an account to "my Maker". Therefore, he had a great responsibility of taking such actions and avoiding actions that could lead to a nuclear war.

I remember as we were on the airplane just before - oh, "therefore," he said, "the answer is for Ike and me to get together at the summit with these fellows," meaning the Russians, of course. Talking with admiral Radford - I guess Admiral Radford said, or maybe I said it, but we both agreed - that with the prime minister in this frame of mind of having to render an account to his Maker, this is no time at all for him to get involved in a meeting with Ike at the summit.

Well, this report was written up, I wrote it up, and I don't know whether you can get hold of that. This is the report of Admiral Radford's conversation I guess it was in May of 1954 with the prime minister, the report to the president and the secretary of state.

Q: That would surely be a State Department -

Adm. A.: I'm sure it's State Department, and is not mentioned in Radford's book here.

Q: The particular episode that you just related to me -

Adm. A.: Here it is, all right, pages 407-409, particularly page 409, of Admiral Radford's memoirs, From Pearl Harbor to Vietnam, although this is not the exact memo that I wrote up on the airplane. Evidently, Admiral Radford derived this memorandum from the report that I prepared on the airplane.

Q: We'll try to find the original memo.*

Adm. A.: I don't know whether you can.

Q: You also have listed at that point and you've already commented on Ridgway and Taylor and Twining, but you have Carney as well.

*Document available through the Office of Naval History.

Adm. A.: I mentioned that Admiral Radford was very conscious of his role as chairman of the Joint Chiefs of Staff, as distinguished from being a former senior U.S. naval officer and vice chief of naval operations. Nevertheless, he was extremely conscious of the importance of the U.S. Navy in its role and in connection with our national security and being able to meet any threat that might co up to the United States. However, he felt that the navy role should be advocated by the chief of naval operations and not by him, even though he was a naval officer, as the chairman. It therefore, irritated him very greatly when Admiral Carney, as the chief of naval operations, did not handle this situation in the Joint Chiefs of Staff to the advantage of the navy as he felt, he, Admiral Radford, felt, as Carney could have handled it. He also felt that Admiral Carney did not pay as much attention to the preparation for meetings of the Joint Chiefs of Staff as he, Admiral Radford, felt he should have.

Admiral Radford felt that Admiral Carney liked to talk so much to cover up occasions when he was not adequately prepared for the subject matter being discussed and wasted the time of the Chiefs inordinately in just talking without coming to grips with the specifi problem that had to be made a matter of decision. Admiral Radford was frustrated. In his, Admiral Radford's opinion, Carney did not contribute as much as he had hoped Admiral Carney would. Also, they were classmates at the Naval Academy and there had always been a certain amount of jealousy between them and differences of opinion because Admiral Radford was a strong advocate of naval aviation and Carney was a very strong nonaviator, spokesman for what you might call the surface navy.

This was a continuing irritation to Admiral Radford. It was irritating also because when broad judgments were written by Radford in connection with a JCS paper or a recommendation to the secretary of defense, the language used always gave the navy an opportunity to justify what Radford felt with valid justifications, and yet would not go as far as the navy would like to see written in a JCS paper to substantiate their case, but that everything that was written really gave the navy an opportunity to justify its forces and its concepts.

So I think you might say that Admiral Radford's dissatisfaction with the work of Admiral Carney as a member of the Joint Chiefs of Staff led him to cooperate with the secretary of the navy, then Charles Thomas, and Mr. Wilson in getting a replacement for Admiral Carney.

Q: After only two years?

Adm. A.: After only two years.

As a matter of fact, one day Admiral Radford came down to the office, sent for me, he'd just been meeting with the secretary of defense and previously with the secretary of the navy, and he told me to look over the list of all navy flag officers and recommend, from me to him, who I felt should be the new chief of naval operations He cautioned me that this was a very sensitive matter and I was to do this work entirely on my own. I got the list of naval flag officers and went over them, and I went back in to Admiral Radford and said:

"In my opinion, there is only one suitable candidate for this position, and that's Admiral Arleigh Burke," who was then I believe commander of cruisers and destroyers in the Atlantic Fleet. He said:

"I agree with you. Now you forget about this."

Shortly thereafter, I noticed that Admiral Burke had come to Washington and, after meeting with the secretary of the navy, came down to meet with Admiral Radford. So there was little doubt in my mind that this was going to be implemented, which it was in a public announcement shortly thereafter.

At the same time Admiral Radford was very anxious to have a change in the army chief of staff and to get General Ridgway out of the picture. He thought that perhaps General Max Taylor, who had had experience in the Far East, would be able to function more effectively as the army chief of staff, functioning as a member of the Joint Chiefs of Staff, than was General Ridgway, the original army member of the so-called good, neat, new chiefs.

Q: Admiral Carney seems to have felt that his personal feud with Secretary Thomas was one of the major factors. They had a feud over communications between Admiral Felix Stump out in the Pacific and Carney, private communications that bypassed the secretary.

Adm. A.: Well, there is no doubt that Radford and Thomas, the secretary of the navy, were close friends and mutual admirers, whereas Carney and Thomas, the secretary of the navy, naturally had differences, which often happens between the CNO and the secretary of the navy.

However, the fact of Carney's actions in the Joint Chiefs of Staff plus the general frustration of Radford of being unable to get the Joint Chiefs of Staff to act more unanimously than they did was an additional factor. Now, which was the most important, I'm not in a position to judge.

Q: Was it an established policy at that point that the CNO had a vice CNO, who was supposed to run the affairs of the Navy Department, and the CNO was supposed to put his principal emphasis on the Joint Chiefs of Staff?

Adm. A.: That was President Eisenhower's direction to Admiral Radford, who had passed it on to the Chiefs, and it was never fully accepted by any of the Chiefs, fully accepted as a concept by any of the Chiefs, because, after all, by tradition, they did have this role as the top naval officer or army officer in the military hierarchy. It always upset Admiral Radford when he would find that the chief of staff or the chief of naval operations was off on some service trip or some other individual, personal activity and let the vice chief attend the Joint Chiefs of Staff meetings when matters of importance were under consideration. Indeed, it was a continuing source of annoyance that that happened so frequently.

Q: The reason I raised the question is because you said earlier that Carney sometimes hadn't prepared himself adequately for things that were coming up before the Joint Chiefs.

Adm. A.: That's right.

Q: And that maybe he was busy running the department.

Adm. A.: That's right, or going on a fishing trip, or going off visiting friends, and so forth. It's a difficult problem and I suppose it continues to prevail, but now I think it is more a custom that the vice chief can recommend - can sit in on the Joint Chiefs of Staff meetings with equal effectiveness. He certainly has the responsibility when he's sitting in there of the chief, but it was an irritation to Radford. I don't think it was so much of an irritation to Twining or some of the other chairmen. But, you see, Admiral Radford had never been the chief of naval operations He'd been vice chief and he'd been Commander in Chief, CinCPacFleet, but he'd never been in the same position. I do believe, though, that Admiral Radford in his broad view, if he had been the chief of naval operations and with General Eisenhower as the president, he would have devoted more of his time to Joint Chiefs work and delegated within the Office of the Chief of Naval Operations more of these activities than did Admiral Carney.

Q: Do you have comments on "Engine Charlie" Wilson, his role as secretary of defense in the Eisenhower years?

Adm. A.: I think Charlie Wilson, from what I saw of him, was fairly good on the business side. I don't think he really understood the military side and I don't think he had a very great comprehension of the political-military factors, the international political factors, the strategic factors that perhaps some other secretaries of defense had. Nevertheless, Admiral Radford enjoyed a very good relationship with Secretary of Defense Wilson, also with Roger Keyes, and Admiral Radford spent a great deal of time explaining the Joint Chiefs of Staff's position to Secretary of Defense Wilson and, although I was never privy to those private conversations, I'm sure that Admiral Radford expressed his concern to Secretary Wilson that Ridgway and Carney frustrated in one way and another the ability of the Joint Chiefs of Staff to function as the president wanted them to function. I think also that Admiral Radford probably expressed that privately to President Eisenhower.

Q: There was a balance in that fashion with a strong chairman of the Joint Chiefs and a secretary of defense who was not cognizant of military matters. This worked to the benefit of the nation in a sense!

Adm. A.: I think it did. I think it definitely did and I think Admiral Radford's relationships with the secretary of state, Foster Dulles, were as fine relations as I've seen or I've known prevail between the chairman of the Joint Chiefs of Staff and the secretary of state. I think that Radford's relationships with the president, with the secretary of state, with the secretary of the treasury, and the secretary of defense were excellent all the way through, and I think they all had great respect for him.

Q: In retrospect, the role of the Joint Chiefs was somewhat more paramount in that time than it has been since.

Adm. A.: That's right, because President Eisenhower had great respect for the Joint Chiefs of Staff. He had great affection for the military services, he deplored interservice rivalry, particularly at the Joint Chiefs of Staff level, and he frequently would say that if the Joint Chiefs of Staff stick together and take a unanimous view of something that is involved in national security, nobody is going to overrule them. He had a better appreciation of the Joint Chiefs of Staff and what they should be doing for the country than any other president that I know of.

Also, Admiral Radford had good relationships with Vice President Nixon and would see Nixon quite frequently.

Q: That was a fascinating scene in which you operated. One more thing, Eddie Layton was there, was he not?

Adm. A.: Eddie Layton was J-2 intelligence of the Joint Staff and a very well qualified intelligence officer on the Joint Staff. He regularly briefed Admiral Radford. I would sit in on those briefings. Admiral Truman Hedding, retired now, was the director of plans on the Joint Staff. Admiral Radford did his very best to build up the strength of the Joint Staff.

Q: He certainly had some brains on it!

Adm. A.: Oh, he had some fine people on it, and he insisted that he would have the review, the approval, of anybody being ordered by one of the services to the Joint Staff and was very irritated if they tried to send somebody down who was not one of their best officers and fairly objective, in his opinion. He had me review the assignment of officers to the Joint Staff and occasionally I would say to Admiral Radford, "I think the army or the navy could find somebody better for this job than the one they've nominated And frequently he'd ask them to send in another nomination, and he had the backing of the secretary of defense in that regard, Secretary Wilson. An ideal setup.

Q: And it was an ideal one for you in which to function, but then you leave the scene in August of 1955.

Adm. A.: I was relieved then by my classmate, Admiral Don Griffin. I'd been there two years, I'd been selected for flag rank, and Admiral Radford suggested that I go out to command the Formosa Patrol Force.

I had been out there in 1955 on the trip with Walter Robertson and Admiral Radford, to Taiwan. I'd been in Hawaii with Admiral Radford and Admiral Stump, and Admiral Radford told me the best place for me to go was out to Taiwan, "You know the area, you can do the best good out there," and it was a fascinating assignment. Then he said, "Maybe you'll come back as chief of staff at CinCPac." I said:

"What I want to do is take command of a carrier division," which of course is another episode.

After we returned from that trip to Taiwan with Radford and Robertson and the incident regarding the offshore islands, my tour of duty was coming to a close and I was ordered by the Navy Department to command of the Taiwan Patrol Force.

Q: Would you give me an estimate of the importance of that patrol force at that time?

Adm. A.: That force was a force composed of land patrol planes, seaplanes, destroyers, with a flag in a large seaplane tender in the Okinawa area. The area of patrol was focused on the Formosa

Strait between Formosa and the mainland and this sensitive area of the offshore islands and extended from the Sea of Japan at Korea down to Indochina, including the Philippines, and it was a fascinating job because, in addition to everything else, you really had the Chinese Navy even if not under direct command you had the primary influence on the Chinese Navy, and the great respect of the Chinese military, including their navy, including Chiang Kai-shek. The fact that I had been out there and knew Chiang Kai-shek and Madame and had met the leaders of the Chinese military forces was a great asset to me.

When I went out I relieved - the flag at that time was in the KENNETH WHITING, which was a seaplane tender, not the largest of the seaplane tenders we had but a smaller one - Rear Admiral Kivette out of the class of '25, who had previously relieved Admiral Truman Hedding when Truman Hedding came as director of plans on the Joint Staff. I relieved in Okinawa, and I did not elect to try to get quarters ashore in Okinawa, although it was possible, and after I left -

Q: Now a very desirable spot, was it?

Adm. A.: It turned out to be very attractive.

We would keep the flagship much of the time in Okinawa, a centralized point, but on the other hand I had the opportunity to make my own schedule and I would make the schedule go from Okinawa to both ends of Formosa, Keelung and Kaohsiung, visit Taipei, then go down to the Philippines, over to Hong Kong, and I would try to get to Hong Kong about every six weeks or two months.

I led sort of a nomadic life because I had a Grumman amphibian, and when my wife came out (she had permission to travel in that amphibian) to go to the ports where I would visit, which was very helpful to me and interesting for her.

The relationships on Okinawa were excellent. The army, General Jim Moore was the island commander, and the relationships that I had with the army and the air force there were excellent. The marines were based in Okinawa and were building up their facilities. A classmate of mine, Joe Ernshaw, had the Marine Expeditionary Force out there. When we would go up to Japan, I had squadrons based in Iwakuni and also in Atsugi, so I would run my schedule to go from one end of the area to the other. Fleet Air Wing 1 had two land-plane squadrons and a seaplane squadron and they would have a special electronics intelligence squadron based in Japan. We would monitor all the shipping in the area, particularly through the Formosa Strait, in sort of intelligence patrols.

I visited the offshore islands frequently. I based sometimes in the flagship, the seaplane tender, in the Pescadores. I remember going over to the Pescadores one time and the old Chinese war lord who was out there, when I came in to make my call, he'd say, "Oh, you're here. I have a very nice Chinese girl for you." And I'd say:

"Thank you very much. I live on my flagship" and he said, "Oh, that's all right."

I deliberately had excellent relations with the Chinese Navy. They were most hospitable, and it was a very interesting tour of duty. My wife came out, flew out, and when we were in Okinawa she would stay at one of the army guest cottages up in Okinawa. Then when I would go over to Taiwan, why, she'd go over there. Sometimes she'd fly from there to Okinawa on one of the local airlines, commercial airlines. My brother-in-law Admiral Wendell Switzer was stationed in the Philippines, at Sangley Point, in command of the U.S. Forces in the Philippines. His wife was my wife's sister. When we got down there, we'd go to Sangley Point, then occasionally we'd go up to Baguio. We went in to Subic Bay, which was being built up at that time, and it was a fascinating tour of duty.

Occasionally we would have to go and pick up planes, seaplanes, that had lost an engine some place. I remember one time having to go to Danang, in Indochina. Another time I had to pick up a plane in the northern Philippines because they were having engine trouble on these planes. It was a very interesting tour of duty.

We had a small operating facility where our patrol planes would base in T'ain-nan on the island of Taiwan, and we had a very small mess there set up by the navy, which was run by a Chinese contract labor force, which the pilots said had the best food in the Orient. It was a very well run organization.

In the chain of command, I was also responsible to Commander, Seventh Fleet, who was then Admiral Pride, who had an additional duty -

Q: Mel Pride?

Adm. A.: Mel Pride - as Commander, Taiwan Defense Command in case the Chinese tried to invade Taiwan or the Pescadores.

Q: Now, the conflict here, the Formosa Patrol Force, the Taiwan Patrol Force?

Adm. A.: It was decided that they would forgo the name of Formosa and everything would be known as Taiwan.

Q: That was in the same year?

Adm. A.: That's right, that was that same year. So we changed our title from the Formosa Patrol Force to the Taiwan Patrol Force. Admiral Pride's title as Commander Formosa Defense Command, to Taiwan Defense Command. Everything became Taiwan.

We had excellent rapport. Admiral Pride got along exceptionally well with the Chinese. Of course, they wanted to have good relations because they wanted more and more equipment of all sorts for their army, their navy, their air force. They could only get so much but we would try to give them what we could.

Q: What was your estimate of their forces at that time? Were they effective warriors?

Adm. A.: They had, I would say, a very effective army force on the offshore islands. They were doing their best to carry on their training, to build up the effectiveness of their forces on the island of Taiwan. Their air force - we had a good U.S. training mission out there in the MAAG on Taiwan for supplying them with better aircraft, and they would have done a reasonably good job in air defense of the island of Taiwan. They could render a measure of air support if they were attacked on the offshore islands. Their airfields were being built up and their radars were being improved. Their intelligence operation was pretty good. Their navy had a high spirit but not very much equipment.

Q: They had some destroyers, did they not?

Adm. A.: They had some destroyers, yes, ex-U.S. destroyers. They were dependent, really, on the Seventh Fleet in the event of hostilities. The Taiwan Patrol Force had a navy designation as Task Force 72 which included Fleet Air Wing One, its planes and tenders plus several destroyers about 4 at any one time. Administratively I was commander of Fleet Air Wing 1, a patrol wing, and Fleet Air Wing 6 was based up in Japan and was not under my command. But we covered all that area from the China Sea down to the South China Sea and off Indochina and the Formosa Strait.

Our squadrons were excellent squadrons basically. We had pretty good equipment, land planes and seaplanes. The electronics squadron, the intelligence VQ 1, I guess it was, was based up at Iwakuni and was a very highly skilled organization.

Q: Was that navy or was it CIA?

Adm. A.: It was navy. I also had good relationships with the CIA in Okinawa, where they had a training facility and there were CIA representatives in various places, particularly Hong Kong. It was an excellent command, fascinating, rewarding in many respects. I had a good appreciation of the situation, total strategic appreciation of the Taiwanese versus the Red Chinese on the offshore islands and the ability to defend Taiwan, provided they had the support of the Seventh Fleet.

I saw the buildup of Chinese ground forces, which was progressing and they were getting better and better all the time. The island of Taiwan is very pretty, tropical. In some places they would have three rice crops a year, and they were also building up their industry which in subsequent years has become a very commendable industry and has built up the economic strength of Taiwan. The feeling against the Taiwanese, of the Chinese in Taiwan towards the Taiwanese, they sort of look down on the Taiwanese, the natives. There was a lack of rapport on the part of the native Taiwanese to the Chinese from the mainland, nevertheless they were being integrated into the whole society.

Q: The same racial stock, aren't they?

Adm. A.: Basically, yes, but they did not have the tradition of the mainland of China. Formosa had been under the Japanese for a long time. There was, you might say, the illusion on the part of all the Chinese from Chiang Kai-shek right down of returning to the mainland. We didn't see the opportunity for them to return to the mainland unless something dramatically changed in the world as a whole. They did not have the capability of going back to the mainland, but they were always building up the forces to return to the mainland, but it was not realistic.

Q: I suppose it was a good morale-builder?

Adm. A.: But it was their morale-builder, yes.

Their customs are definitely oriental instead of occidental, but they were trying to take as much as they could out of our system and our weapons and our equipment as they could get, adapt to it, and use it very well. They were making a lot of progress.

On the other hand, I remember going out to the offshore islands one time on a trip around and there was an old Chinese war lord out there - just a couple of years ago, this was in 1955, when I was there, 1955, 1956, in the early fifties, they'd been building a Chinese wall around the periphery of the island in anticipation of defending the island with an old-fashioned wall, which showed how archaic they had actually been. On the other hand, on another occasion, I went out to one of the offshore islands and they told me how they had good communications with Taiwan and I said, "Well, let's see," and they got instant communication. So they were making progress.

Q: Simultaneously, were there not some nuke warheads there, on the offshore islands?

Adm. A.: Nuclear?

Q: Yes.

Adm. A.: On the offshore islands? Oh, no, not to my knowledge. I don't think so. I would have known it. No, no nuclear warheads. I don't think ever.

Q: This was almost the nadir of the seaplane -

Adm. A.: That's right.

Q: Do you want to talk about the seaplane as an -?

Adm. A.: The only thing the seaplane could do that the land plane could not do better was to land on the water. The navy had a program for a large seaplane, the P6M, and the enthusiasts used the propaganda theme that the oceans of the world will be our runways. It just wasn't realistic. There are many handicaps to operating a seaplane, the smallest of which is the corrosion problem, the rough-water problem. It's so much easier to get effective operation out of a squadron of land planes than out of a squadron of seaplanes, and that became immediately apparent to me out there. We were up more or less up against the technological limit of the seaplane, what we could get out of it. Unless a tremendous amount of funds, which were not going to be made available, could be put into our research and development. It was really, in my mind, the end of the seaplane operations of the U.S. Navy.

It was very pleasant to have my flag in a good seaplane tender like the SALISBURY SOUND or the PINE ISLAND but as soon as we got rid of the seaplanes we could get rid of the tenders as well. We had better planes coming along. The development of the Lockheed, the P-3, far superior, better capable electronically for antisubmarine warfare and for patrol work, reconnaissance work.

So, while we used our seaplanes, looking forward into the future, I did not see that they were any great contribution and would not be in the future, the seaplane as distinguished from the land patrol plane. Furthermore, we had to build up land-plane facilities all around in order to accommodate commercial airliners, land-based planes for the air force, and our carrier planes when we were ashore. So we had adequate land-plane facilities on which to base the land patrol planes.

Q: You have in your notebook a very enigmatic entry at this point. Would you explain it to me? You say "Two plus to three plus and back to two."

Adm. A.: Offhand, I don't recall - oh, this is from my promotion, yes.

Q: It comes right at this point.

Adm. A.: That's the next chapter, you might say.

I had hoped to get command of a carrier division when my tour of duty, which would normally be one year, out there in command of the Taiwan Patrol Force, about a year, and then I hoped to go to sea in command of a carrier division. However, I was told at first that I would come back to Washington for duty in the Navy Department. Then Admiral Radford sent word indirectly to me that I was going to go as the chief of staff, CinCPac, in Honolulu My stepdaughter, who had been working in CIA, had gotten leave and come out to join us, and she and my wife, in anticipation that I would go back to duty in Washington, had made a trip around the world on their own. While they were en route I got the word that I was going to Honolulu as chief of staff to CinCPac, to relieve Admiral Kivette, whom I'd previously relieved as commander of the Taiwan Patrol Force.

Admiral Radford and Admiral Stump had gotten together on

this, in saying that I was going to CinCPac as the chief of staff, and that, as time went on, the Far East command was going to be disestablished, the old MacArthur command that was then being held by General Ridgway, and there would be one command in the Pacific and that the chief of staff of that command would be held by a vice admiral, and that I would be promoted to vice admiral. Well, I poohpoohed that idea at the time -

Q: That's the three plus?

Adm. A.: That's right.

In any event, I was detached, relieved by my classmate Bob Dixon, who was a very, very fine officer and a good friend, as commander of the Taiwan Patrol Force. I arranged for the navy to get a set of quarters on Okinawa in case the new commander wanted to live, keep his family, on Okinawa - the army was very generous in giving us a whole set of quarters there. I made arrangements to get better accommodations for the naval personnel who were going to be based in Okinawa than they'd previously had.

So I was detached and went right back to Honolulu to report in to relieve Admiral Kivette as chief of staff. Going to Honolulu I found very attractive because that would get quarters at Makalapa and my daughter, who was then in college, was coming out for the summer. She came out while Mrs. Anderson was traveling around the world. She came out and joined me out there and also my younger son later came out with Mrs. Anderson. This was in the summer of 1956.

This turned out to be a very, very interesting and challenging tour of duty, primarily characterized by the elimination of the Far East command, setting up a truly joint headquarters in Hawaii for the Pacific command, establishing an overall command structure for the Pacific command, moving the headquarters of the air force and the army from the Far East to Hawaii, and working out the overall contingency plans for the entire new Pacific command. The Joint Chiefs of Staff had made the decision under Admiral Radford's leadership and with the full support of President Eisenhower to eliminate the Far East command under army objections. It was complicated in many ways. It was like putting three of the largest corporations, an airline, General Electric, General Motors, all together in one command, merging, and we did have excellent cooperation locally from General Lemnitzer, who was the retiring commander of the Far East command. He'd been relieved there.

The complications of the United Nations command aspect in Korea, the establishment of local commands, it was a very interesting tour of duty.

Q: The Japanese peace treaty had been signed, too?

Adm. A.: The Japanese peace treaty had been signed, we were going to reduce the U.S. forces in Japan. That was another determination of Admiral Radford's, that we had to reduce a lot of the people all around, get them back to the United States, so that we could constitute a ready reserve that could be used with greater flexibility to meet any conditions that developed in any particular part of the world. He was making headway on that in regard to the Far East, although he was frustrated on reducing the U.S. forces in Europe.

In any event, I came back, I relieved Admiral Kivette at Admiral Stump's joint unified command. Admiral Curts continued to be the Deputy Commander in Chief, Pacific Fleet, and chief of Staff, Pacific Fleet.

Q: Stump continued as CinCPac and CinCPacFlt, didn't he?

Adm. A.: Stump continued as both. We had the headquarters in the old Makalapa headquarters in Pearl Harbor and the first major thing to do was to get a new fully joint headquarters for the joint staff in the islands. We looked over all the islands and finally we picked up the old naval hospital at Aiea Heights, which had been given over to the marines at Camp Smith. I recommended to the admiral that we establish the joint headquarters at Camp Smith because we could do it with a minimum of overhead, the marines could support the general operations of the headquarters itself, we could renovate two floors of the hospital building, and the marines could use the rest of that building and wouldn't need all the space. Well, the marines, of course, didn't like this at all. They referred to the camel getting its nose under the tent, but eventually we got the approval and got it set up, refurnished the building, and got it all set to move up, and then Admiral Stump went on a sit-down strike and wouldn't move up. All the time this was going on, he would say, "What's this? You're building that Japanese whorehouse for me up on the hill?" I said, "No, not Japanese, Korean."

But when the time came to move the staff he went on a sit-down strike and stayed down at Makalapa. It was a very amusing as well as an interesting and challenging period being chief of staff at CinCPac.

Q: I imagine so!

If we could go back for a moment, Admiral, to your Taiwan Defense Command, you have an entry here which indicates Vietnam, Japan, the U. F. and flagships and moral problems, segregated billeting.

Adm. A.: Life in the Far East for the military was considerably different than it was in the United States. Large numbers of our people of all services were young, had no dependents in the area, there were relatively few white girls out there, particularly in Japan. It was a very loose situation. For example, on one side of the airfield at Atsugi half the young enlisted men were what we called brown-baggers, where they were shacked up with Japanese girls, who enjoyed a very good life. They'd come to work in the morning and go back to their little Japanese girl in the afternoon. Generally speaking, it was a rather deplorable situation.

Q: Did not the Japanese people resent this?

Adm. A.: Some of the Japanese people did - yes, it was a carry-over to them of the days of the occupation and it didn't accord exactly with their ideas of foreigners coming in and taking over their girls. The Japanese young men objected to it because they couldn't support the girls the way the American GI could, or the American sailor could. It was just not a very good situation.

Admiral Ingersoll had relieved Admiral Pride as commander of the defense command. I'd known Admiral Ingersoll very, very well, and he was just shocked at what he found out there when he took over, and so we did our very best to try to stimulate a better moral situation in a distinctly difficult climate. On Okinawa, for example, there were small villages there which the blacks of all services took for their own, one particular village - I've forgotten the name of it - the black marines and the black sailors and the black soldiers would not allow a white enlisted man in that area. They monopolized it. It was not a healthy situation. It was the first time I'd ever heard of this, at one of the air bases they would have what was known as a key club. Young air force officers and their wives would go out on a Saturday night to a dance or a ball, and, then toward the end of the evening, they'd throw their keys in and they'd sort of mix up, to see who would go home with whom.

It was a pretty sad situation. We tried to exercise the best influence we could to improve it but it was sort of pushing against some pretty tough waves to try to change that situation out there.

Q: Isn't it noticeable in the effectiveness of the men?

Adm. A.: Yes, it is to some degree. The thing to do is to keep the men as busy as they could be and useful training exercises to improve their overall readiness. But it's very difficult when you have large numbers of marines and large army forces based ashore out there in one spot. It's a very difficult problem to cope with, particularly with the sort of laissez-faire attitude that prevailed in some of the other services.

The venereal disease rate was high throughout the Far East. It was a pretty tough quandary, and the same thing prevailed in Korea, too, among the officers out there.

Q: Had the Japanese at this point begun to talk about getting the Ryukyus back?

Adm. A.: They were talking all this time about getting the Bonins back, getting the Ryukyus back. Admiral Radford resisted them both as far as he could, and I forget the date when they actually got the Bonins back, and then later on they did get the Ryukyus back.

We had in Okinawa the main air base for that particular area we could count on because there was inevitably the prospect of reducing the U.S. occupation forces in Japan, and we had the marines there who were to be available in case of a renewal of hostilities in Korea or the base of anything we were going to have to do farther south in Indochina. So the Ryukyus and Okinawa were very important base areas for the United States in the western Pacific.

On the other hand, we certainly didn't like the idea of having to hold onto the responsibility for civil affairs of all these Okinawans. There were disadvantages to that. I guess it was all resolved as well as could be expected in the changing times.

The morale problems, the discipline problems were real. I think we tried to exercise the best leadership we could, certainly from Admiral Ingersoll's point of view as Commander, Seventh fleet. Admiral Callaghan was up in Japan and I in my own command. I was fortunate in that most of my activities were largely operational and the squadrons and the ships were engaged in their routine patrol and exercise schedules. We had exercises with the Chinese, and it was a twenty-four-hour-a-day operation. We kept track of everything that was going on in the whole area.

So, yes, there was the problem of morals, when you have large numbers of Americans overseas, particularly such as they were in the climate of the Orient, magnified to a far greater degree when we got these large forces in Indochina during the Vietnamese War.

Q: Thank you for that. Now, do you want to jump back again to CinCPac and perhaps talk about Admiral Stump's difficulties in disassociating himself from the two commands?

Adm. A.: He just loved his CinCPacFlt command. He'd never really been brought up in the concept of joint operations. It was a constant irritant to the army in particular that the unified command - there was also a commander of his own principal components, the fleet - they felt that it colored all his judgments as unified commander. He was occupied with his fleet command responsibilities.

On the other hand, I had had this experience over at SHAPE. I recognized what this irritation was. I felt that it was a small price to pay to separate the two commands. I urged all along that the two commands be separated. Admiral Stump did not want to do that, yet when we got the army command in Hawaii, General White and General Kuter for the air force, it was inevitable that they'd have to be separated. It did mean a small price to pay. You'd have to have another four-star naval officer out there.

We were all in complete agreement Admiral Radford, Admiral Stump, the CNO, in complete agreement, that it was most important that the identity of the Commander in Chief, Pacific, be a naval officer. I pointed out that the navy would and should continue to hold that job as a naval officer, so long as the preponderance of forces out there were navy-marine corps, secondly, that the navy did a good job, and third that we always had a logical, well-known, potential substitute Pacific commander-in-chief available. He could come either as the vice chief of naval operations, as has happened in the past, or as a CinCPacFlt commander, who could fleet up and become CinCPac.

Finally, I think that the navy recognized this and later on - I forget just when it was - they separated the two. It was after Admiral Stump left. Could it have been under Admiral Felt?

Q: Yes, Admiral Felt, he had only the single command. Admiral Stump also didn't take too kindly to the State Department personnel?

Adm. A.: Oh, no, political advisers! Oh, he didn't like that at all and I explained that, under the circumstances, it was a small price to pay to have a State Department man there who'd be an adviser to him on political affairs in order to get a more harmonious relationship in support of all the State Department activities in the Far East and back in Washington. It was practiced elsewhere, fully accepted by the army, had been in effect out in the Far East command. it was something that he had to do and I finally recommended that Admiral Stump accept it. I knew he had to, and I nominated a John Steeves who was highly recognized as an effective State Department officer, an ambassador, and that was accepted.

Then came the question of where Steeves was going to live. He said, "Well, you've just got to get him a set of quarters." Well, Stump raised hell about that but reluctantly agreed. Actually, by regulations, he had to pay what would be the equivalent rental value for a house of comparable size, and Steeves moved into the house next door to me as the chief of staff.

Also, we got CIA in there. They moved CIA into the headquarters, which it properly should. We got much better intelligence as a result.

Q: Wasn't there some question as to whether these gentlemen would attend the staff conferences?

Adm. A.: Oh, yes. I think Stump was teasing us all as well as reflecting some of his fundamental views. It was slow going in some respects but we made progress. I think it was a great accomplishment that we set up that joint headquarters up at Camp Smith.

Another thing that was amusing. When we finally got Admiral Stump to move into the new headquarters of CinCPac at Camp H. M. Smith, which was also the marine headquarters on other floors, the admiral would drive up each morning from Makalapa, from his quarters, up to CinCPac headquarters, and there right in the foyer was a picture of General "Howling Mad" Smith. And religiously every morning the commanding officer of Camp H. M. Smith, a marine colonel, would be down there to greet the admiral and say good morning to him, as the admiral would walk in, he'd look up and say, "When are you going to take down that picture of that constipated old bastard?" Deliberately hazing. Stump loved to haze, and if he saw that he could haze you and you got worried about it, then he'd haze you all the more.

One of the things was that he didn't like golf, he didn't play golf, so he'd wait until he found some officer who was out playing golf and he figured he'd delay it just so long - he knew how long it would take to get to the phone from the end of the golf course, then he'd call up and they'd send a car out, the admiral wanted to see him or wanted to talk to him on the telephone. Well, I knew about this, so I just never paid any attention to it when he'd send for me like that.

Another one was he would always go down to the headquarters on Sunday morning. He'd go down to the headquarters on Sunday morning, not that he was getting work accomplished but primarily because he didn't like the sermons of the Protestant chaplain in the Makalapa chapel. We had nine o'clock mass, I being a Catholic and at 10:05 I guess it was, they'd have the Protestant chaplain with his service. Well, just as I was about to go out the door with my daughter and my little son to church one morning, the telephone rang and "The admiral would like to see you." So I just went to church and after church I went down to the headquarters.

"Where the hell have you been?

I said, "Admiral, I went to church."

"What were you doing there?"

"I was just praying that the Protestant chaplain would give a better sermon than the Catholic chaplain."

He just loved to haze people.

One day Admiral Curts and I - he always liked to get us in and talk to us each morning. We had very good relations with Admiral Curts, the chief of staff of CinCPacFlt, and I chief of staff of CinCPac, and the admiral was going to make a trip out to the western Pacific, so we sent for the admiral's flag lieutenant, later Admiral Bernard Forbes, and said, "What's the admiral's schedule?"

He said, "I don't know. He hasn't made up his mind yet." I said, "Well, he's leaving in a couple of days."

"Yes, but he hasn't made up his mind yet."

So we went in to have our morning conference with Admiral Stump and Admiral Curts said to the admiral:

"Admiral, you're going on this trip and you're leaving the day after tomorrow. You ought to make up your mind about your schedule."

He said, "I've made up my mind, but I'm not going to tell that flag lieutenant about it."

Q: You have an entry here that amused me. You called him Friendly Felix, and Curly Curts, and Gorgeous George!

Adm. A.: Admiral Stump was definitely a character.

Q: Oh, yes, I've known Stump.

Adm. A.: And they had these little ridges in the road that were known as Stump's bumps and that was picked up by the whole community. Felix Stump, he was known as Friendly Felix. We'd all laugh about it, the wives would talk about it.

One night I heard the kids referring to Admiral Curts as Curly Curts and I laughed about that. He had a bald head with a few wisps on the top of his head. I laughed about that and the kids laughed evenmore, and I didn't know all the time they were calling me Gorgeous George!

It was very pleasant living, very convenient to get your work done. At noontime I would usually go down to Keeki Beach with my wife for a picnic lunch and a swim. We had the swimming pool across the street, there was sort of an open-air movie theater right down there, the chapel was right down the street. It was very convenient living. The BOQ was nearby. It was a very pleasant place to work and to get work done effectively. We had, I would say, an extremely competent group of army and air force and marine officers who came to work on the joint staff. Admiral Stump did not want to have anybody except a naval officer in a key spot. With a little difficulty I had to persuade him that the secretary of the joint staff could not be a naval officer, should not be a naval officer, and I picked out a very fine air force officer I'd known, Lieutenat Colonel John Got, to come in and he actually did such things as setting up the headquarters based on all his experience in setting up good headquarters. And we got an interior decorator out, bought attractive furniture, fixed up the admiral's office very attractively, and that's when he kept saying I was building a Japanese whorehouse for him up there and I said no, it was Korean. He wouldn't go up and look at it but he had scouts go up and look at it. Very, very amusing.

Well, after we got the command established the question came up of the rank structure and the rank of the chief of staff was earmarked to be a vice admiral-lieutenant general's job. Then we got into another fuss because the army felt very strongly that the chief of staff should be a different service than the commander in chief. Admiral Stump and Admiral Radford supported him completely on this system that the chief of staff should be one who most satisfied the commander in chief's own requirements. They cited the experience in Europe and other parts of the world where the army had commanders in chief and their own chiefs of staff. So it was agreed that Stump could have a chief of staff of his own service at the rank of vice admiral and I was suddenly promoted to the rank of vice admiral, though when I was appointed I wrote to Admiral Burke and told him that I wanted it very clear that after this assignment was over I could revert back to my two-star rank in order to be able to take command of a carrier divison at sea. Admiral Burke said something to the effect well, he didn't think that would happen, but that was what I asked for.

Q: That's the explanation of the two to three?

Adm. A.: That's right.

Q: And two!

Adm. A.: I felt very strongly, and still feel very strongly, that people who go to higher positions should have had earlier lower command experience and not skip it and go to a higher command without having that intermediate command. The same thing is true that I feel that when you select people as rear admirals, they should have had proper commands at sea as captains, and that doesn't always happen these days. It's too bad. Which brings up another subject that we can talk about some time about promotion and rank and assignments.

Q: I'll make a note on that. It does recall something. You said you were going to comment on command as such during the Taiwan Defense Command period.

Interview No. 8 with Admiral George W. Anderson, Jr., U.S. Navy
(Retired)

Place: His residence in the Watergate Apartments, Washington, D.C.

Date: Tuesday morning, 25 November 1980

Subject: Biography

By: John T. Mason, Jr.

Adm. A.: Accelerated promotion first. I believe in the concept of accelerated promotion, of early selection. However, I do not believe that anybody should be selected and promoted early unless he is clearly superior, clearly superior, to those of his contemporaries up for consideration at that particular time. Secondly, I believe that anybody who is so promoted should have the opportunity - who is considered for such promotion, should have the opportunity to fulfill assignments in those billets that are important to long-career development and capacity in the years ahead. In other words, I don't think you should accelerate a captain to rear admiral unless he's had the opportunity to command a major combatant ship, or to select somebody for higher promotion than rear admiral unless he's been able to fly his flag at sea in a combat command. This does not, of course, preclude the assignment of people in specialties, where the sea side of their career is not important at the present time or in the future. In other words, with the navy as it is today, it is desirable to have certain people who specialize in aspects of the shore establishment who don't necessaril have a lot of time at sea.

Also, when I became a young officer, the policy was to assign officers in rotation so that they would get a broad experience. For example, my first duty was in a cruiser. Not only did I qualify as officer of the deck but I was also assigned to the engineering department. Later, when I went into aviation, my first assignment was in a scouting squadron aboard a cruiser, which was a convertible land plane-sea plane. Then I subsequently had duty in patrol planes and fighters in sea assignments. I had the great opportunity to have command of two aircraft carriers, a small one, the MINDORO, and later the FDR, and in my flag career I had my assignment as commander of the Formosa Patrol Force in Fleet Air Wing 1. Then, after I reverted in rank from chief of staff, CinCPac, to have command of a carrier division and then the Sixth Fleet. It provided a well-rounded range of experience at sea.

On the shore side my first assignment ashore was flight training at Pensacola, and after my first sea duty in navy air, I went to the naval air station at Norfolk in the flight-test arrangement there, the flight-test section. Then, the next time I came ashore was to the Bureau of Aeronautics, and I had assignments on the staff at CinCPac, SacEur, SHAPE, and back into Naval Operations and then with Admiral Radford in the chairman of the Joint Chiefs office.

So, I believe in giving people a well-rounded experience, especially those who are generally thought to have a capacity for future value to the navy or the country in higher positions of responsibility. This inevitably means that you have to evaluate the potential of officers at a relatively early part of their career. Admiral Towers used to say you could judge what an officer would be in the future when he was at the rank of lieutenant commander, that he should be able in the rank of lieutenant commander to be earmarked for subsequent high assignment. This means, given the total number of officers you've got in the navy, some people are going to get a broader range of experience at the expense of others for whom there are not that many billets available.

That, in my judgment, while it may put a sacrifice on some individuals who might classify in the average or below-average categories, it serves the best interests of the navy in providing a reservoir of officers coming up for higher positions and more responsible billets for the good of the navy in the future.

So, that, in general, is my concept of the assignment of officers. I realize fully that there are many problems involved in doing this. In my own class - well, all of my class, I guess - we came through the period where we had a great breadth of experience in peace and during World War II, and when I got to the rank of captain, many of my contemporaries had had similar variations in experience which would have qualified them to go higher.

Also, I think you have to recognize that you can only get involved to a limited extent in what I would call the nuts and bolts and the material side of the navy, the technical side of the navy, if you're going to have the experience for operations and staff work and policy-formulation, leading to the higher command positions later on.

Those, in general, are some of my thoughts in this regard.

Q: Then, you approve of this development wherein a man has his rotated sea duty but he comes back to a specialty?

Adm. A.: Yes, I do, particularly in the case of somebody whom you want to mark for higher positions in the Navy Department, as distinguished from the material side, that he goes into plans and operations and policy-formulation, whereas a person who is going to look for the technical specialties goes back into his line of specialty, specialization, whether it be ordnance or engineering of one sort or another, or electronics. I think if you do that you give a great opportunity to the individuals and provide a much greater depth of strength for the navy as a whole.

Also, in going to sea, in my case I always sought if I was in one tour of sea duty in one ocean, I would hope that the next tour of duty would be in the opposite ocean, to get a balance between the Atlantic and the Pacific and the Atlantic Mediterranean and a broader aspect of the whole naval problem we have, particularly on the side of plans, operations, and policy. The balance also comes in between purely naval work and joint activities. I think the day has passed when you can just shoot somebody up to be at the higher levels of the navy who has had no exposure to the operations, the experience, the problems, the capabilities, and the limitations of the army and the air force, and only a purely parochial approach to problems. We've suffered from that in the past, and I think the same principle should apply for the army and the air force; they have to be exposed to joint operations. They, I think, recognized this somewhat before we in the navy did. I think we were slow in recognizing the importance of joint and combined operations and planning. Perhaps the country suffered from it from interservice bickering and competition.

The establishment of the National War College was a very wise idea, and also the inclusion of people from other services in the Naval War College, the Army War College, and the Air University. All this is good for cross fertilization, and meeting people, socializing with them, and broadening your personal relationships.

Q: Charlie Duncan once expressed an idea and I think this was when he was somewhat senior. He felt that the navy would be strengthened in this day with so many sophisticated items of ordnance and so forth if a man could stay at sea for a much longer period of time and not have to be transferred back and forwards for stated periods. He felt that this would be beneficial to the navy, if he could be guaranteed the opportunity to advance in rank.

Adm. A.: No, I think it is probably better to have a normal rotation between sea and shore, provided that they are interrelated in the officer's career program, where he's pointed, what his potentiality in the navy is best judged to be, and I think there the judgment comes from his immediate superiors. There's another thought that I've always had, that it doesn't really matter too much what assignment you have provided that, whatever it is, you do an outstanding job in that particular assignment, and that, in doing it, you learn the job of your next superior up the chain of command, so that you know his job fully and completely and therefore would be able to step into that as you progress in your own assignment. In other words, if you're the executive officer of a ship, you certainly ought to know how to be the commanding officer of the ship. If you're the commanding officer of a ship, you certainly know how to handle a task group in which you're a participant, and, if you're in a shore duty assignment, let's say in plans, you ought to know all the aspects of plans and operations, the next level up. I think that is very important.

Q: That being so, it would not make necessary a very careful career planning, as some men think that you should have?

Adm. A.: Well, the individual is the best person to provide for his own career planning, not the Bureau of Naval Personnel. I remember Admiral Towers saying the best thing to straighten out what was then called the Bureau of Navigation was to detach everybody it in and send people back who had never been in there before. I think that too often, but not always, the Bureau of Naval Personnel has become involved in you might say the corporate system of personnel management, rather than looking out for the strengths that we have in the navy, which can benefit the navy most in the years ahead. You might say that, if the Bureau of Naval Personnel ran the whole show by their policies, you would have a higher level perhaps of mediocrity and less the level of achievement that has been possible over the years by encroachment on the Bureau of Personnel's prerogatives.

Q: There's one other question I want to raise and that has to do with that very small, very exclusive group that achieves the top rank, the chief of naval operations; what about deep selection when it comes to a chief of naval operations. There are differences of opinion.

Adm. A.: I believe that the navy should, as usually it has, have many candidates potentially available to be the chief of naval operations. They can come from a wide variety of assignments, commanders in chief, numbered fleet commanders, or even, at times, somebody on a lower level, perhaps as Arleigh Burke was at that time. Normally, if the chief of naval operations, the outgoing chief of naval operations, is in a position to make the recommendation that would be accepted by the secretary of the navy and then by the president or through the secretary of defense, you will get a very good replacement. Certainly, in my judgment, the higher civilian authorities should not appoint somebody as the chief of naval operations who the outgoing chief of naval operations does not believe suitable for the job. This was one of the mistakes made, in my judgment, by appointment of Zumwalt.

Q: And the outgoing chief of naval operations was opposed to it?

Adm. A.: That's right, and I think he was shown right.

Q: Through the man himself.

Adm. A.: Yes. I believe in the concept of deep selection but, again, I think it is best if you can conduct this in an orderly program over a period of years so that the person who is being deep-selected, maybe not once or twice, maybe three times, will have had a sufficient range of experience. Zumwalt's fault was that he didn't have the proper -

Q: He'd never commanded a fleet.

Adm. A.: No, or never really had a good command at sea.

Q: Now, Burke had some doubts about deep selection in his case. It was a little bit rocky at first, he thought.

Adm. A.: And it probably was a little bit rocky for him, but I think he was the man for it, and if he was a little rocky in his first two years, he was able to extend to six years.

Q: Yes!

Well, all of this is very interesting Sir. I'm glad we put it in at this point. Now shall we go back to the Pacific?

You have in your notebook a cryptic entry, "travels in the Pac command."

Adm. A.: In a command such as the Pacific command, which is really the largest command by area in the world, certainly as it evolved after the disestablishment of the Far East command, but even before because then the commander was also the commander of the Pacific Fleet, it is necessary that the commander in chief have his principal staff members travel around the command, visit the subordinate commanders, and that means that you have to capitaliz on having a good transport airplane that can permit you to travel comfortably around the area with reasonable facility.

The commanders in chief, Pacific, for example, during the war - they didn't have jets at that time, but Admiral Nimitz traveled around quite well in the command. Admiral Radford certainly did. He knew the Far East probably as well as any person in the whole Pacific. Admiral Stump traveled round a great deal, and Admiral Stump permitted me, as the chief of staff, to travel around. In each case, they would take selected members of the staff along with them, come back, and, hopefully, were able to make recommendations for change, if changes were indicated, also to be able to evaluate the performance of subordinates, their relationships with other services, their relationships - this was particularly true of the Pacific command - with the countries in which they were dealing with the military authorities and the political authorities.

I had one very excellent trip. I took that in the summer of 1957. I covered the whole of the Far East. I remember it was a very amusing situation because I visited Taiwan. I knew most of the people out there, anyway, and I got a very, very warm welcome, and that particular trip occurred in August. I had been back to my son's graduation at the Naval Academy in June and just as Mrs. Anderson and I were about to return my daughter announced that she was going to be married, and so Mrs. Anderson stayed back in Washington and this was a very good time for me to make a very thorough trip, which I did. I went all the way down in Southeast Asia and worked my way back. I was in Taiwan and my old friend General Tiger Wan, chief of staff of the Chinese Nationalist armed forces, quite a character, invited me for lunch or for dinner. Well, my schedule was very crowded and the only time that I had available was breakfast, so he invited me to come to breakfast at his quarters with his wife and the three service attachés, army, navy and air force. There were six of us there at breakfast. General Tiger Wan was very expansive and he said in his Chinese, "And how is Mrs. Anderson?"

I said: "Mrs. Anderson is back in Washington. My daughter is going to be married. She went back with me in June."

He said: "Oh, you have not had a woman since June?"

I sort of tried to pass it off and he said: "I have very nice Chinese girl for you." I said:

"Well, General, my schedule is very crowded." And he said, "It won't take long!"

Well, that evening the Generalissimo and Madame were having me for dinner. General Tiger Wan was there, and then he again tried to tie me up, but I said:

"No, I'm leaving for Japan early in the morning."

But those trips were extremely valuable to all of us. The command structure that had been set up was an excellent command structure because it relied on the amalgamation of what you might call two different concepts. One, a primary reliance on the three component commanders: the Commander in Chief, Pacific Fleet, the Commander in Chief, Air Forces, Pacific, and the Commander in Chief, U.S. Army Forces, Pacific. They were the ones who had administrative responsibility for their own services. Their control of the assignment of personnel and of forces within their own services. That was one concept, the service component commander. Then there were the subordinate area commanders which we had for the Marianas, for the Philippines, for Indochina, Japan, depending basically on the problems that were faced on those particular areas, Taiwan, where an officer of a particular service was assigned and he was really the boss of that particular area. It worked very well.

For example, in Korea, the subordinate commander in Korea, an army officer, was also the United Nations commander and, in fulfillment of his United Nations command responsibility, he could go directly back to the Joint Chiefs of Staff and to the U.N. command, which was handled by the Joint Chiefs of Staff. And we envisaged that the same situation would apply if hostilities broke out in Indochina. The senior army officer there was earmarked to be the local commander in the case of U.S. forces.

In the meantime, you had the full power of Air Force, Pacific, and U. S. Pacific Fleet, in support of these local area commanders, but you basically had unified command of good command channels, with the commander in chiefs of the components located in the Hawaiian area, adjacent to CinCPac. It worked out very, very well. We also, as I mentioned, did have a political adviser, John Steeves, while I there, and we had a CIA representative. Now, the CIA never let the CIA men in Hawaii really exercise any control of the CIA activities throughout that command. They reported back to CIA headquarters in -

Q: Was he even cognizant of what they were doing?

Adm. A.: I think generally cognizant. He got the benefit of their intelligence reports but he did not control any of their covert actions, which were handled directly from back in Washington.

Q: What cognizance did your command have, or what authority did you have, over the American representatives at Panmunjom?

Adm. A.: That was handled by the army commander in his capacity as the United Nations commander. I forget who it was at that particular time. He handed that right back to the Joint Chiefs of Staff and the State Department.

Q: There's a notation saying that you visited the Chinese Naval Academy.

Adm. A.: Oh! That was amusing because I went to - I guess it was Kaohsiung, down in southern Taiwan, and Soying, which is right next to it. That's where the Chinese Naval Academy was and Admiral Liang, my good friend who was commander in chief of the Naval Academy, said to me:

"Admiral, I'd like you to see my naval academy," and I said that was fine, so I went in just expecting to look at the facilities. I went into an auditorium and he had the whole body of Chinese midshipmen there. He introduced me and said: "Now, the lecture this morning will be given by Admiral Anderson." I really had to react fast on that one!

Q: But you rose to the occasion.

Adm. A.: Yes, you had to learn to.

Q: Well, now you have a notation saying that in September of that year, it must have been immediately following your trip to WesPac, you went back to Washington.

Adm. A.: I came back to Washington to consult and also to attend my stepdaughter's wedding. It worked out very well. I had a quick trip back, and both operations were quite successful. I touched base with everybody in the Navy Department back here and we had a very nice wedding in Washington, at St. Alban's Church, then Mrs. Anderson and I packed up and left. While she had stayed east, she had rented a house in Tracy Place.

Q: Yes, I know that, and you have a name, Ann Carter Green.

Adm. A.: That's right. It was Ann Carter Green's house which happened to be available at that particular time. It worked out extremely well.

Q: Then you went back to Hawaii?

Adm. A.: Then we went back to Hawaii.

Q: And you have a notation "Felix on Sunday."

Adm. A.: I told -

Q: You told me about that, and Ann Walker?

Adm. A.: Oh, Una Walker. She was a friendly Hawaiian lady, married to the head of (AMFAC) American Factory, I guess it was. They had a lovely place on the other side of the island. They had always been very friendly to the navy, particularly during the war. They invited Admiral Nimitz and his staff out there many, many times, and they continued their friendship with all the commanders in chief. Admiral Radford knew them very well, so did Admiral Stump, and, when I was there, they invited Mrs. Anderson and me over to the other side of the island to spend weekends or to come over for Sunday brunch and a swim. The relationships between the naval authorities and the civilians in Honolulu always were very harmonious.

Q: That was quite fortunate, especially during World War II, wasn't it?

Adm. A.: Yes, it was.

Q: A chance to get away.

Adm. A.: An interesting aspect of this was the composition of the population of Hawaii with large numbers of Orientals and people of foreign extraction, even Portuguese, throughout the islands. With the establishment of the enlarged Pacific command headquarters and the three component commanders, I was very much interested in the intelligence and counterintelligence aspects as well as security. I called all the top people in, including the FBI representatives in Hawaii, CIA, military intelligence, and I told them that it seemed quite obvious to me that this headquarters command and its associated subordinate commands were obviously prime intelligence targets for everybody, not just the communists, but anybody who wanted to know what was going on. And I solicited from them the maximum of their imagination for them to try to envisage how a potential enemy would try to penetrate the headquarters. Obviously, we knew that somebody was going to be doing this The experience of Pearl Harbor and what we found out afterwards showed that that was true, but so far as I know, we never found any indication of how the efforts were being made to penetrate. Maybe it was being done by electronics, spies, whatever, I don't know. But that's a hazard you have when you concentrate a headquarter in a community that is composed of large numbers of people who can easily be penetrated.

Q: The only solution would be to take over one of the islands and make it exclusively yours.

Adm. A.: That's right. Take one of the islands. That wouldn't work either, though. So you have to compromise on a lot of these factors.

Q: Do you want to say something about General Kuter?

Adm. A.: Yes. I had known General Kuter back in Washington during the early part of the war. He was rapidly elevated in rank, as were most of the army air corps officers - Vandenberg, Kuter, Norstad. I'm not talking about the old-timers like Spaatz, Eaker, and Arnold, but, generally speaking, there was accelerated promotion in the army air corps and they were very good people, and General Kuter was an exceptionally able officer.

Q: Freddie Smith was another one?

Adm. A.: Oh, Freddie Smith was a wonderful officer. As you probably know, he was Admiral King's son-in-law.

Kuter had been the Commander in Chief, U.S. Air Forces, Far East, when the headquarters were combined and so he moved from Japan to Hawaii at Hickam Field, established his headquarters there, and established a very effective headquarters. I think we could have had a lot of trouble with the army and the air force components if we had not adopted a very open policy at the joint headquarters. This was a little difficult to put across with Admiral Stump, particularly so since he wanted to retain his command of the Pacific Fleet. That, in itself, posed a little bit of distrust on the part of the other services, but we did keep a very open line of communication with them, and I had gotten all the air force officers who were put on the joint staff, I had checked out with General Kuter in advance, to make sure that they were acceptable to him, and I told them that they should continue to be loyal to their own service, bring into the unified command staff the full benefit of their experience in their own service, but that they had to work for the good of the whole command. There was nothing going on in that headquarters that couldn't be made known to their own service people, unless there was some specific matter which, for security reasons, not interservice politics, that required it, not to talk. And we got a very fine measure of cooperation all the way across the board.

General Kuter ran a very smart command. His wife, Ethel, contributed to it. She was a very dominant service wife. She used to make inspections all around, but they ran a very good command.

Q: You indicate that there was a certain smartness about the whole thing. Was she responsible for part of that?

Adm. A.: I think they cooperated very well as a team.

I remember one day coming into the headquarters - it was before we moved up the hill to Camp Smith. The marines at the Makalapa headquarters were giving what I used to call an Indian scout salute with a bended wrist. I chastised a young marine on duty and instructed him how to make a proper salute and hold his hand properly.

Q: How did that differ from an Indian scout?

Adm. A.: I told the marine, "Now, look, if the Marine sentries and orderlies don't get those salutes straightened out here at CinCPac headquarters, I'm going to send them over to the air force headquarters to learn how to salute." They improved very rapidly!

Q: Do you want to say something about General O'Donnell and developments in Vietnam during that period?

Adm. A.: Yes. Admiral Radford had arranged to have General "Iron Mike" O'Donnell go down to Vietnam from Korea because he felt that General O'Donnell had done a very fine job in supervising the training of the Korean armed forces. Radford felt that O'Donnell was probably as well qualified as anybody to do a similar job for the Vietnamese, even though the French were far less cooperative than the Koreans were. This assignment didn't sit too well with the army, but Admiral Radford, as the chairman, pressed the case and he and Admiral Stump insisted that O'Donnell go down there with the rank of three stars, which the army did not feel that assignment justified down there. In any event, CinCPac's view and the chairman's prevailed and General O'Donnell went down as chief of the MAAG in Vietnam.

Q: Was his connection there ultimately responsible for the contingent of Koreans who came down - this was somewhat later, in the 1960s - to operate in South Vietnam?

Adm. A: I don't think they were particularly connected. Perhaps they were indirectly, but, in any event, General O'Donnell tried very, very hard to train and increase the efficiency and the organiiation of the Vietnamese Army. It was a difficult task, as I say handicapped by the attitude of the French who greatly preferred their own training methods and safeguarding their own prestige. General O'Donnell was a real good, hard-hitting, tough American soldier, and a good man for the job, and I think the Vietnamese liked him, which was the important thing.

Q: He merited the "Iron Mike"?

Adm. A.: Damned right.

Q: What about the Canadian observer? Where does he fit into this picture?

Adm. A.: One of my good friends at the National War College, a classmate there, then a colonel, later a brigadier, Bob Moncell, was assigned in - I forget the title that they had - monitoring the Geneva accords in China. This was composed of an Indian, a Pole, and a Canadian military observer. They were supposed to make sure that the provisions of the Geneva accords were meticulously carried out.

Bob Moncell came back from Indochina, passed through Honolulu, and we had a very nice visit with him. I remember taking him down to the lagoon for a swim and lunch and while we were there we talked about the situation in Indochina. He pointed out the way the communists operate, that they were operating for their own ends, not to implement the Geneva accords, but their own way of how best to implement their own - achieve their own objectives, and, in doing so, in the tripartite administration there, they had control of the Pole and positive influence over the Indian. He pointed out that at one time they had reports of Russian military supplies being brought into the port of Haiphong and the pressure was to get verification of it. They went up there. There were ships obviously being unloaded, Russian ships, and the Pole said he didn't see any Russian military equipment there. The Indian said he didn't either, and there was no minority report allowed from the committee report, majority report, two to one, made a unanimous report, and there was no means of putting in a minority view. He said it was very important that the people who negotiate arrangements such as was done at Geneva recognize fully the machinations of the communists in not leaving any loopholes in the implementation later on at lower levels to see that the agreements, such as were made, were actually being carried out. And this was very true.

Q: His wisdom wasn't observed in the seventies, however, when they had another group of three? Wasn't it a Pole again?

Adm. A.: That's right. The best lesson of the whole thing in negotiating with the communists was set forth in Admiral Turner Joy's book on negotiating with the communists. Unfortunately, I don't think some of our people who have been negotiating, or rather some of them, have ever heard of Turner Joy and his ordeal up there at Panmunjom.

Q: No. That book should be required reading.

Adm. A.: It certainly should.

Q: Why don't you make this a recommendation to the new administration?

Adm. A.: Well, I think that's a very good point. I'll do that.

I did at one time, when I was up before the Intelligence Advisory Board, urge that Kissinger read that book. I don't know whether he ever did, but it's very illuminating.

Q: There was a special study made by Colonel Sleeper. Did this pertain to Indochina? "What is important to the United States."

Adm. A.: Yes. Colonel Sleeper was an air force officer on our staff at CinCPac, highly respected, particularly in the geopolitical field, military field, and he was in the Plans Division in charge of conducting special studies in regard to the Far East as a whole and, I guess, Indochina in particular, and what should be the U.S. reaction. This was not the evolution of a plan. This was rather a study, and I think they did a lot of work on an interservice basis there under the aegis of CinCPac. It was a good study and it's something that we ought to see if we can get a copy of. That would have been done in, completed in, 1957, continuing, I guess, in 1958. Colonel Sleeper is around Washington someplace.

Q: Is he? Is that his rank ultimately, colonel?

Adm. A.: I think he was a colonel. I think he's over there with John Fisher and the American Security Council organization, or one of the think tanks.

It was as objective a study as you could make under the circumstances at that time, and we gave briefings on it to various people who would pass through.

Incidentally, Hawaii was a focal point for visitors going to and from the Far East as well as visitors who just came out from the mainland to Hawaii itself, because there was a great interest in this new Pacific command. At times there was considerable suspicion in the case of certain of the army and the air force people as to how the above was operating the command. We had a large number of visitors. There were a lot of people of high rank and we tried to let them see the presentation of this study of Colonel Sleeper, which really set forth the serious implication in the years ahead of the communist operations out there, in the Far East and particularly in Vietnam.

There was another thing that came up in the case of the command at CinCPac that is a matter of importance, and that was the presumed vulnerability of the CinCPac headquarters in the event of a nuclear attack or a nuclear Pearl Harbor. This was true generally through our military commands, and the national command here in the Washington area, where there was great emphasis on constructing underground facilities. They had done them for relocation of the seat of governmen here in Washington, the Joint Chiefs of Staff in Washington, and all the unified commanders were supposed to have a protected or an alternate headquarters.

We had looked all over the Hawaiian Islands. We thought, perhaps, of digging into the hill under Camp Smith, and decided that the cheapest we could do under the then prevailing circumstances was to take advantage of an underground headquarters that existed, had been built, up near Fort Schofield - Kanea - rehabilitate that as an alternate CinCPac headquarters. We finally got approval to do so and that was under construction during the time that I was there. Unfortunately it did not have as much protection from a direct hit as we would have liked to have had, but it did provide reasonable protection in the event of a near miss of a nuclear weapon The vulnerability as we conducted these studies of how we could exercise command and control revealed that the communications network of telephone lines and cables was extremely vulnerable and presented a major challenge of how you could provide redundant reliable communications in the event of that type of an attack. There were too many focal points that were vulnerable, and I think that subsequent measures have been taken, I'm sure they have been, to make the communications far more reliable.

Q: In that time were there any rumblings in connection with Diego Garcia? Was that even mentioned, in the Indian Ocean?

Adm. A.: To the best of my recollection, there were no mentions of the Indian Ocean. We had our problems of maintaining our forces in the areas to be able to react quickly around Korea our defense of Japan, Taiwan, and the ever-present danger in Indochina, so we were not particularly concerned with the Indian Ocean during my time there.

Q: Did we feel that Pakistan would take care of the situation?

Adm. A.: There was a rather realistic view of Pakistan. Pakistan was friendly to the United States and pretty strong in that part of the world in contrast to India, but we were not too concerned with that part of it. It wasn't on the front burner at that time.

Q: Now, I guess we come to a hiatus, a rather unpleasant chapter. You went to the hospital.

Adm. A.: Oh, well, I had, as we all did in those days, we had to have an annual physical exam and I guess in that time we took our physical exams up at Tripler Hospital, Army Hospital, in Hawaii. I took an annual physical exam and in the course of the exam, the army colonel there who as the head of urology was one of the doctors conducting the different facets of the examination stated he was a little bit suspicious about my prostate and he'd like to keep an eye on it. That was in 1956, and I went out a couple of times early in 1957 and then I guess it was December of 1957 he told me that he'd probably be moving and it was better if he conducted a more thorough examination and took a biopsy just to clarify his view that there wasn't anything serious. So I agreed and went up and went through the process of taking a biopsy. I was released the next day, I guess it was, and was told that there was nothing to worry about. So I went back to the office and the quarters and carried on. Then, early in January of 1958, the surgeon for the Pacific Fleet, Admiral Hays, came up to see me and he said:

"We have some bad news. The slides that were taken of your biopsy are normally processed back to the National Cancer Center in Washington and they decided that they think that one of them is very suspicious. I think you should go up for another examination.

I went back up to Tripler and they decided to take another biopsy. That time their own pathological department (when they take a biopsy they look at it under their own microscopes) - their own pathological department decided that, yes there were some malignant cells and it was a serious condition. So Admiral Hays came to tell me this, and I said, "What do I do?" And he said:

"Well, we think the only thing for you to do is have an operation," and I said:

"If that's your considered judgment, let's go ahead and do it."

He said, "You can't do it here; there's nobody competent to do that."

I said, "Can't you get a civilian from Hawaii to do it?" And he said there was nobody in Hawaii capable of doing it. Apparently, he and the army surgeon general and the doctors at the hospital had all consulted before they came back to me about this, and I said:

"Well, what should I do?" He said:

"You've got to go to Washington."

I said: "Can't they send a doctor out there to do it?" and he said no, they had to have a whole team to do these things. So I said:

"Well, what do I do?"

He said: "Well, you've just got to go back to Washington."

"What are the prospects?"

"We don't know."

So I said: "Well, will you tell Admiral Stump, and, sure, I'll go back to Washington."

Admiral Stump immediately decided that I should go back to Bethesda, he made his plane available, we packed up the smaller mobile things, and I got a very nice send-off from Hawaii, flew back to Bethesda. I went out to Bethesda I guess at the end of January and there they were extremely thorough in the evaluation of the situation. I went through all sorts of tests. Then Dr. Hanton, who was the head of urology, took me personally over to Johns Hopkins and they gave me what their judgment was, that there was a malignancy and the only thing to do, in their judgment, was to operate. They gave me the statistical forecast of what the situation was. They said, "If you don't have this operation, all we can say is that if you're not killed by an automobile accident or an airplane crash or die of a heart attack, you will die of cancer if you don't have the operation."

So I said, "OK, let's go ahead and do it."

They did, out at Bethesda. It was a nine-hour operation, I guess, and turned out very successfully. I had a period of recuperation out there, convalescence there, then they sent me on leave. Then I came back for a reevaluation after my leave - thirty days' leave, we went down to Virginia Beach. In the meantime, of course, I'd reverted to two stars because I'd come in as three-star, reverted to my permanent rank of two stars. Then I got a clear bill of health at the aviation flight physical. That was reported back and very fortunately I got word from Admiral Burke that I had to go through a couple of schools and then I would be assigned command of Carrier Division 6.

Q: Which had been your ambition -

Adm. A.: Which had been my ambition all along.

Q: How long did it take you, this operation and convalescence?

Adm. A.: About two weeks of studies before they were willing to operate, about three weeks in the hospital, convalescence, a month of leave, then back for a check - oh I guess it occupied about three months altogether.

Q: Did you have to take any medication on a continuing basis?

Adm. A.: No. Actually, the length of the operation depended upon the probing all through the lymph glands to make sure there hadn't been any extension, so I felt like I had been pounded by Jack Dempsey. They were simply wonderful out there, Dr. Hanton, and a wonderful nurse, Miss Taves, who took care of me, both within two years were dead themselves, and one of my good friends, Jimmy Flatley, was across the hall. He'd had the suspicion of a tumor of the brain and he died shortly thereafter. So I was very fortunate in the whole thing, wonderful treatment, and I think the Navy Department and Admiral Burke in particular were very considerate in taking the advice of the medical people that it had been a cure. After all, that was in 1958 and here it is twenty-three years later. I have used this experience to tell a lot of people if they do have this type of a problem they should get checks and double checks. I don't know whether you've read this book by Cornelius Ryan, A Private Battle?

Q: No, I haven't.

Adm. A.: It's a marvelous story about his battle with cancer of the prostate. He's the one who wrote A Bridge Too Far, on which he did a tremendous amount of research. Well, he did the same sort of research on the problem of cancer of the prostate while he was suffering through this disease and its prolongation, and he did a lot of consultations here and there. Unbeknownst to his wife, he kept all these notes and tapes on it. She had kept her notes and tapes at the same time, then she found out that he had done it, so she wrote his book for him posthumously, A Private Battle, which is his battle against cancer of the prostate. Very interesting. So I recommended various people about, first of all, the importance of physical examination, and, secondly, getting good, competent medical advice. Now they have more options that are available than I had at that particular time.

Q: Were you very much discouraged when it was first discovered? Did you think your career was coming to an end?

Adm. A.: No, I think I kept an optimistic view right through. They got me up right after this long operation on my two feet and I had all this external plumbing hooked up. I used to talk up and down the corridor and the enlisted men there used to call me "Hot Rod." I started right away trying to get back to health, which I did. As a matter of fact, I came out of the hospital and I had to go out to one of the Tours out to Albuquerque before I went to CarDiv 6. I hadn't played golf all this time - I went out there with a borrowed set of clubs on a strange course and shot a seventy-eight, which surprised me very much. The Lord was very good to me in this whole thing.

Q: Well, so your ambition was being realized at that point, back in 1959? You didn't return to Hawaii at all?

Adm. A.: No, I didn't return to Hawaii until I was chief of naval operations. I went through these preliminary schools that they had. One in particular was nuclear weaponry out there in Albuquerque and I traveled around with some army and air force people Then, let's see, I reported in and took command of Carrier Division 6, which was in the Mediterranean. I took command when the crisis in the Middle East had been brewing for a long time -

Q: You relieved Cooper?

Adm. A.: I relieved Rear Admiral Cliff Cooper in 1958 I guess it was, my chief of staff was Bill Ellis. Twenty-four hours after I took command, the thing blew in Lebanon. I had my flag in the SARATOGA and we were at Cannes. The ESSEX, the other ship of my division was in the eastern Mediterranean, and the flagship of the Sixth Fleet was at Villefranche with Vice Admiral "Cat" Brown, and he got word, it came during the night, to get under way immediately, which we did, and we steamed at high speed toward the eastern Mediterranean. They had good plans for any contingency out there. Of course, we did not know just what the Soviet situation was going to be, so we were in a very high state of readiness. We had our A3Ds, which were capable of delivering nuclear weapons, all loaded and manned.

We steamed at high speed toward the eastern Mediterranean. We shuttled some extra planes over to the ESSEX by air. They were assembling the amphibious force off Cyprus and down towards Lebanon. We got out there and ran the usual air support for the Marines and for the army, when they came in. Admiral Holloway, Sr., had come down from London. He was the overall U.S. commander. Vice Admiral Brown was the Sixth Fleet commander. Under him I had the carriers. We operated in the vicinity of Cyprus and we conducted that operation for a period of about six weeks before we were released from it, having debarked the Marines. The Marines were ashore. We photographed probably every cypress and every rock in all of Lebanon with our photographic reconnaissance planes, maintained constant combat air patrol, and a readiness to give close air support with our combat aircraft, our fighters and our dive-bombers, as required, and our readiness for nuclear war if that situation evolved. We didn't think it was going to, but nevertheless we were prepared for it.

Q: Admiral Burke told me that before you came on the scene there had been ten or twelve actual rehearsals of steaming toward the eastern Med but under the ruse of being an exercise or something of the sort, but the plans had been formulated and -

Adm. A.: The plans were very well formulated, yes. We were well prepared for that operation. How long we could have operated if real hostilities had evolved from the intervention remains to be seen. But the important thing is, as I see it, that when you have a situation of this sort, you must have ready naval forces in the Second Fleet which, if the Sixth Fleet becomes engaged or there is imminence of hostilities, you must be prepared to move reinforcements from the Second Fleet towards the area. You just can't alert forces in one place. You must alert forces generally so that you can provide the reinforcements. This was true also at the time of the Cuban missile crisis later on. You have to take advantage of the mobility and flexibility of naval forces.

Q: Is that what came to be known as the Strike Force that was availab to the Sixth Fleet?

Adm. A.: Well, the Sixth Fleet in its allied command, NATO commanded capacity was known as the Strike Force, southern Europe.

Q: I see.

Adm. A.: No, I'm talking about reinforcement of either the Strike Force, Southern Europe, or the Sixth Fleet, the ships being the same, being able to be reinforced by forces from the Atlantic coast, which come from the Second Fleet. Normally, those reinforcing forces should be moved on over towards the Mediterranean as soon as you know that there is a likelihood of military action, so that you cut down the time available to get reinforcements on the job. Now, you don't have to put them actually into the Mediterranean. You can or you can leave them outside in the Atlantic. You don't have to actually commit them in there. But it gives you a cushion of time and of distance to enable rapid reinforcement.

Fortunately, that was not necessary and, as I say, we operated south of Cyprus. I did have one sort of a critical moment there. We were conducting operations around the clock not only to carry out the requirements of our forces in Lebanon but also normal precautions, defense and training, and we had a flight up in the early evening one night, which included some A3Ds. I was down in the flag mess and I got word that one A3D had come in to land on the carrier, but not caught the arresting wire, and had broken his landing gear. So I went right into CIC, which was adjacent to the flag quarters on the SARATOGA, to check up on this plane. It was in the air and was circling and the pilot had said that he was going over to Cyprus to bail his crew out and then would come back and land his plane aboard. He didn't want to take the chance with his crew with the broken landing gear. So we watched him and got the word, we followed him on the radar, and got the word, "Crew bailing out," and then the plane kept coming on back over Cyprus directly toward the task force, but we coudln't get any further communications with him. I had two night fighters up there. I told them to go up. We weren't certain whether the pilot had bailed out with the rest of the crew or whether he was going to carry out his original intention of coming in to land. In the meantime, the plane was headed for us. It was also headed directly for Egypt. So I had two night fighers up there to intercept him. They flew up very close to determine whether they could identify and see the pilot in the plane or not. The plane was obviously flying then, in retrospect, on automatic pilot.

Q: Kind of a kamikaze?

Adm. A.: It was sort of a dilemma, a kamikaze up there. We certainly could not let that plane go into Egypt, so we had a sort of a cutoff line between the flagship, the SARATOGA, and Egypt, and if we hadn't solved the problem by that time, then we would have to shoot our own plane down, still with the uncertainty whether the pilot was in it.

Fortunately, as it approached that line which was the point of decision to shoot, the plane ran out of fuel, spiraled down, and crashed in the water. We got the word from the RAF who were in Cyrpus that they had picked up the crew because we had alerted them, and we got them back to the ship. But, needless to say, that pilot caught hell for not having made it absolutely clear whether he was going out with the rest of the crew or whether he was on board.

Q: Which is what he did, he went out with the rest?

Adm. A.: He went out with the rest of the crew.

After about six weeks there, the SARATOGA was due to come back. We picked up our routine around the Mediterranean - she was due to come back to the United States because she had been away the previous Christmas and they didn't want to have the same ship and her crew out of the country two Christmases in a row.

Our tour of duty in the Mediterranean was up. We stopped at Gibraltar, had to carry out an exercise in the Atlantic, testing our own air-defense system. You normally don't like to fly what you might say would be precarious or marginal operations when there's only one carrier available, particularly if you do not have landing fields ashore to which you could divert planes in case of a crash on deck or some deterioration of the whole situation. These were fairly marginal. We carried them out but one pilot did get in a bad situation. We did our best to refuel him and clear the crash on the flight deck, which was aggravated by the fact that the big flight-deck dolly got jammed wheels in the landing area, a great big monster for retrieving planes, so we couldn't clear it as quickly as we would have liked to and we refueled as many as we could in the air. We did have a plane go in the water some distance away but fortunately we were able to recover the pilot - I think his name was Phillips - and got him back. But it does point up that you don't normally like to conduct marginal operations where there could be serious difficulties if something goes wrong with your own landing platform.

Q: This operation was in the North Atlantic, was it?

Adm. A.: In the vicnity of the Azores.

Q: From the Azores to -?

Adm. A.: Yes.

Q: Did we have a base at Terceira?

Adm. A.: Yes, we had a base in the Azores. We were doing this at maximum range from the Azores, too, you see, trying to test our own continental air-defense system and warning system.

We came back, then went to Mayport, for our operations around the East Coast and let people have leave. The ship had been home-ported at Mayport. Nothing particularly significant happened. We had the usual training cruises. We had to take the ship finally, just before I left command, back up to put it in the Portsmouth shipyard, and I turned over to my classmate, no, we had our change of command in Mayport and Admiral Moorer took over CarDiv 6 from me in Mayport. I was ordered to command the Sixth Fleet back in the Mediterranean.

Q: Do you want to say something about that air defense command, that whole setup there in the North Atlantic? Some of the naval people I've talked with were involved in it.

Adm. A.: The setup of the Continental Defense Command was a complicated thing, anyway, and it was in a transition period. We were getting into the jets, we were getting into missiles, and the evolution of electronics and radar warnings, anti-submarine warfare were all taking place. So it was a very complicated and very expensive thing to do, anyway, and I think it proceeded about as well, you might say, as could have been expected. It had to be basically a centralized command, and they got good communications in. I think it was progressively improved as time went on, but then for various reasons, I guess largely budgetary as well as the Department of Defense level, they gradually reduced the size of the Continental Defense Command, the number of interceptors and the number of air defense missiles. I don't know what the effect of this was.

Q: That was tied in with what they called the DEW line, wasn't it, across northern Canada?

Adm. A.: Oh, yes, the North Atlantic line. Yes, that was part of the Continental Defense Command, and the Canadians were tied in. That's out in Colorado Springs. I got more involved in that later on, when I became chief of naval operations.

Q: You did at that period when you had the carrier division also operate with the Second Fleet and Smedberg, didn't you?

Adm. A.: That's right, yes. We had problems revolving within the navy itself our own problems for fleet air defense, which was under study at that particular time because it was recognized that we had to greatly improve fleet air defense. I operated under Vice Admiral Smedberg. Admiral Smedberg was a splendid fleet commander, we had an excellent relationship between ourselves.. We had some difficult staff differences on how it was to be done and who was to do things.

Q: You had a difficult operation, exercise, with the air force, too, didn't you, it was aborted or something of the sort?

Adm. A.: I don't recall that. If you could refresh my memory, I might.

The basic question as far as the navy was concerned was whether the air defense should be controlled by the fleet commander, from the fleet commander's flagship, or by the carrier commander's flagship. This was a question of evaluation of who was best capable of doing the job because we both had the same ultimate objective of providing the best defense for the fleet. In that regard, Smeddy was a wonderful person to work with, thoroughly objective, and I thought that I was, too. I didn't agree with some of the theses that were put forward by some of the people on his staff, which were really nonaviation-oriented concepts, that we had better experience in controlling the fighters than they did. But the whole navy was trying to evolve, genuinely trying to evolve, a greatly enhanced air defense at sea, which was a big problem and still is a big problem. It's even more of a problem today, particularly in the opening phases of a war, because if you're in areas where there's a high degree of traffic and you have aircraft capable of launching air-to-air guided missiles at great distances, how are you going to make that decision- who's going to make that decision - to fire the shot to shoot down a possible enemy when you haven't been able to identify him as positively enemy. You might be shooting down a transient aircraft or a friendly plane that hasn't been properly reported. That's the crux of the whole question, how do you make the decision in time to provide for your own defense, to shoot them down at distances where they can't launch their air-to-surface missiles against you? This is as far as the navy's concerned.

Q: To make the decision?

Adm. A.: To make the decision.

Q: Without all the factors being known.

Adm. A.: That's right, yes. Do you do this at the level of the tactical commander or has he got to wait until this goes back up to the White House and some decision comes back on down. It's always going to be a difficult decision, and when you get over in an area like the Mediterranean, where there are so many commercial aircraft, foreign aircraft, potential enemy aircraft, Russians ships, our ships, it's an almost impossible decision.

Q: Bill Martin faced a decision of that sort, something of the sort, with the LIBERTY.

Adm. A.: That's right.

Q: Was Johnny Hyland operating in that Atlantic Air Defense Command when you were there?

Adm. A.: No. Johnny Hyland was the skipper of the SARATOGA.

Q: Oh, he was?

Adm. A.: He took over command of the SARATOGA from Bill Mather. Bill Mather was the first commanding officer of the SARATOGA that I had, then Johnny Hyland took it over, and Tom South was the skipper of the ESSEX.

I had an amusing incident there. I liked Tom South, he was a very attractive guy, a good skipper, later chief of staff to Tom Moorer. I was sitting on my flagship, on the SARATOGA, when the ESSEX was in formation, and I looked over there and thought I would go over and see the ESSEX. So, instead of just saying I contemplated visiting the ESSEX, I sent him a message, "How is ESSEX ice cream?"

Q: Was it worthwhile!

Adm. A.: Then I called for the helicopter, got in the helicopter and went immediately for the ESSEX, and I could see the skipper of the ESSEX sitting in his chair up there writing a message. I was hovering off the flight deck of the ESSEX waiting to give permission to land. So we went over. He was very embarrassed but we had a nice visit and -

Q: Was his supply good?

Adm. A.: Yes, his supply was good, and when I left I sent a message to the ESSEX, when I got back to the SARATOGA, from CarDiv 6 to Commanding Officer, ESSEX, information SARATOGA, "ESSEX ice cream better than SARATOGA's."

We tried to keep a lively, high sense of morale in the two carriers and also to have good morale among our escort ships, the destroyers.

There was a very amusing experience just before I left. We were going out of the Mediterranean to return to the East Coast. Carrier Division 4 under my good friend Admiral Don Griffin was coming in to relieve us, with the turnover in Gibraltar, and there had always been over the years some sophomoric shenanigans when one ship went out and the other one came in. Admiral Brown had done this many years before, and with Admiral Doyle, the incident of whether he would come and make his call, and Admiral Brown said, "What is the uniform?" And Admiral Doyle sent word back, "The uniform is dress blues with shoes." Brown came over to call on Admiral Doyle, coming up the accommodation ladder after he got out of his barge, carrying his shoes in his hand, and he had his flag lieutenant carrying his shoes.

Q: Was this Artie Doyle?

Adm. A.: That was Artie Doyle.

So, with my classmate Don Griffin coming in, I decided that we would break out a system of deception, saying that a visiting party would join the FORRESTAL, his flagship. The party was composed of a Senate staff man, a newspaperman, and a black civil rights leader who had been visiting us in the SARATOGA. They would fly over from SARATOGA and visit the FORRESTAL. I sent Admiral Griffin cautionary notices saying they'd been very obnoxious and I urged very, very VIP treatment so as not to get the party provoked. These were three enlisted men from the SARATOGA who went over there. They went over to Griffin's flagship and were the most obnoxious visitors they could possibly have. They demanded everything and they got it. The black man asked Admiral Griffin, the first thing, whether he'd changed his attitude toward the black people! And the congressional staff man was talking about the number of mess boys they had - oh, it was just a hilarious visit, and they disembarked and came back!

Incidentally, when they finally found out that they - the skipper of the FORRESTAL - I forget who he was - when they found out that they'd been hoaxed this way, it was quite an amusing situation.

Q: It reminds me of boys playing with toy soldiers, but in your case with the fleet!

Adm. A.: Yes. We had previously done one between the ROOSEVELT and MIDWAY. I guess or the CORAL SEA and we had our Protestant chaplain all dressed up as an Arab -

Q: Abscam!

Adm. A.: - And another young officer who was the British exchange officer. We flew them by helicopter into Gibraltar in advance of the arrival of the incoming ship. Admiral Ingersoll, Slim Ingersoll, was the CarDiv commander. They came out in the launch from Gibraltar with the first boarding party when the new ship came in, and they had engraved invitations to attend a cocktail party at the Rock Hotel given by Ali Baba U-Drive It Camel Service, which had activities all around the Mediterranean, and they had a book of testimonials from former commanding officers and admirals who said the Ali Baba U-Drive It Camel Service was very reliable and very helpful for the morale, and this hoax was carried on. It worked to extreme satisfaction. We left and the people on the MIDWAY or the CORAL SEA, we sent them a message back and said, "We trust you enjoyed Ali Baba U-Drive-It Camel Service's cocktail party at the Rock Hotel this afternoon."

We tried wherever we could to keep good spirits up among the crews of the ships and a sense of humor in everything we did because there were so many things that were very, very difficult to do. I would say that this is especially important on aircraft carriers because with the advent of night operations the work days on aircraft carriers were about eighteen to twenty hours, and you've got to keep people in a good sense of humor to maintain their morale if you're going to be able to maintain readiness for round-the-clock operations, which the navy today has got to do.

Q: The next entry you have is SHAPE-X. Did you visit there en route to the Sixth Fleet or what?

Adm. A.: I was invited to attend the SHAPE-X in Paris, the SHAPE headquarters, along with other Americans, particularly those from the Atlantic Fleet who had been invited to attend. I felt very pleased at that because, after all, I was a two-star carrier division commander just having returned from the Mediterranean.

Q: You were also an alumnus, however.

Adm. A.: And an alumnus, and it was a very pleasant experience, which I enjoyed very, very much. I think this was a very good thing that they did at that time and I hope they continue to have it, to have an exchange of people outside of the immediate command of SHAPE who might be going to parts of Allied Command, Europe, particularly the Atlantic Command, SacLant's command, going there, meeting and understanding what the people have to do, and you have a broader perspective of the whole NATO command military structure.

Q: Do you happen to recall the theme of this particular SHAPE-X?

Adm. A.: No, I do not, right offhand. It was the one in the spring of, let's see, 1959.

It was a pleasant trip over as well as seeing the evolution of SHAPE and its progress. I've always been a strong supporter of SHAPE. I religiously attend all the SHAPE reunion dinners here in Washington. It's not only informative but very pleasant. Two weeks ago, we had one over at Bolling Air Force Base and General Rogers, the present SacEur, gave the principal talk. Most of the old people try to attend if they're in this vicinity.

Another thing I did when I was in the eastern Mediterranean—

Q: This was with CarDiv 6?

Adm. A.: Well, when I was Sixth Fleet, when I was CarDiv 6, when I had command of the ROOSEVELT. As a result of my experience at SHAPE, I would arrange for the pilots from the carrier squadrons, if they were in the vicinity of Greece, to go up and fly around in Greece, meet with some of the ground force commanders - the same thing was true of the Southeast Command in Izmir - so that they would have a better appreciation of what the thinking was on the ground, what their problem would be in the air supporting the ground, in the event that they had to come in in any capacity to support the forces of Greece and Turkey, in the event of a Russian invasion and implementation of a contingency plan.

The pilots enjoyed it. I could always get a group of them in a transport plane which the air force or the MAAG would provide, and they appreciated the visit as well as our pilots appreciated it. It sort of tied these people together in something tangible, rather than something just sort of abstract that they might have in a NATO exercise where they wouldn't actually meet people face to face. And I think this is a good part of interservice relationships, interallied relationships.

Q: That was a very imaginative thing to do. Now this is a part of the overall responsibility of command, isn't it?

Adm. A.: That's right. It's a very important part of command. We mentioned keeping a sense of humor and morale, and also to generate the interest, and I'll talk to you more about that when we get into command of the Sixth Fleet. What I consider important principles of command and how you can stimulate good command performance, which ties right into making everybody realize that no matter what their job is, what their billet is, he as an individul is important to the success of the overall operation. But that's another -

Q: That will come in the next chapter.

Adm. A.: Yes, let's talk more when we get into the Sixth Fleet, we'll talk more about my ideas of command, command relationships, the principles of command, morale and personnel administration. This includes, I guess, about everything up to the time I took over the command of the Sixth Fleet.

I was detached, relieved by Admiral Moorer down at Mayport and Mrs. Anderson and I had the opportunity to travel on over to Europe at that time. I guess we went on the UNITED STATES.

Q: A liner?

Adm. A.: The liner, which is a magnificent ship, you know.

Q: Too bad she was decommissioned.

Adm. A.: Oh, too bad. The era passed. But we had a very pleasant trip over, then I made my various calls before actually arriving down in London, to SHAPE, I guess Paris, and then on down to Villefranche, where I reported in and relieved Vice Admiral Ekstrom. I guess we'd better leave that for the next go-around.

Q: There was one question I wanted to raise. Being cognizant of this new development over the last several years and currently under General Kelley's command –

Adm. A.: The Rapid Deployment Force.

Q: Yes, rapid deployment, and this ties in very readily with your description of the –

Adm. A.: Lebanon landings?

Q: Yes.

Adm. A.: Well, to be able to implement a concept of a Rapid Deployment Force, which is nothing more than a better way of implementing contingency plans, you have to be able to use the forces and equipment that are available. You have to consider the factors of time and of distance. The concept is good - airborne troops, airborne resupply - but you cannot meet all your requirements wih the bulk of material supporting equipment, the logistic support you need, by air alone. We found this out very well later on. I guess for every ton of supplies you move over to the Mideast, it took about ten tons for one ton of supplies transported by air, in order to let the air go over and deliver it and then make its way back to get another load. The second thing, of course, is the question of bases.

So either you've got to have material and ammunition and emergency supplies such as food stockpiled at bases in the area or else you've got to have them on ships that are in reasonably close proximity, which I gather is what they're trying to implement. It isn't something that can be created overnight. It takes time to get the ships and get them loaded. It means also immobilizing a certain amount of equipment in an area, which is then not available for some other area, quickly, because you can only handle this immediate resupply operation for one area that is on the top of the burner at the particular time. You certainly can't have these ships loaded with supplies in the Indian Ocean ready to go to the Persian Gulf and have them available for Korea.

Having command, let's say of a carrier division, you are acutely aware of the importance of logistics, mobile logistics. Now, from the days of Admiral Sherman, in the Sixth Fleet in particular, and in the Second Fleet later on, the navy carried on and improved on the concept of mobile logistic support, refueling, rearming, replenishment at sea, and we had that developed to a very high degree in the Mediterranean. The Service Force over there did a fine job. They had introduced the use of helicopters for replenishment, which improved the situation, but it meant that every three or four days you had to refuel fossile-fuel ships, you've got to refuel from tankers, you've got to refuel destroyers from the carriers, larger ships. You've got to keep them up in fuel, and then, at regular intervals, you've got to replenish food supplies and in the event of combat, ammunition. You carried these out as training exercises, they were very important. We do them pretty well but if the ships aren't there or they are sunk enroute, then you're in a bad fix. You've got to protect the replenishment force from air attack and from submarine attack and requirements for defense seem to burgeon, new threats, potential enemies' operations increase, aircraft and missiles and submarines, which means you have to devote more of your own force to defensive tasks and this reduces your offensive capability, and therefore means that you've got to have better weapons, better reconnaissance devices, better tactics, better intelligence, and the ability to effect prompt and decisive decisions in command and control. It's a continuing challenge.

We've made great progress since I had command of Carrier Division 6. We're going to have to continue to do this all the way along the line.

Q: Bill Irvin has a thesis, which he believes in very strongly, that some of the obligations that have fallen on the carrier forces to protect the units of the fleet should call on the smaller units, like destroyers.

Adm. A.: I wouldn't disagree with Bill. I agree with him, but it means you've got to have the weapons to do it and do it realiably, and the surface-to-air missile which is capable of hitting incoming missiles instead of just aircraft. We worked on this for a long time. For every measure, there's a countermeasure, then there are countercountermeasures. It's a tough continuing job that we've got. We'd all like to see that develop to where it's fully reliable.

In the meantime, we've got improved fighters with air-to-air missiles, but then you've got, like in the case of the Phoenix missile, which would be fired at a range of, say, sixty miles, you've still got to come back to what I was talking about before, who's going to make the decision to fire at a suspected target, particularly in the opening phases of a war. And I'll also get into the question of flexibility and deception when we talk about the Sixth Fleet.

Q: Good.

Index to

Series of Taped Interviews

with

Admiral George W. Anderson, Jr., USN (Ret.)

Volume I

AERONAUTICS, BUREAU OF: Anderson relieves P.D. Stroop in Programs and Allocations in 1940, p. 58, pp. 60 ff.; War plan Rainbow V, pp. 64-65; British pass on lessons learned in World War II, pp. 67-68; Pearl Harbor and beyond, pp. 73 ff.; base requirements at the outset of war, pp. 78-79; comments on inadequacy in implementation of plans for aircraft, p. 87; Roosevelt-Churchill plans for plane production, 1942-1943, p. 91; Russian demands for plane allocations, pp. 97-98, 150-151; contract negotiations in wartime, pp. 99-100; program for lighter-than air ships for antisubmarine work, p. 101; Anderson's story of last-minute change of engines for the F6F, pp. 102-103; the story of the P-51 Mustang fighter, p. 105; close cooperation with the Royal Navy on requirements, pp. 105-106.

AIRCRAFT CARRIERS: (late 1930s) a new appreciation of their worth and power, p. 56-57;

ANDERSON, Adm. George W., Jr.: family history, p. 1 ff; family life in Brooklyn, p. 7-9; enters U.S. Naval Academy, p. 9 ff; marriage (1933), p. 46; son, George III born (1935), p. 49; family moves to Albuquerque during Anderson's service in the Pacific, p. 145-6; serious illness of Mrs. Anderson, p. 145-6; her death, p. 179; Anderson marries a navy widow, Mary Lee Sample, p. 179-180; p. 184; family life in Villefranche while Anderson serves with 6th fleet, p. 202; death of his father, p. 215; named as Senior Officer (Navy) on staff of Gen. Eisenhower (SHAPE), p. 212; family life in Paris, p. 225-6; he takes command of CV FRANKLIN D. ROOSEVELT (1952), p. 234; spot promotion to Vice Admiral, p. 328; marriage of step-daughter, p. 342; his experience with cancer, p. 352 ff;

ARNOLD, General Henry H. (Hap): his status with Marshall and King on the Joint Chiefs, p. 155;

BALLENTINE, Adm. John J.: Commander in Chief of the Sixth Fleet, p. 199; p. 203; p. 215; p. 255; p. 259;

BARUCH, Bernard: his position on the question of recognition of Israel, p. 172;

BEACH, Captain Ned: becomes Naval Aide to General Eisenhower inthe White House, p. 264;

BEARN: French aircraft carrier to which U.S. Navy delivered airplanes early in World War II, p. 69;

BROWNING, RADM Miles F.: group commander on new YORKTOWN, p. 52;

BUREAU OF AERONAUTICS: See Aeronautics, Bureau of;

BURKE, Admiral Arleigh A.: with Mitscher on the European trip (1946), p. 165-6; Anderson recommends Burke to Adm. Radford as a replacement of Carney for CNO, p. 301; orders Anderson to command of CarDiv6 after recuperation from illnes, p. 354;

CALDWELL, VADM Turner: exec of Anderson's when he served on FDR in the Mediterranean, p. 246;

CALHOUN, VADM Wm.: Commander, Service Force, Pacific, p. 127; Towers and his staff work with him and change system of logistics in Pacific; p. 128; p. 142;

CANADA-U.S. PERMANENT BOARD OF DEFENSE: background of Ogdensburg Agreement - and post war problems, p. 174-5; Board chaired jointly by Mayor LaGuardia of N.Y. and Canadian General McNaughton, p. 175; later known as the U.S.-Canadian Military Cooperation Committee, p. 176;

CARRIER DIVISION SIX: Anderson commands CarDiv6 in Mediterranean in 1958 following his hospitalization for cancer, pp. 354 ff.; action during the Lebanese crisis of 1958; pp. 357 ff.; Anderson plays a series of pranks on other CarDiv commanders, pp. 366-369;

CARNEY, Adm. Robert B.: becomes CinC, Southern Europe under SHAPE command, p. 221; p. 225; p. 229; p. 232; his attitude towards duties on the JCS, p. 268; Radford's reactions to Carney as CNO and member of the JCS, p. 299-300; p. 304;

COLE, The Hon. W. Sterling: (MC) - Anderson works with him on Unification (1947), p. 170;

CHIANG KAI-SHEK: Eisenhower's proposal to him via Radford and Robertson of State (1955), p. 279-82;

CHUNG, Mom (Dr.): p. 117-118;

CHURCHILL, The Rt. Hon. Sir Winston: p. 83 ff.; his visit to the White house (Dec. 1941) because of his concern for constant pressure on the European front, p. 90-1; New Year's Eve conference and ensuing production figures on aircraft to be manufactured, p. 91; an evening at Chequers in 1954, p. 297-8;

CINC PAC COMMAND: see entries under: Stump, Adm. Felix need for travel in the Pac Command, p. 337; Anderson's trip (1957) - value for a Chief of Staff, p. 338 ff.; restraints on the CIA representative by Washington, p. 340; potential threat of espionage on the Hawaiian Islands, p. 343-4;

CINCINNATI, USS (CL-6): light cruiser in which Anderson served after graduation from Naval Academy in 1927, pp. 26 ff.; life in the Asiatic Fleet, pp. 27-28; Hawaii and the East Coast, pp. 30-31; had a bunch of screwball officers, including CO, Captain Gilbert J. Rowcliff, p. 32;

CLARK, Adm. John J.: offers Anderson (1943) job as navigator of new YORKTOWN, p. 96; p. 112; p. 114; pp. 116-7; his determination to get rid of task force commander Pownall, pp. 119-120; p. 123;

COMMAND RESPONSIBILITIES: Anderson talks about ideas he employed in the Mediterranean, pp. 371-372;

CONCORD, USS (CL-10): light cruiser to which Anderson was assigned as aviator in 1930 after completion of his flight training at Pensacola, p. 33; description of flight operations of CONCORD's O2U seaplanes, pp. 401-41;

CONOLLY, Admiral Richard L.: as Commander in Chief U.S. Naval Forces, Eastern Atlantic and Mediterranean visits Sixth Fleet in late 1940s, pp. 208-209, p. 211;

CURTS, Adm. Maurice E.: Chief of Staff, CinCPac Fleet under Adm. Stump, pp. 325-7;

DAVISON, VADM Ralph E.: Vice Chief of BuAero (1943), p. 94;

DENFELD, Admiral Louis: as CNO, p. 180; p. 182;

DENNISON, Adm. Robert L.: Anderson relieves him on the Joint War Plans Committee of JCS (1945), p. 162;

DIEN BIEN PHU: see entries under:
Radford, Adm. Arthur, and
SEATO;

DOYLE, Adm. Austin K. (Artie): p. 367;

DULLES, The Hon. Foster: Secretary of State, his good relations with Adm. Radford, p. 304;

DURBROW, The Hon. Edbridge: retired U.S. Ambassador on staff of the National War College (1949), p. 187;

EISENHOWER, Gen. Dwight D.: p. 163; p. 169; named (1950) as Supreme Allied Commander in Europe, p. 212 ff.; p. 220; p. 225; his view of the Carney command, p. 230; reaction to the death of Adm. Sherman, p. 230; p. 232; p. 236; tells Anderson he will turn down Navy recommendation that Anderson become Naval Aide in the White House - for a more useful assignment, p. 263 ff.; his practice of weekly meetings with JCS chairman, p. 267; sends Adm. Radford on mission to Taiwan (1955), pp. 278-82; Anderson's summary of the working relationship between President Eisenhower and the Chairman of the JCS, Adm. Radford, p. 286 ff.;

ESSEX (CV-9): commanded by Captain Donald B. Duncan, the new carrier went into commission in 1943 and then operated for a time with her sister ship YORKTOWN (CV-10), pp. 112-116;

F2F-1 FIGHTER PLANE: Anderson assigned as test pilot of XF2F-1 at Norfolk in 1933, receives gift of champagne from manufacturer Grumman, p. 48;

F6F FIGHTER PLANE: made much more effective for World War II operations because of Anderson's work in substituting Pratt & Whitney engine for less powerful Wright engine in XF6F, pp. 102-104;

FECHTELER, Admiral William M.: after succeeding Admiral
          Forrest Sherman as CNO in 1951, writes to
          General Eisenhower to say he wants to put
          Anderson in command of the carrier FRANKLIN
          D. ROOSEVELT, pp. 231, 233-234;

FITCH, Adm. Aubrey: as captain was C.O. of NAS, Norfolk
          in 1933, p. 43; p. 46;

FORRESTAL, The Hon. James: Secretary of the Navy, p. 168;
          an advisor to the Congress on the National
          Security Act (1947), p. 169; pp. 171-2;

USS FRANKLIN D. ROOSEVELT (CVA-42): big carrier which Captain
          Anderson took command of in 1952, p. 233;
          p. 238 ff; training at Guantanamo, p. 239;
          NATO exercise and duty with Sixth Fleet,
          p. 244 ff; Anderson has fun with his chaplains,
          p. 247; Anderson talks about what made her
          a "happy ship," p. 249; calls for general
          quarters on 7 December 1952 and then explains
          reason to crew, p. 250; readiness and respect--the
          two elements Anderson stressed for his ship,
          p. 250; Anderson's philosophy on personnel,
          p. 251; home for Christmas 1952 with stopover
          at Gibraltar, p. 252-5; concentrates on
          night operations of planes in Atlantic,
          p. 255-7; relieved by classmate, Captain
          J.S. Thach, p. 258; Anderson takes ship
          to New York and arranges entertainment for
          officers and men, p. 259-60;

GERMAN REARMAMENT: p. 232-3;

GRIFFIN, Admiral C.D. (Don): p. 148; in command of CarDiv4--
          flag in USS FORRESTAL--the prank Anderson
          played on him and the skipper of the carrier,
          p. 367-8;

GRUENTHER, General Al: Chief of Staff to General Eisenhower
          in NATO, p. 212-3; p. 222; a demanding
          taskmaster, p. 225; p. 228; p. 232; p. 234;
          p. 235;

HALSEY, Fleet Admiral William F., Jr.: makes humorous mistake
          in protocol while commanding carrier division
          in 1938; p. 53-6; Anderson says Halsey messed
          up at Leyte Gulf in 1944, p. 134; Vice Admiral
          John Towers preferred Halsey to Spruance,
          p. 139;

HARMON BOARD: Anderson named with Adm. Tom Hill as navy members to study what would happen in a war with Russia, p. 180 ff; also p. 189-90; (See also entry under SHERMAN, Adm. Forrest on special study he had Anderson make on a similar question);

HINSHAW, The Hon. Carl (M.C.): Forrestal's talk with him-- wanted help in delaying U.S. recognition of Israel, p. 171-2; he was also trying to interest Hinshaw in a national program for research and development of aircraft to save the post war industry, p. 172-3;

HOOVER, Admiral John: tough cookie who had actor Henry Fonda on his staff while serving as forward area commander in World War II, p. 137;

HOPKINS, Harry: his influence on Russian requests for planes, p. 98;

JCS (JOINT CHIEFS OF STAFF): Anderson is taken on by the new Chairman--Admiral Radford to serve as sort of Chief of Staff, p. 262 ff; General Eishenhower's concept of the role of the JCS, p. 266-7; the so-called 'New Look' on size and duties of the respective military services, p. 267-8; the Joint Strategic Survey Committee, p. 273-4; concerns of the JCS on activities of French in Indo-China, p. 275-6; Eisenhower's respect for military augments role of JCS in his administration, p. 304;

JOINT STRATEGIC SURVEY COMMITTEE: see entries under: JCS (Joint Chiefs)

KAMIKAZES: Japanese suicide planes which took U.S. Navy by surprise in Pacific in World War II, forced increase in use of U.S. fighter planes and antiaircraft guns, p. 148-50;

KEYES, Roger: Deputy Secretary of Defense under Charles Wilson, p. 267;

KING, Fleet Admiral Ernest J.: skipper of the CV LEXINGTON (1935), p. 51; p. 87-8; Anderson comments on his rigid security in wartime and how it affected logistics, p. 87-9; p. 107; p. 119; p. 125; p. 139; Anderson returns to Washington early 1945 to relieve Stroop in Plans Division of COMINCH, p. 142; King relieved by Nimitz as CNO, p. 161;

KIRKPATRICK, RADM Charles C.: on the staff of the Chairman of JCS (1952), p. 272; p. 274;

KNOX, The Hon. Frank: Secretary of the Navy--his trip (1943) to Pacific theater, p. 95-6; p. 107;

KOREA: war (1950) makes demands on the resources of the Sixth Fleet, p. 215-6;

KUTER, General Laurence S.: makes transition from being CinC U.S. Air Forces Far East to joint Pacific Command under Admiral Felix Stump in Hawaii during 1950s, p. 344-5;

LAYTON, RADM Edwin T.: did effective job of keeping JCS chairman, Admiral Arthur Radford, informed while serving as J-2 intelligence officer during 1950s, p. 273;

LEAVEY, Major General Edmond: as logistics section head on Admiral Nimitz's joint CinCPac staff in World War II, this Army officer helped identify problems in Vice Admiral William Calhoun's Service Force, p. 127; picked for logistics portion of staff when General Eisenhower formed NATO command in early 1950s, p. 219-20;

USS LEXINGTON (CV-2): carrier to which Anderson was assigned in mid-1930s while a member of squadron VF-2, p. 49-51; ship commanded by Captain Ernest J. King, who was capable but tough, p. 51;

MacARTHUR, General Douglas: p. 126; p. 133-5;

MARIANAS: their strategic importance in pursuit of Pacific war - especially as it pertained to 20th Air Force, p. 153-4;

MASON, Comdr. C. P. 2nd in command to Capt. Fitch at NAS, Norfolk (1933), p. 43; Exec of the new YORKTOWN-asks for Anderson as landing signal officer, p. 50-1;

MAYPORT, Florida: fine naval facilities, p. 254;

McCAIN, Admiral John Sidney: replaced John Towers as Chief of Bureau of Aeronautics in 1942 but preferred pinochle to desk work, p. 93-4; has false teeth swiped by Admiral Halsey during trip to South Pacific, p. 95;

USS MINDORO (CVE-120): escort carrier which Captain Anderson takes command of in 1948, p. 179-80; returns to ship after temporary duty on Harmon Board, p. 182-3; trains three new ensigns as officers of the deck, p. 183;

MITSCHER, Admiral Marc Andrew: as CinC Atlantic Fleet he makes trip to Europe (1946) with Burke as Chief of Staff; Sherman goes along and Anderson, p. 165 ff; taken sick at Malta, p. 166; incident at the Hotel Claridge involving the two flag lieutenants, p. 210-11;

MONCELL, Brig. Gen. Robert (Canadian): military observer in Vietnam on a three man commission to see that Geneva accords were observed, p. 347-8;

MONTGOMERY, Field Marshal Sir Bernard L.: as Deputy to Eisenhower in SHAPE, p. 217; p. 219; p. 223; he leads the SHAPE-X conference yearly, p. 228;

MOUNTBATTEN, Admiral The Lord Louis: p. 85; p. 106; the command dilemma in the Mediterranean as it pertained to him, p. 220-1;

NATIONAL WAR COLLEGE: Anderson enrolls 1949, p. 184 ff; discussion of Russian policy, p. 189-90; the French in Indo-China, p. 190-1; factors of national power, p. 191-2; Anderson writes thesis on Vatican as an Anti-communist force, p. 192-3; the European trip, p. 193-4; the Korean War breaks out on graduation day, p. 196-7; Anderson invited (1952) to address college on activities at SHAPE, p. 235-6;

NATO: see entries under:
SHAPE;
Eisenhower, General;
Gruenther, General;
Radford's views on, p. 276-8; a discussion of what NATO can do, p. 294 ff;

U.S. NAVAL ACADEMY: Anderson enters on July 3, 1923, p. 9-11; hazing methods at the Academy, p. 13; cruises, p. 14-7; value of athletics, p. 19-20; religion at the Academy, p. 21-2; Anderson's early interest in naval aviation, p. 23-4;

NAVAL AVIATION: Anderson passes elimination flight training, 1929, p. 31; p. 32 ff; loyalty to naval aviation, p. 39-40; Anderson as a test pilot, p. 44-5; new horizons in naval aviation, p. 45; effects of the great depression on aviation, p. 47; new planes coming in early 1930s, p. 48 ff; comments of Anderson on suspicions of the Navy as they pertained to the Army Air Corps, p. 154-6;

NIMITZ, Flt. Adm. Chester W.: Sherman becomes Chief of Staff in Hawaii--a new concept of strategy in Pacific, p. 124-5; Towers becomes his deputy CinCPac, CinCPoa (1944), p. 124; Nimitz deals with Adm. Calhoun, p. 127; his anger over Towers' interference in matter of awards and decorations as well as public relations, p. 130-2; p. 134; p. 139; his position on question of directing Spruance in Marianas action, p. 140; takes Oakleigh Thorne as Flag Secretary, p. 157; sets up Sixth Fleet--names Sherman as C-in-C, p. 167-8;

NORFOLK NAVAL AIR STATION: Anderson stationed there in 1933 under Captain Aubrey Fitch, becomes a member of experimental division with responsibility for carrier landing tests, p. 43 ff;

NORSTAD, General Lauris: named by Secretary Patterson and Forrestal to work with Congress on the National Security Act (1946-7), p. 169-70; p. 174;

O'DONNELL, Gen. Iron Mike: Stump sends him to be in charge of MAAG in Vietnam, p. 346;

OKINAWA: see entries under:
TAIWAN PATROL FORCE;

OPERATION OLYMPIC: planning for invasion of Japan done by CominCh headquarters in 1945, p. 158-9;

OUTLAW, RADM Edward C.: as Anderson's executive officer in the USS FRANKLIN D. ROOSEVELT in 1950s, he learned that his shipboard duties came ahead of flying, p. 246;

P-51 FIGHTER PLANE: was put into production for U.S. Army Air Corps in World War II after U.S. Navy learned how well it was performing for British, p. 104-5;

PALESTINIANS: Anderson's observations on their plight in Lebanon in 1950 and 1952, p. 58-9;

PATROL PLANES: Navy's struggle to get allocation of land-based patrol planes in 1942 in order to meet antisubmarine warfare requirements, p. 86-7;

PATROL SQUADRON 44: Anderson assigned to the squadron at Seattle in 1939 as it was due to receive PBYs at Sand Point for rotation duty to Sitka, p. 57-8;

POST WAR PROBLEMS FOR NAVY: p. 159-60; p. 163-5; the Russian threat, p. 164-5; the communist threat to Western Europe, p. 166-7; p. 174-5;

POWNALL, VADM Charles A.: as commander fast carrier task force in later 1943, was criticized by Jocko Clark for lack of aggressiveness and relieved by Rear Admiral Marc Mitscher, p. 119-121;

PRIDE, Admiral Mel: Commander of the 7th Fleet, p. 309-10; p. 320;

PROMOTIONS: Anderson's comments on merits of accelerated promotion, p. 330; need to guarantee well rounded experience,, p. 331-5; deep selection, p. 336-7;

QUEMOY and MATSU: Radford's interest in as Chairman of JCS, p. 272-4; p. 313;

RADFORD, Admiral Arthur: put in charge of aviation training at outset of World War II, p. 78; Navy Rep at Allied Training Conference in Ottawa (1942), p. 80-1; p. 169; as VCNO under Denfeld he called Anderson to Washington to serve on the Harmon Board, p. 180-1; as Chairman of JCS under Eisenhower he takes Anderson as his Chief of Staff, p. 262; his concern about the attitudes of both Gen. Ridgway and Adm. Carney on the JCS, p. 268; his vast knowledge of Pacific great asset on JCS, p. 269; frequent trips at year end to Far

East, p. 270-1; his personal concern about
the French in Indo-China, p. 274-6; his
views on NATO, p. 276-8; his trip with Robinson
of State to Chiang Kai-Shek (1955) at behest
of Eisenhower, p. 278-80; Anderson's estimate
of Radford, p. 286-91; Radford's consideration
for the avowed principles of his subordinates,
p. 292-3; his disappointment in not persuading
NATO countries to allot greater military
force in Europe, p. 293-4; his role in replacing
Carney as CNO after two years, p. 300-1;
p. 305-6; has Anderson transferred from
the Taiwan Defense Command to CinCPac as
Chief of Staff (1956), p. 315-6; his
determination to reduce service personnel
abroad (1956), p. 317;

RAINBOW 5: the plan formulated for war with Japan, p. 64-5;

USS RALEIGH (CL-7): light cruiser in which Anderson enjoyed
bachelor life in early 1930s, flagship of
Rear Admiral W.D. Leahy, Commander Destroyers
Scouting Force, p. 42-3;

RAPID DEPLOYMENT FORCE: some thoughts on deployment, p. 373 ff;

RIDGWAY, General Matthew: his disagreement with certain
aspects of the new look, p. 268; Radford's
desire to replace him on JCS with General
Taylor, p. 301; p. 304;

RILEY, VADM Herbert: 1943 becomes relief for Anderson in
BuAero, p. 96;

ROBBINS, RADM Thomas H.: p. 240; p. 243; p. 245; p. 255-7;

ROBINSON, The Hon. Walter: U.S. State Department--accompanied
And. Radford (1955) to talk with Chiang
Kai-shek--a special mission for the President,
p. 278 ff;

ROOSEVELT, The Hon. Franklin Delano: preparations for visit
to Hawaii for meeting with MacArthur and
Nimitz, p. 133-4;

ROWCLIFF, RADM Gilbert J.: skipper of USS CINCINNATI when
Anderson was aboard, p. 32;

RUSSELL, Admiral James S.: p. 146;

USS SARATOGA: flagship for Anderson in CarDiv6, p. 357; p. 360-2;

SEA PLANES: Anderson comments on Sea Planes, p. 314-5;

SEATO: the origin of SEATO, p. 282-3; the role of CinCPac, p. 284-5; Anderson's comments on the organization, p. 285;

SHAPE: the organization of Gen. Eisenhower's headquarters and staff, p. 214 ff; Gen. Montgomery proves to be an irritant, p. 223; problem of getting the French to accept German rearmament, p. 223; problem of incorporation of Greece and Turkey into the southern European command, p. 223; Gruenther's requirement that staff study French and English, p. 228; interest in the establishment of the Atlantic Command of NATO, p. 231-2; p. 236-7;

see also entries:
EISENHOWER, General

SHAPE-X: yearly conferences led by General Montgomery, p. 228-9; Radford and Anderson attend the meeting in 1954, p. 296; the situation in Dien Bien Phu causes a change in plans, p. 297;

SHERMAN, Adm. Forrest: Chief of Staff to Adm. Towers in Honolulu, p. 122-3; transferred to Nimitz's staff while Radford replaces him on Towers' staff, p. 124; p. 139; becomes Deputy for Plans under Nimitz as CNO, p. 163-4; goes with Adm. Mitscher on European trip in 1946, p. 165; dissatisfied with appearance and conduct of U.S. Navy in Mediterranean (1946)-- goes home to persuade Nimitz to set up Sixth Fleet and to name him as commander, p. 167-8; p. 169-70; p. 174; assigns Anderson the job of doing long-range study of Navy's position in security of U.S., p. 176-7; conclusions drawn in this study, p. 177-8; paper was destroyed, p. 179; p. 200; p. 211; recommends Anderson for staff of Gen. Eisenhower (SHAPE), p. 218; Anderson writes him as CNO to express relief that he did not get a spot promotion to RADM for the SHAPE assignment, p. 220; p. 224; his last European trip to SHAPE, p. 229-30; death in Naples, p. 230;

SIXTH FLEET: Sherman (1946) decides to have a Sixth Fleet
set up--persuades Nimitz (CNO) to name him
as C-in-C, p. 167-8; Anderson ordered to
fleet as Operations Officer (1950), p. 196;
p. 199; a picture of fleet organization
and duties at that date--under command of
Adm. J.J. Ballentine, p. 199 ff; Korean
War drew heavily on resources of the Sixth
Fleet, p. 215-6;

SMEDBERG, VADM Wm. R. III: Anderson's CarDiv6 works under
him as CinC 2nd Fleet, p. 264-5;

SPRUANCE, Admiral Raymond: p. 139-40;

STARK, Admiral Harold, p. 73-4;

STEEVES, The Hon. John: the State Department political
advisor for Adm. Stump as CinCPac, p. 323-4;

STROOP, VADM Paul D.: Anderson relieves Stroop in Plans
Division of CominCh, p. 142; Anderson takes
over his liaison with 20th Air Force Command
in Washington, p. 153;

STUMP, Admiral Felix B.: p. 315; resists the moving of
his command headquarters to Aiea Heights,
p. 318; his difficulties with a Joint Command,
p. 322-3; his difficulties with concept
of POLAD (State Department political advisor),
p. 323-4; 'Friendly' Felix, p. 326; Anderson
promoted to Vice Admiral in order to serve
as his Chief of Staff, p. 328; p. 338;

TAIWAN PATROL FORCE: Anderson takes command in August,
1955, p. 306; the importance of the patrol
force, p. 306-7; p. 310-1; comments on the
Taiwanese people, p. 312; Anderson relieved
by Admiral Bob Dixon and goes to CinCPac
as Chief of Staff, p. 315-6; comments on
morale problems in US personnel in Japan,
p. 319-22;

THACH, Admiral John S. (Jimmy): relieves Anderson on the
FDR, p. 258;

THOMAS, The Hon. Charles: Secretary of the Navy--his role
in replacing Adm. Carney as CNO, p. 300-1;

THORNE, Capt. Oakleigh: came in through Air Intelligence
School at Quonset Pt. to BuAero, p. 77;
p. 156-7;

TOWERS, Adm. John H.: Chief of BuAero (1940), p. 61; p. 73-4; p. 76-7; p. 79; takes Anderson with him to U.K., p. 81 ff; conference with Churchill on allocation of aircraft between U.S. and Britain, p. 83-5; p. 91-3; transferred 1943 to Pacific in command of Air Force, Pac Flt, p. 93; p. 103; p. 107; brings Anderson to his staff as Plans Officer to Commdr. Air Force, Pac Flt, p. 122; 1944 becomes deputy CinCPac--CinCPOA, p. 124; his animosity toward King, p. 125; takes Anderson as assistant in logistics, p. 125; enlists services of Maj. Gen. Leavey, p. 127; Nimitz calls him on carpet for interference in matters of awards, decorations and public relations, p. 130-2; frequent trips to Pacific Islands during consolidation phases, p. 135-6; together with Gen. Leavey sets up bases for B-29s in Marianas, p. 136; directs Anderson to work on problems of smooth replacement of patrol squadrons and carriers in groups, p. 137-9; his efforts to have Spruance change tactics in battle for Marianas, p. 139-40; Towers and Leavey remain based on Hawaii when Nimitz moves to Guam, p. 141-2; p. 142; advises Anderson to take assignment (1945) on CominCh staff, p. 143-4; p. 153; p. 157-8; on General Board in 1947--worked with Secy. Forrestal on Unification, p. 170-1; urged Secy. to advance rank of Anderson to VADM to head Plans and Operations, p. 170-1;

TWENTIETH AIR FORCE: Anderson comments on Air Corps and Strategic Warfare, p. 152; Anderson takes over liaison (1945) with 20th from P.D. Stroop, p. 153; Anderson has suspicions of something pending in the Pacific war, p. 153;

UNIFICATION: post war, p. 161-2;

U.S.-BRAZILIAN DEFENSE COMMITTEE: Anderson a member of this committee -- much less active than the U.S.-Canadian counterpart, p. 176;

VILLEFRANCHE: headquarters for families of the Sixth Fleet officers, p. 202-3;

> See other entries under:
> SIXTH FLEET;

VINSON, Representative Carl: Chairman of House Naval Affairs Committee who did a great deal in the years prior to World War II to build up strength of armed forces, including program for training 50,000 pilots, p. 61-2;

WALSH, The Hon. David I: Senator from Massachusetts, p. 61-2; his opposition to WAVES, p. 79-80;

WILSON, The Hon. Charles: Secretary of Defense in the Cabinet of General Eisenhower, p. 267; comments on him as Secretary, p. 303-4;

USS YORKTOWN (CV-5): Anderson assigned to new carrier upon her commissioning in Norfolk, p. 50 ff; shakedown cruise to Guantanamo, p. 52; joins with ENTERPRISE for fleet exercise in the Caribbean in 1938 under Rear Admiral E.J. King (Commander Aircraft Battle Force), p. 53; involved in development of air group tactics in 1938, p. 54;

USS YORKTOWN (CV-10): Anderson becomes navigator when ship goes into commission under Captain Jocko Clark, p. 96; early operations along with USS ESSEX, p. 112-6; YORKTOWN's planes and complement of men, p. 118; operations against Japanese, p. 119-23;

ZIONISTS: their strong position in the U.S. (1946-7) for recognition of Israel as a nation state, p. 172-3; p. 205